Oriental Interiors

Oriental Interiors: Design, Identity, Space

Edited by John Potvin

Bloomsbury Academic
An imprint of Bloomsbury Publishing Plc

BLOOMSBURY ACADEMIC
LONDON • NEW YORK • OXFORD • NEW DELHI • SYDNEY

BLOOMSBURY ACADEMIC
Bloomsbury Publishing Plc
50 Bedford Square, London, WC1B 3DP, UK
1385 Broadway, New York, NY 10018, USA
29 Earlsfort Terrace, Dublin 2, Ireland

BLOOMSBURY, BLOOMSBURY ACADEMIC and the Diana logo are trademarks of
Bloomsbury Publishing Plc

First published 2017 by PALGRAVE

Reprinted by Bloomsbury Academic

Copyright © Jonathan S. Swift 2017

Jonathan S. Swift has asserted his right under the Copyright, Designs and Patents Act, 1988, to be identified as Author of this work.

For legal purposes the Acknowledgements on p. xiii constitute an extension of this copyright page.

All rights reserved. No part of this publication may be reproduced or transmitted in any form or by any means, electronic or mechanical, including photocopying, recording, or any information storage or retrieval system, without prior permission in writing from the publishers.

Bloomsbury Publishing Plc does not have any control over, or responsibility for, any third-party websites referred to or in this book. All internet addresses given in this book were correct at the time of going to press. The author and publisher regret any inconvenience caused if addresses have changed or sites have ceased to exist, but can accept no responsibility for any such changes.

A catalogue record for this book is available from the British Library.

A catalogue record for this book is available from the Library of Congress.

ISBN: PB: 978-1-4725-9663-5
ePDF: 978-1-4725-9662-8

To find out more about our authors and books visit www.bloomsbury.com and sign up for our newsletters.

CONTENTS

List of illustrations viii
Notes on the contributors xii
Note on the text xvi
Acknowledgment xvii

1 Inside Orientalism: Hybrid Spaces, Imaginary Landscapes and Modern Interior Design 1
   John Potvin

Part One: Representations

   Introduction 21
   John Potvin

2 The Empty Core of Western Aesthetics (Versus the Aesthetics of Eastern Intimacy): A Reading of Interior Spaces and Literary Impressionism in E. M. Forster's *A Passage to India* 25
   Victor Vargas

3 The Exhibitionary Construction of the "Islamic Interior" 39
   Solmaz Mohammadzadeh Kive

4 Orientalism and David Hockney's Male-positive Imaginative Geographies 59
   Dennis S. Gouws

5 The Excessive *Trompe l'Oeil*: The Saturated Interior in *Tears of the Black Tiger* 77
   Mark Taylor and Michael J. Ostwald

Part Two: Gendered and Sexual Identities

Introduction 93
John Potvin

6 Oriental Interiors in Eighteenth-century British Women Writers' Novels 97
Marianna D'Ezio

7 Bachelor Quarters: Spaces of *Japonisme* in Nineteenth-century Paris 111
Christopher Reed

8 Coming Out of the China Closet?: Performance, Identity and Sexuality in the House Beautiful 127
Anne Anderson

9 At the Edge of Propriety: Rolf De Maré and Nils Dardel at the Hildesborg Estate 145
John Potvin

Part Three: Spaces and Markets of Consumption

Introduction 165
John Potvin

10 "Heraldic Fantasies in Blue and Red and Silver": Orientalism, Luxury and Social Corruption in the South Sea Directorial Houses 169
Eric Weichel

11 Promoting the Colonial Empire through French Interior Design 187
Laura Sextro

12 Paradise in the Parlor: Cozy Corners and Potted Palms in Western Interiors, 1880–1900 203
Penny Sparke

13 Traveling in Time and Space: The Cinematic Landscape of the Empress Theatre   219
Camille Bédard

14 "Flights of Unpractical Fancy": Oriental Spaces at Sea from the *Titanic* to the *Empress of Britain*   235
Anne Massey

15 Posturing for Authenticity: Embodying Otherness in Contemporary Interiors of Modern Yoga   251
Lauren Bird

Index   267

LIST OF ILLUSTRATIONS

1.1	Richard Mosse, *Breach*, 2009.	2
1.2	Richard Mosse, *Breach*, 2009.	3
1.3	Richard Mosse, *Breach*, 2009.	4
2.1	Lakshmana Temple 11, Khajuraho, India.	34
3.1	Room 39, Exhibition of Masterpieces of Muhammedan Art, Munich, 1910.	47
3.2	"Oriental Room" at the home of Albert Goupil, Paris, before 1888.	49
3.3	Martin's Collection, General Art and Industry Exhibition, Stockholm, 1897.	50
3.4	Room 9, the Kaiser-Friedrich-Museum, 1909–1910.	51
4.1	David Hockney, *Tea Painting in an Illusionistic Style*, 1961.	64
4.2	David Hockney, *In an Old Book* from *Illustrations for Fourteen Poems from C. P. Cavafy, 1966–1967*.	68
4.3	David Hockney, *Mark, Suginoi Hotel, Beppu, 1971*.	70
4.4	David Hockney, *Gregory Watching the Snow Fall, Kyoto, Feb 21, 1983*.	71
5.1	*Tears of the Black Tiger* "duel" scene between hero gunfighter Dum and gang member Mahesuan.	81
5.2	Digital reconstruction of *Tears of the Black Tiger* "duel" scene showing camera position, character placement, and stage set.	84
5.3	Digital reconstruction of *Tears of the Black Tiger* "hallway" scene showing camera position, character placement, and stage set.	87
7.1	Great Buddha Hall at the Musée Cernuschi, around 1900.	114
7.2	William Bouwens der Boijen, architect, detail of the façade of the Musée Cernuschi in 2012.	115
7.3	Jean-François Raffaëlli, *Portrait of Edmond de Goncourt*, 1888, oil on canvas, 260 × 170 cm (102 × 67 in.).	117

LIST OF ILLUSTRATIONS

7.4 Hugues Krafft, *"Zashiki" et "toro,"* photograph on cardboard, c.1885. 121
7.5 Hugues Krafft, *Jardin miniature,* photograph on cardboard, c.1885. 123
8.1 George Du Maurier, "A Disenchantment", wood engraving, *Punch,* Vol. 71, 29 July 1876: 40. 130
8.2 "Trade Card designed for Mr Marks by, it is stated, Rossetti, Whistler and William Morris," colored wood engraving. 132
8.3 "A Portion of the Dining Room," wood engraving, Wilfred Meynell (ed.), "The Homes of Our Artists," Sir Frederick Leighton's House in Holland Park Road. 136
8.4 Bedford Lemere (1839–1911), "The Peacock Room." 138
8.5 Mr Deming Jarvis's Collection of Chinese Porcelain at Detroit, USA. 140
9.1 *Dervishes,* costumes, lead dancer and choreography by Jean Börlin, with décor by M. Mouveau. 149
9.2 Salon interior of Rolf de Maré's Park Villa, Hildesborg, Sweden, c. 1913. 153
9.3 Interior of Rolf de Maré's salon at 2 Saint-Simon, Paris, c. 1920. 154
9.4 Nils Dardel, *Crime passionnel,* 1921. 158
10.1 William Hogarth, *The South Sea Scheme,* etching and engraving, 1720. 171
10.2 Printed for Carington Bowles, *A monument dedicated to posterity in commemoration of [the] incredible folly transacted in the year 1720,* etching, not before 1764. 172
10.3 Bernard Picart, *A true picture of the famous skreen describ'd in the Londn. journal no. 85 (Satire on the Duchess of Kendall),* etching, 1721. 176
10.4 Model of a lion-dog, porcelain, painted in overglaze enamels; Japan, Arita kilns (Kakiemon type), Edo period, 21.0 cm × 19.1 cm, 1660–1690. 180
10.5 Japanese export porcelain figure of a lion-dog, decoration in overglaze enamels, Arita kilns (Kakiemon type), Edo period, 1670–1700, 12 cm × 14.2 cm. 180
11.1 First page of Lévitan's 1931 furniture catalog depicting the harvesting and transport of French colonial hardwood. The upper frame reads "A harvest of rare species from Koudé, in Equatorial Africa, A.E.F" (Lévitan 1931). 188

11.2 Depiction of an ideal bedroom set displayed at the 1925 Decorative Arts Exposition, as discussed by Magne in *Décor du Mobilier* (Magne 1925). 194

11.3 Page from Lévitan's furniture catalog promoting their award of the *Diplôme d'Honneur* for the furniture designs and displays of the *Salle à manger* and *Chambre à Coucher* at the 1931 Colonial Exposition (Lévitan 1933). 198

12.1 The Interior Decorator, Elsie de Wolfe, lounging on a cozy corner, in her house at 122 East 17th Street, New York, 1896. 205

12.2 Nineteenth-century conservatory in the Gothic style at Orton Hall, Peterborough. 211

12.3 Palm house at Palmyra, Aigburth Vale, Liverpool, 1896. 212

12.4 Dining room in Palmyra, Aigburth Vale, Liverpool, 1896. 213

13.1 Empress Theater, Montreal, 1928. 220

13.2 Rest room on the mezzanine floor, showing the fireplace, Empress Theatre, Montreal, 1928. 224

13.3 West wall, from balcony, Empress Theatre, Montreal, 1928. 225

13.4 Proscenium arch and asbestos curtain, Empress Theatre, Montreal, 1928. 226

13.5 Fountain and part of stage, Empress Theatre, Montreal, 1928. 230

13.6 First-class stairway of the Champollion steamship (1924), decorated with a painting of Jean Lefeuvre. 231

13.7 Usherettes of Grauman's Egyptian Theater, Hollywood, California, c.1922–1923. 231

14.1 Charles Edward Dixon R.I., *Orient Line to Australia*, poster, lithograph printed in ten colors on paper laid on board and varnished, c. 1912. 237

14.2 Elsie MacKay, The Verandah Café, *Viceroy of India*, 1929. 244

14.3 Elsie MacKay, First Class Smoking Room, *Viceroy of India*, 1929. 245

14.4 Edmund Dulac, Cathay Lounge, *Empress of Britain*, Canadian Pacific Line, 1931. 246

15.1 Yoga practice room, HappyTree Studio, Montreal. 252

15.2 Altar space of the yoga practice room. 253

15.3 Promotional image from HappyTree online gallery. 258

15.4 Tree Mandala commissioned by S. Jowett for HappyTree Yoga Studio, 2012. 262

NOTES ON THE CONTRIBUTORS

Anne Anderson is Honorary Associate Professor at the University of Exeter and an Associate of the Leeds Centre for Victorian Studies. With a first degree in archaeology and a PhD in English, Anne was a senior lecturer at Southampton Solent University for fourteen years, where she specialized in the Aesthetic Movement, Arts and Crafts, Art Nouveau and Modernism. During 2009 to 2010, Anne worked on *Closer to Home*, the re-opening exhibition at Leighton House Museum, Kensington. In 2013, Anne curated *Under the Greenwood: Picturing the British Tree* for St Barbe Museum and Gallery, Lymington. Anne's career as an international speaker has taken her all over the world, including Spain, Germany, Australia, New Zealand, Canada and the USA. She has contributed chapters to: *The Places and Spaces of Fashion, 1800–2007* (2009); *Material Cultures, 1740–1920: The Meanings and Pleasures of Collecting* (2009); *Rethinking the Interior c.1867–1896: Aestheticism and the Arts and Crafts* (2010); *Fashion, Interior Design and the Contours of Modern Identity* (2010); *Bodies and Things in Nineteenth-Century Literature and Culture* (2012); *Domestic Interiors: Representing Homes from the Victorians to the Moderns* (2013); and *Crafting the Woman Professional in the Long Nineteenth Century: Artistry and Industry in Britain* (2013).

Camille Bédard is an architectural historian based in Montreal whose interdisciplinary approach combines architecture, art and curatorship. She completed her BFA in Art History at Concordia University's Institute of Co-operative Education in 2011, with a final Co-op work term at the Tomi Ungerer Museum, International Centre for Illustration of Strasbourg. In 2012, she did an internship in the Department of Architecture and Design at the Museum of Modern Art, New York, working, among others, on the catalog of the exhibition *Henri Labrouste: Structure Brought to Light* (2013). Camille graduated from the Post-Professional Master's in Cultural Mediation and Technology at the School of Architecture of McGill University in 2013. Her research focuses on historical movie theaters, the affective experience and role of movie-going in urban sociability. Passionate about Montreal's built environment, she is a co-curator of Points de vue, a socially engaged, activist, and community-based platform which organized a series of urban laboratories and exhibitions at the Darling Foundry in 2014. Camille also works for the creative workshops of the Musée d'art contemporain de Montréal.

Lauren Bird is a doctoral candidate in Art History at Queen's University and a practicing studio artist. Her research explores embodiment as influenced by interior spaces and the representation of colonial subjects, with particular interest in sites of resistance and hybridity. Her dissertation explores Orientalism, performance, and embodiment in the pre-war works of Diaghilev's Ballets Russes.

Marianna D'Ezio completed a PhD in English Literature at the University of Rome "Sapienza." She lives and works in Italy, where she has been Adjunct Assistant Professor of Italian at the University of California (Rome Study Center) and is currently Adjunct Professor of English (Language, Translation, and Literature) at UNINT University for International Studies of Rome. Her research interests focus on eighteenth-century literature and travel writing, with special attention to women writers; her monograph on British writer Hester Lynch Piozzi *(Hester Lynch Thrale Piozzi: A Taste for Eccentricity)* appeared in September 2010. She also edited a collection of essays on eighteenth-century literature for Cambridge Scholars Publishing and published a book of English grammar for Italian students (Mondadori, 2010). Alongside teaching and researching, she is also a freelance translator: her latest published translations are Charlotte Brontë's *Jane Eyre* (2011), Meghan O'Rourke's *The Long Goodbye* (2012), Bram Stoker's *Dracula* (2014), and Jane Austen's *Sense and Sensibility* (2014), all for Giunti Editore of Florence.

Dennis S. Gouws is Professor of English at Springfield College and Director of Arts and Education at the Australian Institute of Male Health and Studies. He serves on the executive board of *New Male Studies: An International Journal*, on the editorial board of *The International Journal of Family Research and Policy*, and on the advisory board of *The Foundation for Male Studies*. His recent publications include "A Male-Positive Introduction to the Victorian Manhood Question" in *New Male Studies: An International Journal*; "Orientalism and David Hockney's Cavafy Etchings: Exploring a Male-Positive Imaginative Geography" in *The International Journal of the Arts in Society*; and "Boys and Men Reading Shakespeare's *1 Henry 4*: Using Service-Learning Strategies to Accommodate Male Learners and to Disseminate Male-Positive Literacy" in *Academic Service-Learning Across Disciplines: Models, Outcomes, and Assessment*. Dennis is currently designing a male studies curriculum to be offered by the Australian Institute of Male Health and Studies in 2016.

Solmaz Mohammadzadeh Kive is a doctoral candidate in the History of Architecture at the University of Colorado. She has practiced, researched and taught as an architect and architectural historian. She is currently writing her dissertation on the role of architecture in exhibitions of "Islamic art."

Anne Massey is Professor of Design at Middlesex University. She has supervised seven MPhil/PhDs to completion, and examined ten, on aspects of twentieth-century visual culture. She is currently supervising seven research projects, including an Arts and Humanities Research Council-funded CDA with the National Maritime Museum. She is the founding editor of the academic journal *Interiors: Design, Architecture, Culture*, published by Berg since 2010. She has written seven single-authored books and co-edited three, as well as contributing to three edited collections. She published *Designing Liners: Interior Design Afloat* in 2006. She has researched and lectured widely on the subject of the Independent Group, including *The Independent Group: Modernism and Mass Culture, 1945–59* (Manchester University Press, 1995) and *Out of the Ivory Tower: The Independent Group and Popular Culture* (Manchester University Press, 2013). She was guest editor for "The Independent Group Issue," *Journal of Visual Culture* (August 2013).

Michael J. Ostwald is Dean of Architecture at the University of Newcastle, Australia. He is a Visiting Professor at RMIT University and a Research Fellow at SIAL (Melbourne). Michael has a PhD in architectural theory and history, he completed postdoctoral studies on Baroque Geometry in Montreal and Cambridge (Mass.), and he has a higher doctorate (DSc) in design mathematics. He is on the editorial boards of *ARQ* (Cambridge), and *Architectural Theory Review* (Taylor and Francis), and is Co-Editor in Chief of the *Nexus Network Journal: Architecture and Mathematics* (Springer). His most recent book is the two-volume edited collection *Architecture and Mathematics: From Antiquity to the Future* (2014).

John Potvin is Associate Professor in the Department of Art History and Director of the PhD Humanities Program at Concordia University, Montreal, where he teaches on the intersections of art, design and fashion. His research explores the relationships between subjectivity, interior design and space, as well as the complexities that cut across contemporary and historical art and fashion. His work also addresses the ways the male body, masculinity and male sexualities, in particular, are performed, represented, understood, critically evaluated, memorialized and perceived through various design and visual cultures in Europe since the late nineteenth century. In addition to numerous articles, he is the author of *Material and Visual Cultures Beyond Male Bonding* (Ashgate, 2008), *Giorgio Armani: Empire of the Senses* (Ashgate, 2013) and *Bachelors of a Different Sort: Queer Aesthetics, Material Culture and the Modern Interior in Britain* (Manchester University Press, 2014). In addition to these books, he is also editor of *The Places and Spaces of Fashion* (Routledge, 2009) and co-editor of *Material Cultures, 1740–1920: The Meanings and Pleasures of Collecting* (Ashgate, 2010) and *Fashion, Interior Design and the Contours of Modern Identity* (Ashgate, 2010). His current project, *Deco Dandy: Modernism, Nationalism and*

Sexuality in 1920s Paris, is the result of his most recent three-year Social Sciences and Humanities Research Council of Canada Grant and explores the fashion, painting, performance and interior design cultures of the much-neglected inter-war dandy.

Christopher Reed is Professor of English and Visual Culture at the Pennsylvania State University. His most recent book is the co-authored *If Memory Serves: AIDS, Gay Men, and the Promise of the Queer Past* (2012). His other books include *Art and Homosexuality: A History of Ideas* (2011), *The Chrysanthème Papers: The Pink Notebook of Madame Chrysanthème and other Documents of French Japonisme* (2010), *Bloomsbury Rooms: Modernism, Subculture, and Domesticity* (2004), *A Roger Fry Reader* (1996), and the anthology *Not at Home: The Suppression of Domesticity in Modern Art and Architecture* (1996).

Laura Sextro is a lecturer of Modern European and World History at the University of Dayton. Laura received a master's degree from New York University and a PhD from the University of California at Irvine in French studies and history, respectively. In addition to teaching courses on French history, European imperialism and women's history, she has recently presented on the use of French colonial wood in French modern furniture design and is currently working on the impact of French curricular development on inter-war Indochinese decorative art instruction and production. Laura was recently awarded a humanities grant at the University of Dayton to develop course-collaboration between introductory classes in history and art history and a grant from the National Endowment for the Humanities in 2014 to participate in the summar institute "World War I and the Arts," hosted by the University of Cincinnati.

Penny Sparke is Professor of Design History at Kingston University, London. Educated at Sussex University and Brighton Polytechnic, where she studied French Literature and received her doctoral degree in 1975 for a study of *British Design in the 1960s*, respectively, she is the author over a dozen books on various aspects of twentieth-century design. Between 1982 and 1999, she taught on, and subsequently led, the History of Design program run by London's Royal College of Art and Victoria and Albert Museum. Her best-known publications include *An Introduction to Design and Culture in the 20th Century* (re-issued in 2004 as *An Introduction to Design and Culture, 1900 to the Present*); *As Long As It's Pink: The Sexual Politics of Taste* (a study of the relationship between gender and modernism); *Italian Design*; *Japanese Design*; and, most recently, *A Century of Design*, *A Century of Car Design*, *Elsie de Wolfe: The Birth of Modern Interior Decoration* and *The Modern Interior*. She has also curated a number of exhibitions and broadcast widely on her specialist area. She lives in Putney, London.

Mark Taylor is Professor of Architecture at the University of Newcastle, Australia. He is an editorial advisor to *Interiors: Design, Architecture, Culture* and regularly reviews papers and book manuscripts for international publishers. His writing on the interior has been widely published in journals and book chapters, he was the editor (with Julieanna Preston) of *Intimus: Interior Design Theory Reader* (2006), editor of the four-volume collection *Interior Design and Architecture: Critical and Primary Sources* (2013) and (with Anca Lasc and Georgina Downey) editor of *Designing the French Interior: The Modern Home and Mass Media* (2015).

Victor Vargas is originally from Texas (BA, University of Texas). He started off at the graduate level in English studies with an interest in Chicano literature (MA, Texas State University) before moving onto postcolonial Anglophone studies at Claremont Graduate University (PhD, 2012). He has presented at many academic conferences, including several that involve the study of literature and religion, at Lancaster, Leiden, Tübingen, UC Berkeley. His dissertation dealt with the influence of the "Eastern esoteric" and the Occult movement of the nineteenth century on British and Irish modernist literature. He has taught at various California colleges. He is currently a lecturer at San Jose State University and De Anza College.

Eric Weichel is a recent PhD graduate from the Art History Department in Queen's University, and currently holds a SSHRC Postdoctoral Fellowship at Concordia University, Montreal. Over the past four years, he has taught several popular classes for the Center for Initiatives in Education program at Carleton, and has also taught undergraduate courses in Art History and Classical Studies at Concordia, Queen's, the Queen's-Blyth program in Italy, and at the University of Guelph. He has received research awards from Oxford and Yale, presented at a wide range of international and national conferences, and published in a number of edited volumes and refereed journals. Eric also curated an exhibition on eighteenth-century French prints for the Carleton University Art Gallery, and was a research assistant at the prestigious Rembrandt Specialist conference at Herstmonceux Castle, Sussex. Eric's research interests include dance, fantasy and ritual in palace societies; gender and sexuality in eighteenth-century art and culture; literature, mythology and the body in British painting, 1660–1914; landscape and country house studies in British North America; cross-cultural interaction and alternative forms of patronage in the visual and material culture of aristocratic women; notions of Francophilia, fashion and self-performance in portraiture; chinoiserie, orientalism and narrative in ceramic design; history and nationhood in the historiography of the academic tradition; gardens, landscape and the performance of grief and grieving, and a wider interest in the art and architecture of ancient Egypt, the Greco-Roman world and Pre-Hispanic Mesoamerica.

NOTE ON THE TEXT

The author and publisher gratefully acknowledge the permission granted to reproduce the copyright material in this book.

The third-party copyrighted material displayed in the pages of this book is reproduced on the basis of "fair dealing for the purposes of criticism and review" or "fair use for the purposes of teaching, criticism, scholarship or research" only in accordance with international copyright laws, and is not intended to infringe upon the ownership rights of the original owners.

Every effort has been made to trace copyright holders and to obtain their permission for the use of copyright material. The publisher apologizes for any errors or omissions in the above list and would be grateful if notified of any corrections that should be incorporated in future reprints or editions of this book.

ACKNOWLEDGMENT

The editor would like to acknowledge his undergraduate research assistant Thomas Collins for his hard work in the final stages of this book, his sharp eye, attention to detail and for indexing.

1

Inside Orientalism: Hybrid Spaces, Imaginary Landscapes and Modern Interior Design

John Potvin

In his unsettling photographic series *Breach* from 2009, Irish-born photographer Richard Mosse set out to capture the effects of the US-led invasion of Iraq that began in 2003. At first glance, the direct frankness of Mosse's photographs appear as straightforward documentation of war, an idea that the photographer himself shies away from. Rather, these unconventional pictures, in many ways, function as both a distillation of a well-rehearsed and yet current relationship between East and West as well as a provocation to see foreign occupation in different and novel terms, namely through the effects on the built environment and interior space. Mosse's project does not set out to record the destruction of war on the landscape and people, but rather the devastation wrought on the interiors and poolside landscapes of Saddam Hussein's stately residences as occupied by US armed forces. Although Mosse only managed to visit six of the eighty-one palaces that comprised Hussein's impressive real estate portfolio, the resulting series is at once both ambivalent and ambiguous, precisely because it represents a modern Oriental despot's (read: modern-day dictator's) removal, rather than the homes of average middle- or lower-class Iraqi citizens. In these pictures, various forms of power inscribe themselves onto the surface design of the interiors. These grand palaces that visibly betray the effects of war are transformed through occupation to service as makeshift housing for foreign soldiers; a vivid reminder that the function, meaning and lived-in nature of interior space changes—sometimes quite rapidly and destructively—over time. Now in despotic opulence, American soldiers rest in opulent thrones or on the edge of jewel-toned tiled swimming pools [see Figures 1.1–1.3]. Through these pictures, our fervent fantasies of Oriental spaces are destroyed, buttressed only by sandbags and machine-guns. The fantasy of the sultan's harem now replaced by a battalion of soldiers whose desert-storm colors are juxtaposed with gem-toned walls, ceilings and pools.

In these photographs, the Oriental picturesque (Nochlin 1989: 50–51) gives way to the Oriental sublime, where the mask of seductive surfaces and fantastical scenes is removed to reveal a more horrifying aspect of the West's relationship with the East. The power of these images lay, at least in part, in the evocative way they juxtapose destruction and devastation with, where still visible, the opulence of a putatively decadent Orient. Inadvertently, they serve as the material and visual evidence of the overthrow of the enemy, of despotic rule, and in the absence of his body, the *Oriental interior* becomes indexical. In her ground-breaking essay "The Imaginary Orient," Linda Nochlin sets out to explore a series of intersecting "absences" present in French Orientalist painting from the nineteenth century. Focusing largely on

FIGURE 1.1 Richard Mosse, *Breach*, 2009.

FIGURE 1.2 Richard Mosse, *Breach*, 2009.

the work of Jean-Léon Gérôme, Nochlin argues that depictions of the Orient share in common:

1. a sense that time stands still, or in other words that history or temporal change have yet to impose themselves on these places and spaces;
2. that within the images of the Orient as spectacle, the Westerner functions as a dispassionate, disinterested and disengaged bystander outside the frame of representation;
3. the way artists, through the guise of realism, cloak the fact that these are aesthetic representations rather than born out of scientific certainty and authentic evidence; and
4. a denial that labor and industry comprise an integral part of the Orient.

In sum, Nochlin asserts that "[n]eglected, ill-repaired architecture functions [. . .] as a standard topos for commenting on the corruption of contemporary Islamic society" (1989: 38). In *Breach* Mosse reverses and unsettles the order of things. In his pictures, absences are replaced by a tangible Western

FIGURE 1.3 Richard Mosse, *Breach*, 2009.

(armed) presence, labor is represented in the form of plebeian or crass interior design, documentary evidence is coupled with subjective disclosure, while history is made evident in the site-specific struggles over the built environment. For Mosse, the choice of subject was a way to reveal the sediments of history:

> Well you have Saddam's palace, all of the marble, the artificial lakes, the grand columns, the plastic chandeliers, and the murals. Then the Yanks take over. You have the layers of US troops and their personal effects, their bits and bobs, baseball pennants, Wrestlemania posters, camouflage netting. You can see the military's provisional plywood architecture within the gaudy vaulted palace domes. You can just see, very simply, the strata of history in front of your eyes, like archeology.... But the traces of people are there in the interiors and landscapes that I choose to photograph.
>
> (in Birnir 2009)

In Mosse's compelling photographs, in other words, we enter inside, or at the very center of, Oriental interiors.

Interiors, not unlike bodies, are never neutral, but sites and sources of morality, scrutiny and voyeuristic pleasures; they function, to borrow from Henri Lefebvre's tripartite notion of space, as everyday practices (perception), representations (conception) or imaginary realms (the lived). This way of looking into space allows for the multiple possibilities that the study of the interior has to offer in its various and endless real and imagined forms. For, as Mark Crinson notes:

> The more radically disjunctive notion of space, the emphasis on the multivalent use, appropriation, and co-optation of space that Lefebvre alerts us to, is consonant with the emphasis in postcolonial theory on culture as an active process of translation and interpretation.
> (2002: 81)

This volume does not place more value on one part of Lefebvre's spatial triumvirate, as all three aspects of interior space and design form an integral and defining component of the creation, promulgation and experience of the modern interior as it comes into contact with Orientalism. Interiors are at once prescriptive, descriptive and inhabited. This intersection between the protean modern interior and the various impacts and influences of Orientalism over time reveal much about how space creates knowledge and meaning for a given time, place and community. As both a volume and as a broad spatial project, the *Oriental interior* is necessarily transdisciplinary in scope, relying on the expertise, approaches and knowledge of numerous types of people. The chapters that comprise this volume take this into account, and, as such, a definition of the Oriental interior is necessarily loose and broad, especially when one considers the vast and differing influences and fascination the East has held in the West. Moreover, the spaces or representations of interiors each chapter considers might be characterized as "incomplete" in their Orientalist program. Rather, Oriental interiors as we present them here are products of hybridity, offering alternative spaces betwixt and between polarities associated with East and West. Each interior weds Oriental decorative idioms to a Western design syntax to create a unique and novel language for the modern interior.

Since the publication of Edward W. Said's ground-breaking *Orientalism* thirty-five years ago, numerous studies have explored the West's fraught, long-lasting fascination with the so-called Orient. These studies have largely focused their critical attention on the literary and pictorial arts. Additionally, they have more often than not neglected the importance interior design, space and material culture have played in the formation, performance, perception and reception of the Orient in the West. *Oriental Interiors* specifically seeks to explore the importations and adaptations of an expansive yet amorphous Orientalism into the far-reaching landscape of interior design. What these interiors (imagined or real) share in common is a desire to elaborate a commingling of East and West that at once subverts and maintains cultural stereotypes while offering something new. Notions of morality and difference, and their sustained impact on aesthetic and cultural forms, underscore the volume's emphasis on hybridity and intersectionality. As a theoretical starting point, *Oriental Interiors* wishes to view these interiors and their authors beyond a moralizing template that has long portrayed the East as victim, with the West acting as its invasive and omnipresent oppressor. This is not to suggest that tensions, inequities and violence are absent from these exchanges. Importantly, if "we maintain a static dualism of identity and difference, and uphold the logic of the dualism as the means of explaining how a discourse expresses domination and subordination, we fail to account for the differences inherent to each term" (Lowe 1991: 7).

Rather, the purpose here is to rethink and dismantle polarizing perspectives and conceive of the various case studies as products that forge new spatial, subjective and conceptual possibilities. As Homi Bhabha posited in "The Third Space," hybridity, the guiding principle of this volume, provides for "new positions to emerge. The third space displaces the histories that constitute it" (1990: 211). With its pitfalls and possibilities, Orientalism has always offered a different and differing alternative global landscape, far beyond the us–other scenario that has largely plagued East–West relations. Bhabha's notional third space opts out of providing nothing short of "a liminal site between contending and contradictory positions. Not a space of resolution, but one of continuous negotiation" (Hernandez 2010: 95). The hybrid nature inherent in the modern interior in general, and the examples explored in depth in this volume more specifically, entertain some form of dialogical spatial and material practice. Interior design, this volume asserts, possesses the conceptual and concrete possibilities of a so-called third space, one to be explored beyond restrictive assumptions and cultural boundaries.

The notion of authenticity is a rather loaded and much contested concept, especially if one considers the equally loaded term of inspiration as it concerns cultural production. Nevertheless, I make brief mention of authenticity here as an important source of tension, as all too often it serves as a filter as much as a fulcrum through which objects, peoples and spaces are constructed, perceived and rendered meaningful. Authenticity is largely a product of perception and representational strategies rather than an expression of lived and lived-in experiences. In my own work on Turkish baths (*hammam*) in nineteenth-century London, for example, I was fascinated by the way the creation of a supposedly authentic space within a pre-existing British architectural structure allowed for a particular type of an enactment of gendered and racial performances. Rituals associated with proper towel use, for instance, in the British *hammam* may prove authentic while simultaneously pointing to a perceived effeminacy precisely because of its Oriental flavor (Potvin 2015). As a result, I suggest that Oriental interiors are the result of an ongoing, endless series of hybrid becomings, always in the process of taking *place*; they are the resulting flux of constant and ongoing tensions, negotiations, ebbs, flows, bursts, presences and absences. "By foregrounding heterogeneity," Lisa Lowe suggests "to open spaces that permit the articulation of other difference—themselves incongruous and nonequivalent—not only of nation and race but also of gender, class, region, and sexual preferences" (1991: 29). This speaks to the twined topic of this book, Orientalism and interior design. In their own unique ways, both remain unfinished products and terrains, always changing, shifting and evolving, responding to the impacts and trajectories of global, regional and local economies, cultural forces, subjective needs and consumer impulses. This volume explores the interest in Orientalism by questioning how subjectivity and space are products of travel, fantasy and cultural exchange as much as colonial conquest, gender contest and prohibited sexual appetite.

The design and spatial landscape of Oriental interiors necessarily runs the full gamut of expression and experience. On the one hand, some interiors either deploy motifs as surface treatments or introduce furnishing accessories into a pre-existing aesthetic program or, on the other, fashion, design, bodies, music and/or food are deployed to aggrandize, attenuate, enhance or particularize the exoticism, authenticity and/or pleasures of so-called Oriental space and design, forming what we might liken to a *Gesamtkunstwerk*, that is, the interior as a total expression or work of art. At either extreme, the space's culture is transitive, the product of a constellation of cultural translation and transnational communication. Interiors are rarely static, but evolve over time. They expose shifting tastes and trends, material conditioning and the moral implications of aesthetic interventions.

Oriental interiors are also tied into inchoate or particularized expressions of gender, race, class and sexuality; in these spaces, identities and interiors play off each other, each informed by and informing the other. This volume will, as a result, attend to the complex ways in which identities are performed, negotiated and designed, and subjectivities given spatial specificity. All too often, studies in the field rely too heavily on architectural approaches, obscuring the spatial, cultural and subjective dynamics of interior design as proscriptive, ideal and lived-in experiences. This has meant that as a field of study, interior design continues to be undernourished. This volume seeks to fill a gap in the burgeoning field of interior design as much as Orientalist studies, the latter having itself misplaced the significance of the interior within its expansive purview. It demonstrates how the design of the interior exposes numerous political, social, economic, cultural, commercial, emotional, psychic, sexual and gendered registers. In the case of the Oriental interior, it reveals more about the subjective processes of design than providing knowledge of the sources of origin of the objects, designs and even bodies included in these spaces.

Excellent texts already exist on the various experiences and expressions of Orientalism and architecture (see, for example, Beaulieu and Roberts 2002; Crinson 1996 and 2002; Hernandez 2010) as they also do in fashion studies (Bolton 2015; Geczy 2013; Martin and Koda 1994). Oddly enough, Orientalism and the interior have yet to be the subject of a sustained study. To date, only Emmanuelle Gaillard and Marc Walter's sumptuously illustrated coffee-table tome *Exotic Taste: Orientalist Interiors* (2011) tackles the topic. The book's agenda is made clear in its one-page introduction:

> This book explores the way in which such aspirations found fertile ground in the private domain during the 18th and 19th centuries, and introduces people—learned princes or wealthy artists and poets—who presided over the creation of these exotic interiors, capable still of transporting us to faraway places.
> (Gaillard and Walter 2011: 7)

Aside from the high-gloss allure of the book, its authors focus on the exotic enticement and splendor, rather than the mundane and the possibilities of the everyday.

The study of the interior is a young and blossoming field of enquiry, and, of course, of broadening interest. As a result, it cannot rely on scholarly precedents from within its borders, and must turn to a larger frame through which to explore the material. Methodological singularity, therefore, does not inform this volume. Rather, multiple vantage points and positions are taken up to display the diversity of *Oriental interiors*. While the chapters have been grouped into three unique sections governed by a principal thematic framework—modes of display and representation; gendered and sexual identities; spaces and markets of consumption—it is important to recognize that there is much that overlaps between each part, especially in light of the multivalent nature of the material.

With these three themes as a guiding force, the volume attempts, nevertheless, to be as comprehensive as possible, while not exhaustive by any means, by including discussions of potted palms, painting, cinema, furniture design, literature, ocean liners, yoga, rugs, china, porcelain and museum staging and displays, amongst others. This volume takes up and moves forward John M. MacKenzie's aesthetic interdisciplinarity which attempted to push the dialog beyond the still-prevalent preponderance of literary-based Orientalist studies, as well as examine "the extent to which the Orientalist thesis can be revised in more positive and constructive ways [...] to consider the relationships among different cultural forms, both elite and popular in character" (1995: xiv) without falling prey to periodizing tendencies still prevalent in some aesthetic disciplines. Temporal and broadly conceived tidy categories tend to reflect artificial systems of classification and disciplinary regimes more than they expose the ongoing, ever-changing, multilayered and multivalent relationships between the Orient and Occident.

Like the East, the West is itself not a homogenous or monolithic entity, but an untidy assortment and continuous series of at times overlapping and yet differing expressions and collections of "imagined communities." As such, through its case studies, this volume shows how perceptions, conceptions and lived expressions of Orientalism must be cared for through their unique articulations rather than as symptomatic of a univocal self/other relationship. The various chapters offer the exploration of numerous environmental sites, from theaters and yoga centers to private homes and ocean liners, from a range of countries that includes France, Canada, Britain, Sweden, the USA and Thailand. Although each chapter attends to different, unique and compelling case studies, my hope is that they shed light on different strategies to approach similar if not equally unique material. With this rather expansive purview as a point of departure, one key aim of the volume is to provoke further dialog and entice future study of the affect and effects of Orientalism on the modern interior and the way subjects inhabit and design a notional Orient.

Designing Orientalism: Beyond the frame of colonialism?

The so-called Orient has proven fertile ground for the West's construction of what Said has referred to as "the imaginary geography" (1985), a result of human imagination rather than forces of nature. Within the spectrum of interior design, Oriental space comprises a clear and recurring locus of fascination (harem, public baths, mosque, despot's palace), which give space to stereotypical typologies (the sexless eunuch, the wanton harem concubine, the helpless slave, the merciless barbaric warrior, the tyrannical despot). The collusion of the interior with steadfast stereotypes of the Oriental Other provides a sort of "theatricality as sophisticated as it is unsought, a sort of involuntary *mise-en-scène*" (Lefebvre 1991: 74). However, if we consider Oriental interiors as at once perceived, conceived and lived in, we might be better equipped to engage in a more meaningful discussion of how objects, spaces and bodies are brought together through various forces, or put in other words, how the Orient and its material and design culture becomes a mode of orientation. As Sarah Ahmed asserts: "The Orient becomes what we would call a 'supply point'. Lines of desire take us in a certain direction, after all. Desire directs bodies toward its object" (2006: 114). By viewing the interior as a spatial mode of orientation, a series of questions necessarily emerges. Who and what populates the landscapes of Oriental interiors? How do subjects and objects interact and what spaces and sensations do they enliven? Can emplacement and embodiment, within the context of the Oriental interior, be read beyond the confines of colonialism? If we think of Orientalism as part of a colonial project or imperialist program that wrenches objects and people from their origins, and if we couple this with the modern interior, which is itself a result of a constant flux of unfinished becomings, thanks in part to a capitalist imperative, what does this pairing suggest? How might the commixing of interior and Orientalism, the two germane forces of this book, enliven news ways of thinking through transnational, cross-cultural exchanges and influences? How might this coming together, this intimate proximity, lead us to imagine new ways of conceiving, perceiving and living space in a global landscape that guarantees only constant flux, change and even instability?

Design and space reveal a matrix of competing, rather than homogenous, interests, associations and practices, a contest that takes place at both the subjective and public levels. "Acts of domestication are not private; they involve the shaping of collective bodies, which allows some objects and not others to be within reach. After all, if the direction toward objects such as the Orient is shared, then the West as well as the Orient takes shape as an effect of this repetition of the 'orientation toward'" (Ahmed 2006: 117). The interiors explored throughout this book do not operate merely as representations of the Orient in the conventional sense, but are guided by a concern for taste and an acknowledgment that, perhaps, the so-called Orient got some things right in its design of objects and spaces. Holly Edwards notes that, for Americans, the Orient contributed to their "sense of self-worth." Painting, collecting and interior design were not separate enterprises for the turn-of-the-century artist or designer, but together served as sites of "enthusiasm, opportunities for creating selves and setting of aesthetic appeal and social charisma. All of these activities make up what we might term Orientalism, capaciously encompassing product, performance, and person" (Edwards 2000: 30).

As Mackenzie beautifully asserts: "The western arts in fact sought contamination at every turn, restlessly seeking renewal a reinvigoration through contacts with other traditions. And both Self and Other were locked into processes of mutual modification, sometimes slow but inexorable" (1995: 209). Contamination, of course, possesses both positive and negative connotations in the way it points to notions and the trials of difference as much as it acknowledges the fluidity, hybridity and polymorphous nature of inspiration, adoption, appropriation and the circuitous circulation of ideas. "Perceived oriental forms, however misinterpreted, were a repeated source of inspiration, offering new routes out of architectural reaction. What emerged were not copies, the constant bugbear of the architectural commentator, but new styles infused by the design values and sometimes the spirit of another age or culture" (MacKenzie 1995: 101–102). In this instance, what ensues are acts of cultural translation. The concern for taste, style and *savoir-faire* cannot be underestimated, nor can the ways in which the so-called Orient provides a means to expand and/or restrict one's pretentions to them. In many of our cases, Orientalism provides a mode to develop a discriminating taste or a discernibly unique sense of style largely enabled through the gendered networks, intellectual theories and commercial systems of collecting.

Mary Louise Pratt designates "contact zones" as spaces (domestic or otherwise) where different bodies and cultures are brought together, and "where cultures meet, clash, and grapple with each other, often in contexts of highly asymmetrical relations of power" (1991: 34). Each chapter is united by a belief that we are better served when not focused on the differences between East and West, but rather when thinking through the comminglings, imbrications, overlappings and combinations; in other words, the products of hybritiy of these zones of contact. For, as MacKenzie claims:

> It is difficult to discover in any of the arts at whatever period sets of clearly delineated binary oppositions, sharp distinctions between the moral Self and the depraved Other. Rather has the whole experience been one of instabilities and fusions, attraction and repulsion, an awareness of characteristics to be peremptorily rejected as well as devoutly embraced.
>
> (1995: 211)

We have all too often viewed the Oriental project as one rooted in univocality, wherein the colonizer has affected and impacted the colonized, leaving the former untouched, unscathed, unblemished. However, we would do well to recognize how "colonizeds" too are "participants in the production of counter narratives or resistant images, rather than solely as mute objects of representation" (Beaulieu and Roberts 2002: 3). The pioneering work of Julie Codell and Diane Sachko Macleod, to cite only one example, has shown how Britain's notions and theories of the aesthetic were themselves transformed through the colonial experience, largely for the better (1998). Not all forms and functions of Orientalism, or what we might call Orientalisms, are derogatory, hostile, pejorative, condescending, essentialist, reductive or deprecating. As Rana Kabbani boldly, and importantly, claims: "I have come to feel very strongly indeed that in order to arrive at a West–East discourse liberated from the obstinacy of the colonial legacy, a serious effort has to be made to review and reject a great many inherited representations. For these inherited representations are so persistent, and so damaging (they are continually being reinvested with new life)" that they compel us "to see beyond them, to our common humanity" (1986: 12–13). This volume sets out to begin to chart new zones of contact—without falling pray to steadfast colonial tropes and typologies.

In his scathing indictment of Said's *Orientalism*, *THE Guardian* journalist Jonathan Jones argued that the book begot more "prejudice," "bigotry" and "hatred" than it generated knowledge of the East. For Jones, what is perhaps most remarkable about the book is how it, unwittingly, shows how "Europeans and Americans in the 19th century knew more about the cultures of the Middle East than we do now" (2008). As a result of this supposed lack of knowledge, he simply asks, "I think there was real curiosity and admiration. But where has it gone?" (2008). While slightly simplistic in his own reading of Said's text and historical differences between "then" and "now," the spirit of this volume is one fueled by a "real curiosity" about the men and women who designed interiors, collected objects and fashioned their lives through a deep sense of "admiration" for the so-called Orient. A project such as this one does not have to foreclose on "romanticism" (Jones 2008) while remaining steadfast in its critical analysis.

Consuming subjects: Artists, designers, writers and therapists

The creation, circulation and consumption of the modern interior and domestic ideals were in large part aided by and the product of various forms of popular media, whether in the form of photographs or guidebooks and manuals (see Colomina 1999; Rice 2007). This fact is strikingly similar to the expansionist nature of Orientalism, as Said argues throughout *Culture and Imperialism* (1993). As an amorphous entity, the Orient was the progenitor of new circuits of objects, expanding economies and networks of cultural influence. In these instances, there is a certain type of imperialism at work, one fueled by normative notions of gender, race, class and sexuality that are all too readily adopted and disseminated in the material and visual cultures of commodity markets. The chapters in this volume both showcase conventional adherences to normative structures and ideals as well as explore how individual agents sought to transform and/or subvert normative codes of the interior and Orientalism. The subjects included here also largely occupy spaces and positions of privilege and advantage within the power relations inherent in the networks and systems of consumer goods and objects.

Whether Pierre Loti's extravagant transformation of his family's rather bourgeois Rochefort estate into a lush, exotically charged seraglio of opulence, James Abbott McNeill Whistler's lush decorative scheme for the Peacock Room or Lord Fredrick Leighton's splendid and much celebrated Arab Hall [see cover], artists and writers have long turned to the Near and Far East as a conduit for creativity and opulence as much as a site for the abandonment of conventional codes of living. Yet, the sense of eclecticism that tended to dominate the nineteenth century in many countries lent itself well to the seamless inclusion of Oriental elements. In her eloquent discussion of Proust's interiors, Diana Fuss notes how a

> tension between masculine and feminine interior décor accentuates an even stronger opposition in the bedroom between Occident and Orient, between the room's matching French rosewood chest, wardrobe, and

mirrors and its more colorful Ceylonese cabinet, Chinese screen, and Oriental rug. Heavy Second Empire furniture invoking the militarism of the Napoleonic West provides ballast to more delicate Oriental furniture connoting the exoticism of the Far East.

(2004: 165)

Countless fashion designers too have long been fascinated with the East as a source of inspiration for their collections, but also for their own domestic interiors or those of others. Paul Poiret was perhaps the first designer to deploy the mystical and mythical associations of the Orient as a fulcrum for his revolutionary fashion house. However, Poiret also initiated a home design firm, Maison Martine, which seamlessly wedded contemporary modern motifs with Oriental decorative details. More recently, Giorgio Armani has refurbished his boutiques around the world featuring a bamboo scheme as the central motif to conjure a translucent, ultra-lux Japanese garden. His interest in the design motifs of Asia, in particular, has also heavily imposed itself upon his extensive and luxurious Armani/Casa range of home furnishings and furniture design that often fuses his other source of inspiration, the Art Deco era of Paris and Shanghai (Potvin 2010). On the other side of the world, Donna Karan has created special retail outlets, Urban Zen, beyond her namesake boutiques, to assemble a vast array of objects from Italian linens to Balinese furniture and Vietnamese handwork. Urban Zen was inaugurated with the goal of providing a space and product that enables "conscious consumerism," and where mind, body and spirit are connected and balanced (see urbanzen.com).

The irony of enterprises such Karan's and the more recent surge of interest in spatial design practices like *feng sui* is their focus on the spiritual and religio-ritualistic aspect of the Orient. In more recent decades, we have witnessed the proliferation of guidebooks and consultants proselytizing the ancient wisdom of *feng shui*. Non-Chinese homes in the West have attempted to adopt certain key and defining aspects of the system to ensure positive energy flow and deliver productive domestic and economic results. In many ways, the system and its sudden proliferation, seemingly an overnight sensation, harkens back to the 1990 publication of *In the Oriental Style: A Sourcebook of Decoration and Design*. In it, its authors take considerable pains to describe the three primary religions, or philosophies, that have come to dominate the visual and material culture of Asia, or as they describe it, the "look of the Orient" (Freeman et al. 1990: 19). Collectively, Taoism, Confucianism and Buddhism have furnished loci of inspiration for the look. In an all too often seen trope, they claim that "[t]he look of the Orient is dedicated by this cultural and religious heritage alongside the preoccupations of everyday life; unlike the peoples of the West, most Orientals see their religion, philosophy and faith as an intrinsic part of ordinary life" (Freeman et al. 1990: 39). In discussions of Orientalism and its interior design, there is, not surprisingly, not only a conceptualization of the proper use of space, but also an inevitable discussion of time whose elasticity is magnified by supposedly differing experiences of the past, present and future. For as *In the Oriental Style* describes:

> Some Westerners bemoan the apparent rapid passing of the old ways, but the truth is that much of Oriental life is based upon a sense of pragmatism coupled with a genuine belief that past, present and future are a continuous stream—to fight against this current is futile, but instead one must keep moving to ensure the best for the future.
>
> (1990: 39)

The influence of the East on interior design, well beyond the contemporary fashion system, seemingly functions as an antidote to the ever-increasing secularization of the West. Within this decorative ethos, the home, in particular, becomes a space of peace, calm and respite, imbued with near-mystical healing and transformative powers. Oriental motifs in the late twentieth and early twenty-first centuries have moved far away from the perceived pleasures of the seraglios of sexual liberation and lush decadence that the Near and Middle East once conjured. Notions of excess and decadence have long plagued Orientalist descriptions, often fueled by evocative travelogs. Part of this image was stimulated by marketing and advertising techniques which claimed "that the purpose of exotic objects was a manifold endeavor, providing the home a veneer of cosmopolitan luxury and the owner an opportunity for fantasy. It also seems to have masked a desire to reconfigure the spaces of social interaction [in which. . .] exoticized spaces carried an erotic charge and invited people to succumb to desires of all sorts" (Edwards 2000: 32). In other words, the exotic nature the Oriental interior provided for was transformative as much as a liberating form of othering, an antidote to "rigid norms of Victorian society" (Edwards 2000: 32). Department stores like Liberty's in London and the Bon Marché in Paris, amongst others, were large-scale outlets that fueled the Orientalist craze and provided important sources of objects that could help transform the bourgeois home into a space of pleasure and delight with just a soupçon of exoticism (see Cheang 2007). For their part, American department stores in the early part of the twentieth century constructed Oriental bazaars to showcase wares imported from the East, providing consumers with escapist tableaux and immersive spaces.

In her brief discussion of Orientalism, objects and the home, Sara Ahmed makes a clear distinction between the objects that occupy the space of Sigmund Freud's office and home versus those repositioned in diasporic homes. The latter, she claims, form a sort of hybridity (rather than a nostalgic longing for a no longer present homeland), one that now occupies a space alongside objects acquired in the new place of residence. This is the result of "the comings and goings of different bodies as they remake homes in what at first might feel like rather strange worlds" (Ahmed 2006: 150). Indeed, there is a qualitative difference between the homes of collectors and travelers, like Freud, and those of a diaspora displayed by exile. But, do they both not form hybrid experiences, performances, designs and perceptions within the subjective expression and experience of the interior? Even if original meanings are lost in the acquisition, as she claims, new meanings, no matter how problematic modes of acquisition may have been, are created and enlivened as the subject inhabits space along with these objects; this interaction is replete with meaningfulness and burdened by associations. Are objects so sacred, whether from the Orient or Occident, that their meanings must be limited to a singular, solitary one? In no way am I condoning nefarious or violent acts of acquisition or appropriation; simply, I wish to question what takes place, after the fact, in those moments when we dwell in the home or other spaces with such (variously acquired) objects. What meanings, performances, identities and designs are produced in this state of hybridity that seemingly knows no beginning and no end? In other words, by hybrid interiors I do not wish to suggest the commixing of supposedly discrete authentic sources endowed with pure origins that necessarily create an entirely new, perfectly balanced and harmonious object, space or identity. In her rich and evocative discussion of Freud's home and office, Fuss exposes Freud's Oriental interiors in which objects helped to orient the care for and performance of subjectivity to take shape (2004). In the interior of Freud's study, the infamous couch surrounded by exotic objects from far-off locations helped to facilitate psychoanalytic readings of the subjective self. Interiors and object choice betray specific facets of individual subjectivity or household interests and needs as much as expose larger cultural, political and economic networks and markets. Meaning is variously produced through differing gestures of assembling, collecting and designing material objects (Potvin and Myzelev 2009). Hybridity, as it is being positioned here, takes into consideration the networks, systems, mechanisms and markets that allow this meeting to come into being in the first place. Often, the exchange does not always come equally from two unique sources, but rather from various productive forces that engender new hybrid circumstances, new ways to perceive, conceive and live.

After all, in the world of interiors, reception and perception is everything.

References

Ahmed, S. (2006), *Queer Phenomenology: Orientations, Objects, Others*, Durham and London: Duke University Press.

Beaulieu, J. and M. Roberts (2002), *Orientalism's Interlocutors: Painting, Architecture, Photography*, Durham and London: Duke University Press.

Birnir, A. (2009), "The Architecture of War: A Look at Saddam Hussein's Palaces" (June 12): http://flavorwire.com/25071/the-architecture-of-war-a-look-at-saddam-husseins-palaces-richard-mosse [Accessed March 14, 2014].

Bolton, A (ed.) (2015), *China: Through the Looking Glass*, London and New Haven: Yale University Press.
Boone, J. A. (2014), *The Homoerotics of Orientalism*, New York: Columbia University Press.
Çelik, Z. (2002), "Speaking Back to Orientalist Discourse," in J. Beaulieu and M. Roberts (eds.), *Orientalism's Interlocutors: Painting, Architecture, Photography*, Durham and London: Duke University Press: 19–42.
Cheang, S. (2007), "Selling China: Class, Gender and Orientalism at the Department Store," *Journal of Design History*, 20(1) (Spring): 1–16.
Codell, J. F. and D. Sachko Macleod (1998), *Orientalism Transposed: The Impact of the Colonies on British Culture*, Aldershot: Ashgate.
Colomina, B. (1994), *Privacy and Publicity: Modern Architecture as Mass Media*, Cambridge: Cambridge University Press.
Crinson, M. (1996), *Empire Building: Orientalism and Victorian Architecture*. London and New York: Routledge.
Crinson, M. (2002), "The Mosque and the Metropolis," in J. Beaulieu and M. Roberts (eds.), *Orientalism's Interlocutors: Painting, Architecture, Photography*, Durham and London: Duke University Press.
Dobie, M. (2001), *Foreign Bodies: Gender, Language, and Culture in French Orientalism*, Stanford: Stanford University Press.
Edwards, H. (2000), *Noble Dreams, Wicked Pleasures: Orientalism in America, 1870–1930*, Princeton: Princeton University Press.
Freeman, M., et al. (1990), *In the Oriental Style: A Sourcebook of Decoration and Design*, New York: Bulfinch Press.
Fuss, D. (2004), *A Sense of an Interior: Four Writers and the Rooms that Shaped Them*, New York and London: Routledge.
Gaillard, E. and M. Walter (2011), *Exotic Taste: Orientalist Interiors*, New York: Vendome Press.
Geczy, A. (2013), *Fashion and Orientalism: Dress, Textiles and Culture from the 17th Century to the 21st Century*, London: Bloomsbury.
Hernandez, F. (2010), *Bhabha for Architects*, New York and London: Routledge.
Jones, J. (2008), "Orientalism is not racism," Art and Design, *guardian.co.uk* [Accessed February 9, 2009].
Kabbani, R. (1986), *Europe's Myths of Orient: Devise and Rule*, New York: Macmillan.
Lefebvre, H. (1991), *The Production of Space*, D. Nicholson-Smith (trans.), Malden, MA, and Oxford: Blackwell.
Lewis, R. (1996), *Gendering Orientalism: Race, Femininity, and Representation*, London and New York: Routledge.
Lowe, L. (1991), *Critical Terrains: French and British Orientalisms*, Ithaca, NY: Cornell University Press.
MacKenzie, J. M. (1995), *Orientalism: History, Theory and the Arts*, Manchester and New York: Manchester University Press.
Martin, R. and H. Koda (1994), *Orientalism: Visions of the East in Western Dress*, London and New Haven: Yale University Press, 2013.
Mithcell, T. (1992), "Orientalism and the Exhibitionary Order," in N. B. Dirks (ed.), *Colonialism and Culture*, Ann Arbor: University of Michigan Press: 289–318.
Nochlin, L. (1989), "The Imaginary Orient," in *The Politics of Vision*, New York: Harper and Row: 33–59.

Potvin, J. (2005), "Vapour and Steam: The Victorian Bath, Homosocial Health and Male Bodies on Display," *Journal of Design History*, 18(4) (Winter): 319–333.

Potvin, J. (2010), "Cross-Dressing Fashion and Furniture: Giorgio Armani, Orientalism and Nostalgia," in J. Potvin and A. Myzelev (eds.), *Fashion, Interior Design and the Contours of Modern Identity*, Aldershot and Burlington: Ashgate: 225–244.

Potvin, J. and A. Myzelev (eds.) (2009), *Material Cultures, 1740–1920: The Meanings and Pleasures of Collecting*, Aldershot and Burlington: Ashgate.

Pratt, M. L. (1991), "Arts of the Contact Zone," *Profession*, 91: 33–40.

Rice, C. (2007), *The Emergence of the Interior: Architecture, Modernity, Domesticity*, New York and London: Routledge.

Roberts, M. (2002), "Contested Terrains: Women Orientalists and the Colonial Harem," in J. Beaulieu and M. Roberts (eds.), *Orientalism's Interlocutors: Painting, Architecture, Photography*. Durham and London: Duke University Press.

Said, E. W. (1978), *Orientalism*, New York: Vintage Books.

Said, E. W. (1985), "Orientalism Reconsidered," *Cultural Critique*, 1 (Autumn): 89–107.

Said, E. W. (1994), *Culture and Imperialism*, New York: Vintage Books.

PART ONE

Representations

Introduction

John Potvin

The problem for the photographer or writer visiting the Middle East, however, was not just to make an accurate picture of the East but to set up the East as a picture.
(Mitchell 1992: 305)

From three-dimensional international world fairs and curated museum exhibitions to two-dimensional painted interior landscapes by Ludwig Deutsch and Frederick Arthur Bridgman, from the prose found in Lady Mary Wortley Montagu's vivid travelogs to the cinematic evocations such as *Shanghai Express* (1932) or *Lawrence of Arabia* (1962), the Near and Far East have proven fertile ground for creative expression. Whether to conjure the fantastical or create systems of classification, representations such as those mentioned above have provided a clear orientation in the construction of the Orient. In scholarly discussions and surveys of Orientalist representations, one important aspect that has all too often been glossed over or neglected entirely by historians are the interiors, the spaces that continue to inform our impressions and images of the so-called Orient. Yet, it is precisely these interiors that have evoked vivid imagery, wild sensations, illicit fantasies and deepest fears, while also informing the West's own sense of the exotic, taste, style, glamor and luxury.

Turkish baths and harems, Japanese tea-rooms, Moorish palaces, Ottoman mosques, Chinese gardens, Bedouin tents and Indian mausoleums, to name but a few examples, have all served as important settings for countless representations as much as sources of inspiration for design strategies in the West. Colonial expression is all too evident in the depictions of these interiors;

visual, literary and material manifestations of colonial penetration and control. What happens, however, within landscapes of representation where East meets West and boundaries are blurred? Each chapter in this first Part takes as its starting point a completely different form of representation to answer this question. However, what these chapters share in common is an exploration of the representation of the interior and the interior as mode of representation. Underlining their enquiries is a sense that the Oriental interior as a locus of cultural hybridity threatens any representational integrity the West might claim for itself or fervently cling to.

In his chapter, "The Empty Core of Western Aesthetics (Versus the Aesthetics of Eastern Intimacy): A Reading of Interior Spaces and Literary Impressionism in E. M. Forster's *A Passage to India*," Victor Vargas interrogates who has the right over representations of the colonialist interior and its interpretation. Through the prism of literary impressionism, Forster provided an innovative form of modernism by representing the intimate space of Indian interiors. Vargas boldly claims that it was also colonial, rather than an exclusively urban, cosmopolitanism favored by writers like Virginia Woolf, which helped the Bloomsbury Group to unleash its impressionist aesthetic modernism. For Vargas, Forster's novel exposes the colonial Orient as a space of aesthetic innovation as much as an agent for the observation of the West, providing the author with visual inspiration and an admiration of an alternative sense of intimacy well beyond known European forms.

From world fairs to contemporary museum exhibitions, the Orient has been placed on display, often burdened by cultural assumptions and long-held representations. These displays are themselves forms of representation. In his analysis of nineteenth-century world fairs and Orientalist cultures of knowledge, Timothy Mitchell asserts that the

> image of the Orient was constructed not just in Oriental studies, romantic novels, and colonial administrations, but in all the new procedures with which Europeans began to organize the representation of the world, from museums and world exhibitions to architecture, schooling, tourism, the fashion industry and the commodification of everyday life.
>
> (1992: 289)

For her part, Solmaz Kive explores the representation of Islamic architecture and artifacts from interior decoration within the space of Western galleries and museums. In her chapter "The Exhibitionary Construction of the Islamic Interior," Kive unpacks how the visual impact on the interior spaces constructed in exhibitions such as the 1931 Exhibition of Persian Art in London reproduced the all too common romanticized trope of *The Arabian Nights*. As she shows, museums, both past and present, recreated the image of the Islamic interior as unified and homogenous, wherein Oriental carpets were used to conjure a putative authentic space. In this way, these common decorative domestic objects serve, like the flying carpets of *The*

Arabian Nights, as a metaphoric mode of transportation. The immersive quality of these carpet displays, she argues, also challenge the visual and tactile detachment endemic to the white-cube interiors that comprise the modern museum and gallery space.

Since the nineteenth century, objects such as carpets have long been deployed by painters to fashion seemingly legitimate and authentic Orientalist depictions of Eastern interiors. Carpets were used to reconstruct spaces as varied as harems, mosques and private domestic interiors. In "Orientalism and David Hockney's Male-Positive Imaginative Geographies," Dennis Gouws provides a different impression of the traditionally female spaces of the harem interior. Not unlike countless artists before him, Hockney imagines the spaces of the Orient as the loci of a different expression of eroticism. In his paintings, the harem is remodeled as a site not of women nor for a cross-sex male desiring gaze, but of and for an all-male intimacy and homosociality. Gouws posits that Hockey's pictures challenge a traditional colonial authorial presence while also subverting Western heterosexist depictions of the East by creating what he identifies as an "a male-positive imaginative geography."

For Mark Taylor and Michael J. Ostwald, the Oriental interior is brought into perspective through subversion and saturation. In "The Excessive, *Trompe L'Oeil*: The Saturated Interior in *Tears of the Black Tiger*," Taylor and Ostwald explore Thai film *Tears of the Black Tiger* (2000) through the lens of Jean Baudrillard's critique of Orientalism. Within the Oriental interiors that film director Wisit Sasanatieng constructs in the now cult-status film, the aesthetic device of *trompe l'oeil* sets in relief traditional binaries marking the cultural and emotional coordinates of East versus West. Somewhere between critique and homage, American western, European romance and Thai action films and romantic melodramas, Sasanatieng constructs an interior that is contaminated by its own hybridity. Rich in its representational complexity, the film moves us beyond conventional postcolonial critique into unchartered territory.

Reference

Mitchell, T. (1992), "Orientalism and the Exhibitionary Order," in N. B. Dirks (ed.), *Colonialism and Culture*, Ann Arbor: University of Michigan Press: 289–318.

2

The Empty Core of Western Aesthetics (Versus the Aesthetics of Eastern Intimacy): A Reading of Interior Spaces and Literary Impressionism in E. M. Forster's *A Passage to India*

Victor Vargas

The Bloomsbury aesthetic of E. M. Forster that such critics as S. P. Rosenbaum and Ann Banfield identify in their analysis of the modernist movement of literary impressionism has long established the philosophical and aesthetic interconnectedness of the inner circle of the Bloomsbury group while countering readings of the development of any particular member as independent of the intellectual and artistic group they came to be identified with. This, of course, includes Virginia Stephens, Quentin Bell, E. M. Forster, and judging from the letters with the latter, Leonard Woolf. To that discussion, I've added analysis of the Bloomsbury aesthetic within the colonial context, in particular the influence of Indic spirituality and the literary thematic development of subterranean spaces in more than one literary member of Bloomsbury (Vargas 2013). Here, I'm referring to images of tunnels below the London Tube that Virginia Woolf refers to in Rachel Vinrace's colonial-set death-bed dream sequence in *The Voyage Out* (1915), or to the "ancient song" bubbling up from "a mere hole in the earth" beneath Regent Park's Tube in *Mrs Dalloway* (1925: 77). This tripartite of "imperial" literary impressionism, images of subterranean realms and touches of non-Western esotericism that Virginia Woolf flirts with in *The Voyage Out*, *The Waves* (1931), and *Orlando* (1928) also play out in the other Bloomsbury literary figure whose literary expression of dialog between the English and the Indian became more politically prominent as a statement against colonialism. However, that "subterranean space" so central to what became E. M. Forster's final fictional narrative is emblematic of a spiritual and personal intimacy ultimately elusive of European forms (aesthetical, legal, relational). The many critical readings that focus on an absence at the core of *A Passage to India* (1924) speak from the negative and disoriented reactive frame of the European characters to the Marabar caves, and perhaps I should add also speak from the position of Western literary criticism too, which seems ill-equipped to read texts that encode broad political and cultural statements as subtexts beneath literary works concerned with the esoteric or occult (as with W. B. Yeats). Of prominence in the realm of cultural criticism here is Edward Said's well-known "intimate estrangement" critique of Forster, which reads the deferred friendship in the ending scene of Forster's novel as constructing "an Orient destined to bear its foreignness as a mark of its permanent estrangement from the West" (Said 1993: 188). That "foreignness" beyond the grasp of the Westerner is actually part of a conception of (Eastern) intimacy in human relations, though I don't believe Forster felt himself incapable as an Englishman of experiencing this while in India. *A Passage to India*, a novel about East/West relations, involves an accusation of rape against a native by an English woman when the two ventured into an ancient cave system that hummed with the disorienting echo of "ou-boum." Adela Quested, the Romantic seeker of a spiritually syncretized India ("[Emperor] Akbar's new religion"), meets her aesthetic and spiritual death in the fantasized violating touch of a disorienting aesthetics (in the colonial impressionism of the novel), and in a spirituality older even than the Buddha. To ponder what happened in the Marabar caves is to ponder the nature of Eastern spaces that have imparted a spiritual intimacy as old as the geologic forming of the land.

In the late birth of Brahma Gokul Ashtami festival scene of *A Passage to India*, a European character unexpectedly provides an Indian doctor visual access to an elusive element of an Indian religious festival that the Indian had sought but failed to detect. Providing access to this perspective inverts a failed informing of the Westerner by the same Indian character earlier in the novel concerning Western aesthetics and Post-Impressionism in interior design. However, the point of concern in *A Passage* may be a spiritual or yogic experience occurring "before space" (Forster 1924: 208), as the Marabar caves are framed, but it is also one on the nature of structured spaces themselves and the issue of intimacy.

While Fielding's "joy of forms" experience, as he travels back through the "Grand Salute" of Venice, speaks to the broad culturally orienting capability of European spaces, the analysis to follow of the novel will show that Forster also construes them as lacking intimacy (and as a hollowness). But the irony in providing visual access to Aziz of this religious ceremony is that Fielding is an atheist while Aziz is from a culture that Fielding deems as having monstrous aesthetical form, or at least of form not compatible with either European or Mediterranean form. What's interesting is that Aziz's visual-access scene is subsequently followed by a literary expression Edward Shanks described in the 1930s as "one of the most extraordinary feats of impressionism in modern literature, the festival of the birth of Brahma [Gokul Ashtami]" (Shanks 1927: 14). But the construing of Indian-set spaces in *A Passage to India* and the Bloomsbury aesthetics of literary impressionism are far from contradictory. The conjoining of Eastern esotericism and Western avant-garde aesthetics suggests that for Forster the two were relational. In fact, literary impressionism is as much about probing the sense datum involved when spaces are experienced as it is about experiments in perspective, as literary impressionism is chiefly known for. The novel's probing of the way in which Indian beings experience domestic spaces in sometimes problematic ways is as prominent of an aspect in this narrative on colonialism that is, at its core, a story of how certain English characters react to the most intimate of spaces—the Marabar cave. The strangeness for romanticized British tourists such as Adela at Marabar speaks not to a strangeness of Eastern esotericism but to a strangeness of intimacy itself.

While Edward Shanks in *The London Mercury* locates a ground-breaking impressionist explosion late in the novel, its salience can also be seen early on when Aziz first encounters the elderly British traveler Mrs Moore and mistakes her for one of the pillars supporting a Mosque's interior: "one of the pillars of the mosque seemed to quiver. It swayed in the gloom and detached itself. Belief in ghosts ran in his blood, but he sat firm. Another pillar moved, a third, and then an Englishwoman stepped out into the moonlight" (Forster 1924: 20). Images of misperceived interiors occur in every section of the novel. When Mrs Moore notices a wasp on the tip of a peg as she attempts to hang her jacket, the narrator informs us that "[p]erhaps he [the wasp] mistook the peg for a branch—no Indian animal has any sense of an interior. . . . it is to them a normal growth of the eternal jungle" (Forster 1924: 35). The wasp and mosque pillar scenes from *A Passage to India*, though, are also a probing of the Bloomsbury aesthetic exploration of the real and the spatial. In these two scenes involving Mrs Moore, we encounter the notion that structured spaces for Indian beings can be "mistakenly" informed by realms that are usually separated in the Western construction of spaces, such as the domestic and the natural, or the natural and the supernatural, as in the Mosque scene. Aziz's mistaken view of Mrs Moore as a ghost in the Mosque, of course, foreshadows her assumption to a goddess-like status later in the novel when she dies then becomes a mantra in the mouths of Chandraporean natives marching through the street. While Aziz reads the future ghost of Mrs Moore, his visual frame is impressionistic.

For the colonizers and their colonial interiors, though, there are strict boundaries between aestheticized spaces and the natural as inferred in Forster's second pronouncement on the 1924 British Empire exhibit at Wembley, "The Doll House," where the exhibit's central Queen Mary's Doll House is described as "the apotheosis of non-being" (Forster 1996: 49). It is a misreading to conjoin both the Marabar cave and the Wembley Exhibit's central Queen Mary Doll House as representative of narratives with absence at their core. Despite critical readings of the Marabar cave along those lines (such as the one offered by Gillian Beer in "Negation in *A Passage to India*" where "Nothingness" predominates the novel), the resulting sickness that Aziz, Adela, Godbole and Mrs Moore suffer from their experience of either hearing of the Marabar caves, as in the garden courtyard tea scene from the "Mosque" chapter, or of physically encountering them, speaks to the presence of some transmissible aspect (Beer 1980: 155). The disorienting reaction to a sort of physical overabundance that is Mrs Moore's reaction at the cave's entrance is counter-posed by the reaction Adela has to the negation of desire inside as she ponders a distancing from any sort of bodily connectedness to Ronny: "She and Ronny . . . did not love each other . . . The discovery had come so suddenly that she felt like a mountaineer whose rope had broken" (Forster 1924: 152). She'll revisit this dissociative reaction from desire in the courtroom when her body trembles again as a negative assessment is made of her appearance from the courtroom gallery: "Her body resented being called ugly, and trembled" (Forster 1924: 219). On the other hand, Mrs Moore's disorienting reaction, as we'll see shortly, results in a widening of vision. But this vision is a context foreign to the British, who seek a more "definable" and "accessible" expression laden with meaning from Oriental spaces or structures in general. As he surveys Fielding's room early in the novel, Aziz describes the Western aesthetics of design as "the architecture of Question and Answer." The Marabar caves offer neither.

While one race is deemed as lacking the appropriate context to operate in aesthetically structured spaces, the other is seemingly dependent on privileged space to gather its cultural social understanding, a notion that is questioned with the empty core of Wembley. When Fielding, initially a sympathizer with the colonized, encounters spaces laden with assimilable cultural meaning (Venice, in particular) in his "joy of forms" return passage to Europe late in the novel, he retreats from things Indian. Entry into pre-cognitive esoteric spaces is deemed as unreadable (Marabar), while entry into spaces laden with cultural context represents an overabundance of meaning. The "Salute holding the entrance" of the structures of Venice (Grand Salute) is conveyed with a feeling of cultural immediacy, but then this is undermined as the narrator suggests that entry into such spaces entails a withdrawal of intimacy (from his Indian friends). Fielding's reaction in trying to convey the meaning of Venice in his postcards to Indian friends is an attempt to enact something that doesn't exist, or rather, the mystery of absence in *A Passage to India* is not in relation to Marabar but to the absence at the core of Western aestheticized spaces presumably laden with cultural meaning. Adela too will re-enter Western forms (the colonial legal structure) and resume the posture of bended knee in prayers before the Christian god, returning "after years of intellectualism" (Forster 1924: 211).

The nature of European form, with its attendant presumptions of definable spirituality and politics, is brought to mind for Fielding: "but something more precious than mosaics and marbles was offered to [...Fielding] now [back in Europe]: the harmony between the works of man and the earth that upholds them, the civilization that has escaped muddle, the spirit in a reasonable form, with flesh and blood subsisting" (Forster 1924: 282). The result is that he assumes once again the perspective of an Englishman and the cold perspective of a colonial European. This is supported by postcards Fielding writes to Aziz from Venice, "so cold, so unfriendly that all [Indian friends of Aziz] agreed that something was wrong" (Forster 1924: 293). The "joy of forms" passage is an extensive commentary on the relation between Western architectural aesthetics to spatio-cultural meaning, or on the Western "sense of place."

Its culturally mediating implication is also apparent with Adela Quested's simple and presumptuous search for the "realness" of a foreign place in her desire to see the "real India:" "In her ignorance, she regarded him [Aziz] as 'India', and never surmised that his outlook was limited and his method inaccurate, and that no one is India" (Forster 1924: 72). In the absence of a guiding touch towards the "real India," Adela fantasizes a violating touch. Marabar offers only a touch that comes without expectation and without explanation. In cultural terms, for Adela and the "romanticized" British tourist, absence in the spiritual and aesthetic realm is violating. Not only does Marabar as an Oriental space lack the sort of social contextualizing that the Grand Canal Salute of Venice offers Fielding, it lacks aesthetic orientation (readability), as Godbole notes in pointing out the absence of "ornamentation," or of Parvati and Shiva sculptures as at the caves of Elephanta which offer a spiritual context. In this defraying of romanticization, as "no one could romanticize the Marabar because it robbed infinity and eternity of their vastness," Forster offers Marabar as an Oriental space beyond the interpretive, though not beyond political inferences (Forster 1924: 150). Marabar, however, is not without internal form and order like architectural spaces, nor does it lack repetitive dimensions: "A tunnel eight feet long, five feet high, three feet wide, leads to a circular chamber about twenty feet in diameter. This arrangement occurs again and again" (Forster 1924: 124). The "structured" nature of Marabar highlights the several references in the novel and in the manuscript where Forster analogizes elements seemingly in line with architectural forms: "The sky too has its changes... Clouds map it ... up at times, but it is usually a dome" (Forster 1964: 3).

Not all English characters come away with a sense of having been violated by their exposure to Marabar. Neither do all regain, once having been altered by it, a sense of "meaning" from re-exposure to things European (whether architectural forms or colonial infrastructures). When Mrs Moore encounters the Marabar caves, she retreats from a European sensibility into an advanced enlightened state that can be described as ascetically Eastern in nature: "She had come to that state where the horror of the universe and its smallness are both visible at the same time—the twilight of the double vision in which so many elderly people are involved" (Forster 1924: 207). Her change in perspective begins with her first entry into an Indian structure, this after having escaped during a play's intermission in a performance space in the administrative Anglo-Indian enclave of Chandrapore. Here, I'm referring to her conversation with Aziz in the Mosque, where, once having removed her shoes, she remains in a facially obscured "purdah [Moslem covering]:" "She was now in the shadow of the gateway, so that he could not see her face" (Forster 1924: 20). Mrs Moore is then metonymically aligned with a tributary stream from the sacred Ganges river, which she has just indirectly experienced with Aziz in the form of the externally replenished cleansing absolution tank situated between them during their conversation: "A sense of unity, of kinship with the heavenly bodies, passed into the old woman and out, like water through a tank, leaving a strange freshness behind" (Forster 1924: 29–30). The Oriental space of the Mosque combines the aesthetic, the natural and the supernatural.

In yogic "conversion" narratives, if you will, there is a spatial/geologic and mantric context, which is what entry into the Ganges signifies and which the privileging of narratives of guru's bestowing of mantras upon initiates in the Himalayas has mythologized. Forster mentions in his BBC talk how Hindu temples themselves are oriented towards the "world mountain," or the Mount Meru that Sheldon Pollock highlights as the cosmological center of the Sanskrit cosmopolis. Mrs Moore's metonymic entry into the Ganges and her coming to represent a mantra later in the mouths of protesting servant-class Indians outside the courthouse during Aziz's trial speaks to an ascetic assumption on her part: "It was revolting [to Ronny] to hear his mother travestied into Esmiss Esmoor, a Hindu goddess. 'Esmiss Esmoor Esmiss Esmoor Esmiss Esmoor Esmiss Esmoor . . .'" (Forster 1924: 225). She will not survive much into her passage beyond the Ganges's end (the Indian Ocean). When Mrs Moore initially hears of the Marabar caves in another conversation with Aziz a few pages later, after the Mosque encounter, her emotional reaction is more diffuse as she becomes "terrified over an area larger than usual" (Forster 1924: 150). Oriental spaces extend beyond the frame of their physical context. This sickness from hearing of Marabar is referred to several times subsequent to the garden party, with even "Aziz and old Godbole . . . both ill after" (Forster 1924: 239). Adela's version of the "cave illness," or "hallucination" as she suggests to Fielding in a post-trial discussion, also began at the garden house gathering and prior to the lingering sonorous "devoid of distinction" echo, or the suggestively yogic "ou- boum" vibration that the cave will emit upon their visit (Forster

1924: 147). It will end for her beneath the specter of the half-naked native courtroom fan-operator oblivious to the equally hallucinatory impressions of the legal proceedings ("scene of the fantasy") (Forster 1924: 231).

The negative sensory reaction to the first mention of Marabar caves by both English and Indian is to a space temporally beyond the historical interpretive narrative frames of both Indic spirituality and even of European romanticized cosmologies of the subcontinent (à la the Theosophical Society's lost continent of Lemuria):

> But India is really far older. In the days of the prehistoric ocean, the southern part of the peninsula already existed, and the high places of Dravidia have been land since land began, and have seen on the one side the sinking of a continent that joined them to Africa, and on the other the upheaval of the Himalayas from the sea. They are older than anything in the world. ... There is something unspeakable in these outposts [Marabar]. They are like nothing else in the world, and a glimpse of them makes the breath catch. They rise abruptly, insanely, without the proportion that is kept by the wildest hills elsewhere, they bear no relation to anything dreamt or seen. To call them "uncanny" suggests ghosts, and they are older than all spirit. Hinduism has scratched and plastered a few rocks, but the shrines are unfrequented, as if pilgrims, who generally seek the extraordinary, had here found too much of it. Some Saddhus did once settle in a cave, but they were smoked out, and even Buddha, who must have passed this way down to the Bo Tree of Gya, shunned a renunciation more complete than his own, and has left no legend of struggle or victory in the Marabar.
>
> (Forster 1924: 123–124)

In prior works, Forster constructed spaces harkening to an earlier time, or as Gregory Bredbeck frames it in regard to his reading of Forster's short stories and the novel *Maurice* (1971), "a nostalgic time before, a time which embodies the fantasy of an escape, not a refinement" (Bredbeck 1997: 51). *A Passage to India* may not represent a "refinement" in Bredbeck's sense, but it's nevertheless laced with political and social inferences. Intimate Indian spaces, domestic or religious, set apart from an outside world and informed by the supernatural, are framed as expressing the real, while spaces outside of that, including the Anglo-Indian administrative enclave, occupy a realm of the fantastical. British colonial infrastructures such as those concerned with tourism, built partly on romanticized "Eastern" trek narratives from which Adela springs, exhibit the fantastical while also being a conduit for avant-garde literary aesthetics. The double vision or double-ness that English and Indian characters exhibit is related to a change in perspective from Indic geo-spiritual and spatial interactions (Marabar, Mosque, Ganges). Mrs Moore's version of the double vision seems to resemble Western impressionist perspective as she "watched the indestructible life of man and his changing faces, and the houses he has built for himself and God, and they appeared to her not in terms of her own trouble but as things to see" (Forster 1924: 209). The extensive scope of vision, from "smallness" to "universe," mirrors the extensive reach of the Marabar cave hand sky gesture that Fielding envisions later in the novel. But it's also the access to a broader scope and a related double-ness that is deemed as the crucial element in Aziz's presumed guilt: "And then came the culminating evidence: the discovery of the field-glasses on the prisoner ... The facts will speak for themselves. The prisoner [Aziz] is one of those individuals who have led a double life" (Forster 1924: 222).

While perspective is broadened from interacting with the Marabar cave and Indic spiritual spaces, as with Mrs Moore's reaction in the Mosque or Aziz's subsequent vision of the floating clay god during the Gokul Ashtami festival, attempts to appropriate Western aesthetical concepts of perspective entail mis-readings. Dr Aziz attempts to identify a Western-oriented space in Fielding's room, and is deemed as having trespassed onto Western terrains of the critique of aesthetics. This occurs in an early scene from the novel when he queries Fielding as to Adela's possible "Post-Impressionist" outlook. However, the Englishman's reaction of exasperation "suggested that he [Aziz], an obscure Indian, had no right to have heard of Post Impressionism—a privilege reserved for the Ruling Race" (Forster 1924: 66). Issues of impressions and defining an individual reappear late in the novel beyond discussions of Western aesthetics. Partly driven by commentary on a "sense of perspective" and cross-cultural issues, the narrative probes the relation of impressions and the colonial by exposing notions of power in "privileged perspectives"—this, when Fielding reproves Aziz for misjudging intentions in the former's offer of help to Adela (post-trial) with statements that, in the Englishman's opinion, are filled with "dismay and anxiety" (Forster 1924: 273). This discussion mirrors at the individual level the privileged communal perspective from the opening scene of the novel where the narrator notes how the Anglo-Indian colonial administrative enclave purposefully overlooks the entirety of Chandrapore: "Inland, the prospect alters. ... Houses belonging to Eurasians stand on the high ground" (Forster 1924: 8). Aziz attempts to assess relationships between the English post-trial and takes umbrage with Fielding's reaction, as the Indian doctor responds: "Have I not lived my whole life in India? Do I not know what produces a bad impression here?" (Forster 1924: 273). Fielding's retort, that Aziz's assessment is of "a scale" out of proportion, posits the perspective of intimacy itself as a thing of privilege. The Indian's inability to navigate the interior human spaces of intimacy, for "which no Indian animal has any sense," recalls Mrs Moore's misplaced wasp earlier in the novel.

Indians "misread" the interiors of intimacy and spaces, but *A Passage to India* is also about how Europeans misread nature, from the misreading of Marabar to the misreading of the boar as ghost or ghost as boar in the car accident during Adela and Ronny Moore's outing. But the concept of space in the Indian context is also fluid with no definable boundaries, where even native residents and their houses are connected to the sacred stream, of which "[t]he very wood [of structures] seems made of mud, the inhabitants of mud moving" (Forster 1924: 8). With the crashing of the wood from Aziz and Fielding's boats, colliding on the native state pond during Gokul Ashtami, the letters of Ronny and Adela themselves release into the flowing mud. The accusatory word floats off. It's a metaphoric release that frames the pond portion of the ceremony in a pre-literary sense, and that allows Aziz to capture a vision of the godly between lake trees. But these scenes of visual and aesthetic fluidity also highlight how to read impressionistically is to misread altogether, English or otherwise. Here, the novel questions its very form for accessing intimate spaces.

Despite these misreadings of the intimate and of perspective, there is a correlation between intimate gestures and unveilings. Aziz's "unveiling" of his wife to Fielding in the form of having shown him pictures of her without purdah—an intimate gesture that will later be trounced on by legal authorities as they ransack Aziz's house—as well as Fielding's continued presence in the homes of Indians, becomes the conduit for his scope of the Marabar caves's hand sky gesture. Fielding's vision of the Marabar cave's "fingers" touching the universe is inversely in the mode of Adela perceiving a touch at the individual level inside the cave. For both Mrs Moore and Fielding, access to intimacy inversely allows for a comprehension of Indic vastness. It's these two characters' "strange and beautiful effect" on Aziz that elicits true intimacy, and which sets his assessment of their friendship apart from the sort of "overrated hospitality" that, according to the novel's narrator, "Orientals" are prone to mistake "for intimacy" when interacting with the English, "not seeing that it is tainted with the sense of possession" (Forster 1924: 142).

At heart, then, *A Passage to India* is about a concept of space that exceeds, either Western aesthetical interpretive perspectives, or even of the Eastern esoteric sort, from a more primitive expression that represents Godbole's telepathic attempt to "impel" Mrs Moore and her wasp at Gokul Ashtami. As strange as Fielding's geo-spiritual vision is of the universal hand gesture that the Marabar cave extends, so too is this telepathic moment from Godbole, from a spirituality foreign to Brahmin Hinduism and more in line with the "popular cult" variety that Radhakrishnan and other modern social and political reformers attempted to extricate from Hinduism. It's also the sort of Indic folk spirituality which Anthony Copley claims in *A Spiritual Bloomsbury* (2006) really captivated Forster, and that may be a closer expression of the spiritual quality of the Marabar caves- something missed by critics reading mainstream Hinduism in Forster (Copley 2006). Regardless of which sector of Indic esotericism Forster believed was being expressed in Gokul Ashtami or that he consigned to the Marabar caves, what's most interesting is the linking of an impressionist visual mode with the fluidity of Eastern spaces.

Scenes of communal intimacy, as in the Gokul Ashtami festival, certainly correlate with Forster's own politics; he once noted, in elucidating the West's

FIGURE 2.1 Lakshmana Temple 11, Khajuraho India. © Antoine Taveneaux. Image available at http://commons.wikimedia.org/wiki/File:Lakshmana_Temple_11.jpg under a Creative Commons Attribution-ShareAlike 3.0 Unported license.

privileging of the state (political) over friendship, that "personal relations mean everything to me" (Bradshaw 2007: 211). In his travelog, *The Hill of Devi* (1953), Forster infuses the actual Gokul Asthami experience with openness and an almost over-determined aesthetical frame (and which is word for word replicated in the novel), as when his employer the Rajah worships the dancer: "The Rajah and his guests would then forget that this was a dramatic performance, and would worship the actors" (Forster 1924: 303). In Forster's BBC talk from 1929, he is emphatic in his admiration for Hindu art and architecture, and opposed to the sort of characterization of it from the likes of Lord Macauley, who in 1843 described the whole of Indian art as "hideous, and grotesque and ignoble" (Miller 1992: 1). Forster goes on to describe the "world-mountain" of some Hindu "temple group in the middle of India," as well as their exterior wall expressions of "all the complexity of life—people dying, dancing, fighting, loving and creatures who are not human at all, or even earthly" (Lago and Hughes 2008: 431). His further description of the inner "cavity"- or "cell"-like interior of the Khajraho temple complex [Figure 2.1], an arrangement that evokes an intimacy with god that is elusive of the congregationally oriented structures of Christianity, Islam and Buddhism, links Hinduism with an expressiveness of the smallest of sacred spaces to the celestial. A sense of veiled intimacy is also conveyed in the scene Edward Shanks focuses on, wherein we find that the Krishna cult members of Gokul Ashtami were of the nature of whom "some call the real India" and for "whom anything outside their villages passed in a dream" (Forster 1924: 283–284). The fact that Fielding facilitates an Indian's experience of Gokul Asthami speaks to the intimacy with which Forster may have believed it was possible for an Englishman to have in a colonial jungle village, and may also be reflective of a personal intimacy from his extended stay in India—this, despite the novel's ending of defrayed intimacy between Fielding and Aziz: "'Why can't we be friends now? ... No, not yet'" (Forster 1924: 322).

If a greater scope from the minute to the universal is possible, then by inference the minuteness of intimate relations exceeds the capacity for closeness on the part of European relations. This would fit with David Roessel's reading of Forster's "Salute to the Orient" and "Graves," where intimacy and friendship in the East is a stronger bond than nationalism, while the opposite is the case in the West. The novel figures this notion repeatedly, of acclimating a broad scope as a result of intimate relations between the English and the Indian. Confronted with a smear on a global vision of Empire, Forster strives to cleanse it by envisioning another global scope, one stemming from the most minute of gestures. Fielding's two visits to Indian homes result in intimate views—the one of Aziz's wife without veil and the post-trial dinner party's view of the "gestures well-bred Indians make ..., the social equivalent of Yoga" (Forster 1924: 251). Similar images correlating the minute to the universal occur in other sections of the novel, such as with Fielding's vision of the Marabar caves as a hand gesture covering the entire sky.

Fielding lost his usual sane view of human intercourse, and felt that we exist not in ourselves, but in terms of each others' minds—a notion for which logic offers no support and which had attacked him only once before, the evening after the catastrophe, when from the verandah of the club he saw the fists and fingers of the Marabar swell until they included the whole night sky.

(Forster 1924: 250)

In other words, Fielding's vision is of a scope beyond the realm of European structures, as Marabar or Indic spirituality affords both an intimacy beyond European intimacy and a universal relational gesture beyond the gesturing of such European figures as Ferdinand de Lesseps gesturing out from the Suez Canal, which Forster elucidates in the opening image of arguably his most politically anti-colonial of writings, "Salute to the Orient." Within Forster's colonial writings, the symbolic nature of the canal structures of the "Grand Salute" of Venice and the gesturing statue of de Lesseps contrasts with that of the Ganges river, whose sacred waters not only take in the dead but also feed such spaces as absolution tanks in Indian holy sites. The aesthetics of Indian spaces is not of man's ingenuity on nature but of nature's entrance into intimate spaces occupied by men. In reverse fashion, Eastern spaces in *A Passage to India*, and its interconnected quality, comment on the interior spaces of man in the final paragraph conversation between Aziz and Fielding:

"Why can't we be friends now?" said the other, holding him affectionately. "It's what I want. It's what you want." But the horses didn't want it—they swerved apart: the earth didn't want it . . . the temple, the tank, the jail, the palace, the birds, the carrion, the Guest House, that came into view as they emerged from the gap and saw Mau beneath: they didn't want it, they said in their hundred voices "No, not yet," and the sky said "No, not there."

(Forster 1924: 323)

References

Beer, G. (1980), "Negation in *A Passage to India*," *Essays in Criticism*, XXX(2): 151–166.
Bredbeck, G. (1997), "'Queer Superstitions': Forster, Carpenter, and the Illusion of (Sexual) Identity," in R. K. Martin and G. Piggford (eds.), *Queer Forster*, Chicago: University of Chicago Press.
Copley, A. (2006), *A Spiritual Bloomsbury: Hinduism and Homosexuality in the Lives and Writings of Edward Carpenter, E.M. Forster, and Christopher Isherwood*, Lanham, MD: Lexington Books.
Forster, E. M. (1924), *A Passage to India*, London: Harcourt, Brace & World.
Forster, E. M. (1996), *Abinger Harvest and England's Pleasant Land* (ed. E. Heine), London: Andre Deutsch.

Forster, E. M. (2007), *The Cambridge Companion to E. M. Forster* (ed. D. Bradshaw), Cambridge and New York: Cambridge University Press.
Forster, E. M. (2008), *The BBC Talks of E. M. Forster, 1929–1960* (ed. M. Lago and L. K. Hughes), Columbia: University of Missouri Press.
Miller, B. S. (1992), *The Powers of Art: Patronage in Indian Culture*, Delhi: Oxford University Press.
Roessel, D. (1990), "Live Orientals and Dead Greeks: Forster's Response to the Chanak Crisis," *Twentieth Century Literature*, 36: 43–60.
Said, E. (1993) *Culture and Imperialism*. New York: Knopf, Random House.
Shanks, E. (1927), "E. M. Forster," *London Mercury* (July).
Vargas, V. (2013), "Six postures to literary enlightenment: In the yogic realms of Woolf, Lawrence, and Yeats," dissertation, Claremont Graduate University.

3

The Exhibitionary Construction of the "Islamic Interior"

Solmaz Mohammadzadeh Kive

> *A "flying carpet" straight out of the Arabian Nights will soon float over the Louvre's collection of Islamic art, one of the most spectacular in the world . . .*
>
> French Embassy in London (Canetti 2011)

"Islamic art" became the subject of public displays only in the late nineteenth century. Nevertheless, many of the objects, installation techniques and institutional principles were rooted in the nineteenth-century systematic displays of what were considered ethnographically or aesthetically valuable. In these earlier exhibitions, the selection, presentation and arrangement of objects, in tandem with props and settings, usually evoked an image of a mysterious culture filled with luxury and sensual delight, yet frozen in the past.[1] Beginning with the first international exhibition in London in 1851, the reviews of these exhibitions endlessly alluded to the *Arabian Nights*. John Tallis's multi-volume review of the *Great Exhibition*, for example, described an apartment "in the style of an Indian palace" in which, he claimed, "was realised all that the *Arabian Nights*, and other romances have detailed with respect to their gorgeous and costly luxury" (1852: 33).[2]

A Thousand and One Nights, better known as the "Arabian Nights," is a set of tales within a frame story, which was first translated from Arabic into French by the famous Orientalist Antoine Galland (1646–1715) in 1704, and soon after was translated into other European languages and spread throughout the "West." The book, according to Galland, represented "costumes and manners of the Orientals" (in Warner 2011: 163).[3] Although this cultural image was also reproduced by many other media, the popularity of the *Nights* made it a common trope for an exotic "Orient," which was at the same time irrational and stunted and yet filled with luxury and sensuality.[4]

For the nineteenth-century exhibitions of Islamic art, which were close to the entertainment industry, the evocation of the mystery and luxury found in the *Arabian Nights* was often regarded as one of the main attractions. According to scholar and art dealer Meyer-Riefstahl (1880–1936), what the public expected from the exhibition of "something 'truly Oriental'" was "a mixture of waterpipe smoking, sensuous perfumes, belly dancing, jangling jewellery of gold-coins, half disguising veils, thick draperies, swelling female forms and carpets, which in their folds show a forgotten unreadable manuscript with unspeakable obscene miniatures" (in Kroger 2010: ff 91–92).

In the early twentieth century, however, the ethnographic connotations of the earlier exhibitions were criticized in the name of the individual value of objects, which were now elevated to the status of *art*. In 1910, one of the earliest exhibitions of so-called "Islamic art," and perhaps the most influential one, the Munich exhibition of *Meisterwerke Muhammedanischer Kunst* [*Masterpieces of Mohammadan Art*], proudly renounced the imagery of the bazaar[5] and the *Arabian Nights*. For its organizer, Friedrich Sarre (1865–1945), the aesthetic value of Islamic art would be regained through the exhibition of objects as individual works of art within a neutral gallery space (Troelenberg 2010: 8). The Munich exhibition had a lasting influence in that following exhibitions of Islamic art almost unanimously abandoned explicitly ethnographic displays. Nevertheless, many of the effects of the earlier exhibitions remained pervasive and evoked the same imagery. For example, the 1931 *International Exhibition of Persian Art* in London, which did not use ethnographic displays, was nevertheless perceived as "a re-creation from 'The Arabian Nights'" (in Wood 2000: 116).

As the popularity of the *Arabian Nights* has diminished since the mid-twentieth century, so has its dominance in the reviews of Islamic art exhibitions. In fact, the recent gallery of Islamic art in the Louvre is one of the rare instances of a contemporary practice that has revived the clichéd allusion to the *Arabian Nights*. However, the stereotypical image of a life of mystery and heady pleasure, to which it once served as a shorthand, is still occasionally evoked through the exhibitions of Islamic art. For instance, the guide to an exhibition, *Islamic Art in the Metropolitan Museum*, reads: "What should become clear to even the casual observer is that the people for whom this art was produced sought to surround themselves by beauty" (Komaroff 1992: 2).

In early exhibitions of Islamic art, I suggest, the popular trope of the *Arabian Nights* served a dual function: first, as a fairy tale, it suited the dominant perception of the museum as another world to which the visitor traveled; second, as a depository of harem and bazaar imagery, it specified the world in which these objects were created and consumed. The latter, in turn, was grounded in the essentialist understanding of a homogenous timeless culture called the "Orient," or the "Muslim world." These three elements of the popular culture, I would argue, were supported by early twentieth-century curators and historians of Islamic art. When the museum practice of historicizing the gallery space was coupled with the themes of homogeneity and superficial beauty grafted onto the notion of "Islamic art," the result was an immersive atmosphere, which easily lent itself to the cultural image that had been created elsewhere.

This chapter explores some spatial and visual techniques through which the cultural images once epitomized in the *Arabian Nights* are still being recreated in many temporary and permanent exhibitions of Islamic art. I suggest tracing these techniques in the interstice of the scholarship on Islamic art and museum practices of the late nineteenth and early twentieth centuries. I begin with a brief review of the nature of the aesthetic value ascribed to Islamic art to underline two themes of "superficial beauty" and "unity." This is followed by a discussion of three modes of employing gallery space to communicate historical context: providing intellectual direction; evoking images of an original setting; and creating a spatial effect. Then, discussing the traces of these late nineteenth- and early twentieth-century practices, I will hint at their adaptations in some contemporary examples. I argue that while the two first sets of techniques mainly focused on reproducing the unity of Islamic art and ascribing it to a Muslim world, the third led to an *Arabian Nights* effect, which was, and still is, created through an immersive sensualized gallery interior. I conclude by suggesting a reconsideration of the idea of museum display as a means of understanding other cultures.

The concept of "Islamic art"

A scholarly counterpart of the idea of luxury and headless pleasures dominant in the *Arabian Nights* imagery, I suggest, can be traced back to the late nineteenth- and early twentieth-century art historian's perception of Islamic art as a superficial beauty devoid of a meaning. In fact, the notion of "Islamic art," as the artistic production of *one* homogenous Muslim civilization was a modern, Western construct. The objects had been collected in the West for centuries. However, they had not been conceptualized as "Islamic" or as "art," nor had they been placed on public display. They first appeared publically in the mid-nineteenth-century international exhibitions and under national or ethnical banners, such as "Indian," "Turkish" and "Arab" arts. Soon after, the objects of aesthetic value were collected by museums of applied arts, which in the early twentieth century shaped the departments of "Islamic art" of numerous European museums.

One of the first museums to systematically acquire and exhibit Islamic objects was the South Kensington Museum (now the Victoria and Albert Museum).[6] Founded after the successful *Great Exhibition* of 1851, its mission was to improve the public taste and educate craftsmen. When the museum consulted William Morris (1834–1896) on the acquisition of an Ardabil carpet, he declared that: "it would be a crime to let it go" (in Stanley 2006: 13). This enthusiasm was common among many theorists of ornament and decoration, including some highly influential figures of the time, namely John Ruskin (1819–1900) and Owen Jones (1809–1874). In *The Grammar of Ornament*, Jones admired "the presence of so much unity of design, so much skill and judgment in all the works … of all the other Muhammedan contributing countries," which he contrasted with the West's modern products that confessed "general disorder everywhere apparent in the application of Art to manufactures" (1910 [1856]: 77).

Nevertheless, this enthusiasm for ornament and decoration in objects of utility was informed by a romantic interest in the past. Elsewhere, Jones emphasized that "the many beautiful works displayed in the Exhibition of 1851 showed that the unvarying principles which they have held for a thousand years are still powerful amongst them" (1854: 15). To this notion of a still, a-historical culture, Ruskin added the idea of an innocent "intuition." For example, while praising Indians' "love of subtle design," he claimed their ornament was not derived from an understanding of nature. Rather, "[t]he fancy and delicacy of the eye in interweaving lines and arranging colours … seems to be somehow an inheritance of ignorance and cruelty, belonging to men as spots to the tiger [sic.]" (in Howard 1999: 45).

Since Islamic artifacts entered the museum for their aesthetic value, early scholarship tended to focus on form and style at the expense of intellectual meaning and cultural relevance. Although in the early twentieth century, Islamic objects were elevated to the status of *art*, the former association with intuition and ignorance did not totally vanish. In 1965, the Islamic art historian Basil William Robinson (1912–2005) claimed that "the beauties of Persian painting are all on the surface." Thus, he suggested approaching them with a "child-like naïveté," since "the simpler we approach, the quicker and truer will be our appreciation" (in Wood 2000: 126).

The association with surface beauty was somewhat inherent in the notion of "Islamic art." On the one hand, by becoming *art*, Islamic objects were subjected to the principles formed within the paradigm of Western art. As Avinoam Shalem remarks, when mimesis, or faithful reproduction of nature, which had been known as "the ethos of Western visual culture," was applied to non-representative forms of Islamic art, the latter was "condemned by this measure to be either iconoclastic or ornamental" (2012: 15).

On the other hand, in the Western conceptualization of *Islamic* art in association with religion, "Islam" becomes an art category. However, many of the objects grouped under this class do not have a religious association. Nevertheless, despite the secular nature of many of these objects, religious belief is commonly held as the essence of Islamic art, rather than its political/cultural context (Shalem 2012: 6).[7] In a typical manner, the Metropolitan Museum of Art describes "the Nature of Islamic Art." To justify the use of the term "Islamic art" in reference to the works that were not "created specifically in the service of the Muslim faith," it underlines the omnipresence of "the Muslim faith." It claims: "[a]s it is not only a religion but a way of life, Islam fostered the development of a distinctive culture with its own unique artistic language that is reflected in art and architecture throughout the Muslim world" (2001). This essentialist approach not only supports the idea of a homogenous "Muslim world," but also removes the meaning and cultural relevance of objects. As Wendy Shaw argues, the commonality among Islamic arts, most of which are not religious objects, could not be explained by the term "Islamic." Thus the claimed *unity* is accounted for in terms of solely formal aspects (2012: 3–10).

In the early twentieth century, when the scholarly view of Islamic art was coupled with the practice of historicizing gallery space, some spatial design techniques were developed which were not aimed at (re)creating a space from the *Arabian Nights*. However, as they were founded on the above-mentioned perception of Islamic art, they resulted in similar effects. Criticizing the 1975 permanent installation of Islamic art in the Metropolitan Museum of Art, Amy Goldin wrote: "Almost everything about the spacious Islamic galleries proclaims this art as a feast, a come-as-you-are party that requires no special effort" (2011 [1976]: 184). In the last three decades, many historians of Islamic art have problematized an essentialist, generalizing approach, which has led to the idea of *superficial beauty*.[8] However, the over-emphasis on aesthetic value has not been removed from exhibitions. At the same time, as will be discussed below, the idea of an *"Islamic" unity* is occasionally supported by exhibition techniques, which in collaboration with other strategies intensify the fairy-like, *Arabian Nights*-inspired, beauty once ascribed to Islamic art.

Historicizing the gallery interior

Inasmuch as the evocation of the *Arabian Nights* imagery was in debt to the perception of the museum as another world, the spatial techniques of constructing this world were rooted in the museum practice of historicizing gallery space itself. Since the first purpose-built museums, architecture had served the idea of traveling into another time and place.[9] By the mid-nineteenth century, however, the systematic classification of objects into historical and regional collections required specification of galleries. At the same time, since it was interpreted as the frame within which the objects would gain meaning, the design of the gallery's space became a means of facilitating the comprehension of exhibitions. Accordingly, the gallery interiors were considered as the contexts of communicating the specificity of different regions or historical periods.

As Christopher Whitehead notes, in mid-nineteenth-century Britain, two distinctive sets of techniques of historicizing the gallery interior were under debate (2005: 38–58). The first approach considered variations in revivalist styles as a means of conveying the difference of historical contexts. Following the same logic as the historiographical ordering of the works of art, the stylistic decoration of the gallery's interior was intended to help visitors locate the artworks in their historical and geographical context. Even though this romanticized reconstruction borrowed many techniques of scenic decoration from the early nineteenth-century leisure spaces (such as the circus and the theater) and the domestic tradition of art display, the main intent was pedagogical, namely providing visitors with intellectual orientation. Thus, archaeological or stylistic precision was subordinated to the overall evocation of a time and region (Whitehead 2005: 40–41).

The second approach was developed around the same time. It was introduced to Britain by the director of the Royal Museum in Berlin, Gustav Friedrich Waagen (1794–1868) (Klonk 36–37). Underlining the intimate connection of art objects with their original contexts, this trend employed the gallery space as a substitute for those origins (Whitehead 2005: 38–39).[10] Waagen argued that objects were "especially regulated and conditioned by architecture, for which they are calculated, and which serves to explain them." From this, he concluded that museums had to "realise in some degree the impression produced by a temple, a church, a palace, or a cabinet, for which those works were originally intended" (in Whitehead 2005: 39). The resulting gallery space did not simply *refer* to the original context; rather the ideal was, in Waagen's words, "to cause the spectator ... to forget that the [objects] no longer occupy their original places" (in Whitehead: 52). Unlike the revivalists' intent at providing *intellectual* directions, here the reproduction of the origin would ideally invite visitors to *experience* an imaginary travel to another time and place. The indulgence in this experience could be so strong that in 1853, during a parliamentary debate in London, the suggestion to imitate the space of a Catholic church for Italian paintings was accompanied by the reassurance that this identification would not affect the believers: "We are not at all afraid of a 'conversion' to the superstition, by the reconversion of the picture to its proper poetry" (in Whitehead 2005: 40).

In the late nineteenth century, Wilhelm von Bode (1845–1929)—the future Director-General of the Royal Museums in Berlin—introduced an alternative way of producing historical context, which shared many features with the above-mentioned approaches in Britain. Echoing the earlier discussions in London, he suggested that "in all material aspects, such as lighting and architecture, [the gallery interior] should resemble ... the apartment for which it was originally intended." To this, he added that "the character of the several epochs [should be] realised in furnishing and decorating these rooms" (Bode 1891: 512). However, though his emphasis on context resembled the two above-mentioned approaches, Bode's method used a different set of techniques and required another mode of experience. He rejected stylistic decorations. Instead, historical effect was created through the integration of paintings and sculptures with objects of applied art in the same gallery (Baker 1996: 144). Although since the mid-nineteenth century the gallery interior was expected to condition the perception of objects, now objects were used as measures of creating a spatial "effect." On the other hand, inspired by the domestic interiors, he used colors and decoration not to create stylistically accurate settings, as the revivalists did, but to make an emotional impact (Klonk 2009: 55–60).

The rejection of decoration and the use of light colors may resemble the so-called "white-cube" of the modern art museum, which was introduced in the 1920s and 1930s.[11] However, Bode's method emphasized the overall effect over the individuality of artworks, which was the main governing principle of the latter. I suggest, the "white-wall" trend of Islamic art exhibition must be understood in terms of the contextual effect (or atmosphere) introduced by Bode.

The above-mentioned three sets of interior design techniques were, and still are, employed in many temporary and permanent exhibitions in order to produce a context specific to Islamic art. In what follows, I argue that while some modifications of the first two approaches function as the historical reference to support the idea of an *Islamic* space produced by the museum institution, various modifications of Bode's techniques create immersive atmospheres which in collaboration with the former may result in the *Arabian Nights* effect.

The *Islamic* gallery

Many exhibitions of Islamic art have borrowed from the above-mentioned exhibition design practices not only the idea but also the spatial techniques of communicating historical contexts through the gallery's interior. Although in contemporary practice of exhibiting Islamic art there is no one dominant approach, there are nevertheless some spatial techniques that many of these exhibtions have inherited from the late nineteenth- and early twentieth-century practices.

Firstly, the adaptation of the revivalist approach to the exhibition of Islamic art can be found in the use of the so-called "Islamic arch"—an abstracted pointed or horseshoe arch. When used in recent practices in Muslim countries, abstract arches have been loaded with various layers of associations. Usually related to the changing interpretations of national identities, different arches have been employed in a variety of building types. In the West, however, the use of the elements of the so-called "Islamic architecture," such as arches and domes, is almost exclusively limited to the religious buildings.[12] Thus when used in a museum exhibition, the arch is little more than a visual translation of the homogenizing term "Islamic." It supports the same underlying assumption of a *religious* commonality that unites the variety of objects. Unlike revivalist decoration, the Islamic arch does not provide the content of a claimed unity, which is left to be filled by visitors' pre-existing images (perhaps formed by Orientalist paintings, the

Arabian Nights or more recently the literature on terrorism). On the other hand, when interpreted against the broader museum context in which historicized decorations indicate the progressive development of styles, the formal consistency of the arch in the galleries of Islamic art suggests a timeless, a-historical essence to this art.[13]

The second approach, the imitation of the original setting of objects, has been embraced by many curators of Islamic art, perhaps with little criticism. One of the most common instances of this approach can be found in the installations of *mihrabs*—or praying niches—which are often carved into gallery walls. To provide a correct optical perception of building fragments, capitals are placed above the eye level and dado panels bellow it. This approach can be found in the earlier exhibitions, such as the 1932 installation of the Pergamon Museum in Berlin, as well as many recent ones, such as the renovations of the Islamic galleries in the Metropolitan Museum. In the latter, fourteenth-century columns have been integrated into the "Moroccan Court" built by contemporary artists. As a result, in addition to presenting their original function, these columns also mimic that function.

This interest in reconstruction of the original setting also can be found in many instances of laying carpets on the ground. In the Munich exhibition of 1910, the floor of a large peristyle hall was covered by carpets to resemble praying halls of mosques [Figure 3.1] (Troelenberg 2012: 16). The same approach has been consistently adopted, almost whenever the space allows. In the recent renovation of the Victoria and Albert Museum's "Jameel Gallery," the large Ardabil Carpet is set on the floor at the center of the room, for "it was designed to be used and appreciated at ground level." This interest in facilitating optical perception even resulted in an attempt to place the carpet "beneath a glazed floor" (Salway 2006: 84).

In fact, the majority of Islamic objects, including the carpet, indicate use value. Thus, while imitation of *visual* context might be sufficient for evoking the original setting of medieval religious paintings and sculptures, when the same idea is applied to the objects of Islamic art, the result is ethnographic display. Questioning the suitability of museums for Islamic art, a prominent historian of Islamic art, Oleg Grabar (1929–2011), suggested, "they are in fact to be seen as ethnographic documents, closely tied to life, even a reconstructed life" (2005 [1976]: 16). Whether called "ethnographic" or not, the imitation of an allegedly original context constructs the external reality that it claims to imitate.[14]

Although functioning at different levels, the aforementioned spatial techniques—intellectual referencing and imitating the original setting—support each other. Visual icons, such as arches, suggest unity of Islamic art and connect it to a generalized, stereotypical *Islamic mind*. When visitors are invited to imagine an "original" setting, the alleged specificity of this origin furnishes that stereotype with a reality effect, ascribing these objects to the external "Muslim world." These two sets of techniques by themselves do not produce an *Arabian Nights* effect. However, they connect the sensual

FIGURE 3.1 Room 39, Exhibition of Masterpieces of Muhammedan Art, Munich, 1910. After Sarre and Martin, *Die Ausstellung von Meisterwerken*, published by Bruckmann 1912, vol. 1.

experience created by the third to a homogenous Muslim world. The latter is perhaps the most effective component of this collaboration. In many exhibitions of Islamic art, as will be discussed below, techniques of object installation are coupled with gallery design to create what have been called the "Islamic effect," "atmosphere" or "ambience." The result, I will argue, has been oftentimes an immersive atmosphere, which, in the words of a *New York Times* commentator, "alternately lulls and excites the senses" (in Wood 2000: 116).

The immersive atmosphere

The Munich exhibition in 1910 is unanimously regarded as a turning point in the display of Islamic art in museums. Informed by the contemporary approaches to art gallery space in Berlin and Vienna, it displayed objects in allegedly neutral settings. Soon after, this so-called "white-wall" trend became the dominant mode of exhibiting Islamic art until the late twentieth century, and by some accounts up to the present day.[15] Following the common art museum practice, objects have been relatively isolated from each other and placed against neutral backgrounds. However, the principle of singularity of the artwork, which governed the "white-cube" of the modern art gallery, does not govern the "white-wall" of Islamic art. Rather, objects are often reintegrated within an atmospheric interior, which turns the visual distance into a tactile intimacy. In other words, even though the distance among objects in the contemporary exhibitions of Islamic art has increased, the distance between the observer and the work, fundamental for the experience of the individual work that Walter Benjamin (1892–1940), and many after him, have discussed under the notion of "aura," is often absent. Not only has the use value attached to many Islamic objects maintained a trace of an everyday experience, but also, I would argue, many Islamic art exhibitions tend to intensify the atmospheric quality of space at the expense of the singularity of objects.

The immersive atmosphere of Oriental carpet exhibitions has been often remarked on. Shared with harems, mosques and bazaars, the carpet was a common design feature in Orientalist paintings. Thanks to its richness of color, size, material and historical associations, the carpet has served many collectors, dealers, artists and designers in their attempt to create an "Oriental interior." However, I argue that the effect created in the museum is also the result of its method of installation.

As David Roxburgh argues, the early exhibitions of Islamic art borrowed from private collections the techniques of creating an authentic Oriental effect through "a seemingly random array." In private collections, the value of the individual object would be gained from the whole to which it belonged (2000: 11–20). In the corresponding mode of exhibition, the totality of the collection was gained by an inclusive space created through the extensive use of carpets and textiles throughout the space. In Albert Goupil's "Oriental room" in 1888 [Figure 3.2], described as "some place from *The Thousand and One Nights*" (in Roxburgh 2000: 13), carpets created a homogeneous rich background against which many diverse objects were unified. A similar technique was repeated in many public exhibitions, as can be seen in F. R. Martin's collection in the *General Art and Industry Exhibition* in Stockholm in 1897 [Figure 3.3].

This practice of carpet installation was adopted by the twentieth-century museums. When the earlier practice of covering all wall surfaces with paintings had long fallen out of favor, carpets were still hung close to each other and occasionally remained the background to other objects. The 1904 installation of Islamic art in the Kaiser-Friedrich-Museum, Berlin, was arranged under Bode and Sarre. As a photograph from the installation reveals [Figure 3.4], the lower parts of many carpets were covered by other objects, perhaps partially as the result of space limitations. The background quality of carpets was reinforced by the emphasis on upper alignment, which gave it a linear silhouette in harmony with the cornice to emphasize the carpets' role as wall. In 1932, when the Islamic art collection was moved to the Pergamon Museum and extended from three rooms into seventeen galleries, some carpets on the wall were still covered behind showcases to the emphasis of their background value. The wall-like quality given to the carpet reached its climax in the Museum of Asiatic Art in Dahlem, which housed

FIGURE 3.2 "Oriental Room" at the home of Albert Goupil, Paris, before 1888. *Catalogue des objets d'art de l'Orient et de l'Occident, tableaux, dessins composant la collection de feu M. Albert Goupil, 1888.*

FIGURE 3.3 Martin's Collection, General Art and Industry Exhibition, Stockholm, 1897. After F. R. Martin, *Sammlungen aus dem Orient in der Allgemeinen Kunst- und Industrie* Ausstellung, 1897.

the Islamic art collection of Western Berlin after the Second World War. Here, the division within the single-space gallery of Islamic art was made by carpets, which, unlike the rest of the exhibition, did not follow a chronological order (Kroger 2012: 179–181).[16]

The practice of covering the wall with carpets might be reminiscent of the nineteenth-century art galleries where walls were virtually draped by paintings. However, unlike the latter, which, inviting the eye to penetrate into the scene, creates a perceptual depth that could counteract the absence of three-dimensional space, the surface produced by the expansive and flat pattern of carpets resists any sense of depth.[17] In addition, the scanning suggested by this surface-effect reinforces intimacy and removes distance. As a result, the cubic space of the exhibition collapses into planes, creating an immersive space uncommon in the exhibitions of Western art. At the same time, the tactile pleasure produced by the eye's move over the surface is coupled with the carpet's material as well as its domestic association to sensualize the gallery's space. This quality is occasionally referred to in the reviews of the exhibitions of Islamic art. Discussing the 1932 installation in the Pergamon Museum, Oskar Bie concluded: "Islamic art touches like a fairytale from the *Arabian Nights*" (in Kroger 2010: 106, ff 26).

The immersive space is not exclusively produced by carpets. Resembling Bode's schema, often the composition of objects in tandem with lighting

FIGURE 3.4 Room 9, the Kaiser-Friedrich-Museum, 1909–1910. Credit: bpk, Berlin / Zentralarchiv der Staatlichen Museen zu Berlin / Art Resource, NY.

produce a unifying effect, which has been intensified since the postmodern return of color to the gallery space (Klonk 2009: 16–17). The extreme sensuality of the space in the Museum of Islamic Art in Doha,[18] has been created by color, light, material and other architectural measures, none of which are specific to Islamic art or architecture.[19] This space, in the words of its interior designer, Jean-Michel Wilmotte, is "a theatrical atmosphere in the best sense of the term—an atmosphere that truly allows the objects to be seen and appreciated" (in Jodidio 2008: 201). The theatricality of this impressive work of interior design is in part produced by the dark space, which has been long used in movie houses and theaters in order to collapse the space between the viewer and the stage to let him or her indulge in the staged imaginary world.

It is perhaps not a mere coincidence that at the same time that objects are exhibited in greater isolation, gallery interiors with rich colors and dark spaces compensate for the lost unity. The immersive spaces are not simply by-products of an attempt at producing appealing exhibitions. Rather, the reintegration of objects into one totality is indispensable to the unity imposed by the notion of Islamic art in which the commonality among objects is not accounted for in terms of artistic features but is based on an alleged cultural homogeneity.

Conclusion

As the guidebook of the Munich exhibition of 1910 explained, to appreciate the artistic value of Islamic objects, the exhibition "avoid[ed] having the rooms which would contain the Islamic artworks somehow arouse the impression that they were buildings, halls, chambers of the Orient." However, for the audience used to historicized gallery space, "they also had to provide a spatial framing, which [would] not appear alien to the exhibits, or even contradictory in stylistic and colouristic terms" (in Troelenberg 2012: 21). In other words, while historical reference could evoke the existing imagery of the *Arabian Nights*, the absence of any historical reference would result in the same effect by suggesting a timeless art which best suits the fairy-like space. For over a century, the curators of Islamic art have had to face this conundrum, the roots of which, I posit, must be found in the institutional principles of the museum.

On the occasion of the opening of the Louvre's gallery of Islamic art, its biggest single donor, Prince Waleed Bin Talal of Saudi Arabia, emphasized the significance of Islamic art to "tell the West about real Muslims, about real Islam, and how peaceful our religion is" (in Iqbal 2012). Many curators of Islamic art in Western museums have expressed a similar urge to emphasize its beauty. Regarded as the positive side of Islamic civilization, Islamic art has become a means to counteract the existing negative image of Muslims (McWilliams 2012: 153). However, this over-emphasis on aesthetic value, particularly when the specificity of historical context is absent, has resulted in an image of a culture of luxury and heady pleasure. On the other hand, these too positive messages, focused on the *past* of the so-called "Muslim world," which is in sharp contrast with the negative images circulated in the present, could give the exhibitions of Islamic art an even more *Arabian Nights* quality.

These good intentions are premised upon the idea that exhibiting the art of other people can and must lead to understanding them. While for Western art, contextualization is a means of understanding the *artwork*, the arts of the "others" (most of which initially entered the museum as ethnographic objects) have remained a means of understanding their *cultures*. Although the contemporary exhibitions of Islamic art are in intention far different from Orientalist ideology, the self-appointed, selective exhibition of the objects of the "other" as means of understanding them re-produces and reaffirms an existing image of the Orient in a manner not dissimilar to the discursive media once noted by Edward Said (2003 [1978]: 20–22).

Some critics associate the *Arabian Nights* effect to the absence of context and over-emphasis on beauty. According to Grabar,

> Adjectives such as "exquisite" and "splendour," frequently used to describe objects of Islamic art displayed in museums, suggest associations with a mythical East more than they associate works with any culturally intrinsic meaning. When nothing else can be said about it, Islamic art

is—even today—supposed to dazzle its viewer into pleasure, mimicking the imagined pleasures of the harem, the bazaar, or other adventures in *A Thousand and One Nights*.

(2005: 24)

Based on similar criticisms, a growing trend in the exhibition of Islamic art underlines the significance of historical context as the main missing component, the absence of which leads to the *Arabian Nights* effect. Accordingly, a few exhibitions have refused the still dominant trend of creating aestheticized gallery space.[20] However, some supporting components of that effect, particularly the very assumption of an underlying "unity" are inevitably reinforced by the exhibition of "Islamic art" as one collection. Perhaps as long as the notion of "Islamic art" maintains the idea of unity and the museum discourse encourages reading objects as "traces, representations, reflections, or surrogates" (Preziosi 1998: 509), the evocation of the *Arabian Nights* can never be totally removed or too distant.

Notes

1 In the early international exhibitions, the romantic fantasy of an exotic "Orient" was usually coupled with the imagery of the contemporary retarded, static Muslim culture(s) in sharp contrast to the progressive West. Ethnographic displays, which were particularly popular in the entertainment arena, are the prime example of this dual relation (Çelik 1992).

2 The rather gross generalization upon which the stories that took place in eighth-century Baghdad could be a point of reference for the contemporary India was the underlying principle of many exhibitions of Islamic art and by extension the notion of "Islamic art" itself.

3 In his introduction to the French translation of the *Arabian Nights*, Galland claimed that "All the Orientals, Persians, Tatars and Indians, can be distinguished here and appear just as they are, . . . And so, without having suffered the weariness of going to look for these peoples in their country, the reader will have the pleasure here of seeing them act and hearing them speak" (in Warner 2011: 163).

4 See Edwards (2000).

5 The trope of the "bazaar" also referred to commodification of art, which was intensified through the mode of exhibition that clustered objects in groups. In the 1920s, Walter Benjamin theorized a similar idea. According to him, "There are relations between department store and museum, and here the bazaar provides a link. The amassing of artworks in the museum brings them into communication with commodities, which—where they offer themselves en masse to the passerby—awake in him the notion that some part of this should fall to him as well" (2002 [1927]: 415).

6 The interest of the South Kensington Museum in Islamic art was based on its pedagogical significance for improving the public taste and educating

craftsmen. Accordingly, although it was one of the first museums to exhibit objects of Islamic art, in the absence of the notion of "Islamic art," objects were spread throughout the museum in material-based exhibitions. It was only in 1950 that a gallery was allocated specifically to "Islamic art" (Stanley 2006: 21).

7   As Blair and Bloom put in one of the earliest criticisms to the notion of "Islamic art," it is "a convenient misnomer for everything left over from everywhere else. It is most easily defined by what it is not: neither a region, nor a period, nor a school, nor a movement, nor a dynasty" (2000:153). Discussing many problems of this unity, the authors conclude, "'Islamic art' is a poor name for an ill-defined subject" (174).

8   For a history of the self-criticism of Islamic art historians, see Necipoğlu (2012).

9   See Ameri (2007).

10 Whitehead considers this method as a "passive" one. To him, the "adaptation of the interior to the correct viewing of the artwork" is facilitating the perception of objects rather than influencing it (38–39). However, I would argue, when seen in the context of art-ethnographic distinction which is usually applied to non-Western and medieval art, what Whitehead calls "passive" very directly suggests an ethnographical nature for the object. This can be well observed in Waagen's discussion, which connects objects to the "national existence, religion, manners, geographical characteristics of country, climate, &c." (in Whitehead 2005: 39).

11 See O'Doherty (1986) and Klonk (2009: 135–212).

12 For a discussion on the use of the dome in the West, see Avcioglu (2007). In his review of the "Jameel Gallery" of Islamic art in the Victoria and Albert Museum, Richard Tillinghast suggests: "The ideal ceiling for a room full of Islamic art would be a dome, given the importance of domes in mosque architecture . . ." (2007: 293). He does not explain the relevance of the mosque to objects with little ecclesiastical function.

13 Some of the recent exhibitions have challenged this approach. For instance, the Metropolitan Museum's exhibition of "Arts of the Arab Lands, Turkey, Iran, Central Asia and Later South Asia," as its name indicates, offers a variety of arches (both constructed and reconstructed) throughout its galleries of Islamic art.

14 For the production of "Orient" through ethnographic displays, see Timothy Mitchell (1992).

15 See Roxburgh (2010) and Weber (2012).

16 Treating carpets as walls may resemble the architectural theorist Gottfried Semper's (1803–1879) idea that the origin of the wall was found in textiles. For Semper, however, the carpet was a horizontal element on the floor. In *Style in the Technical and Tectonic Arts* (2004 [1860–1863]), he distinguishes tapestry and drapery from "floor dressing." According to him, the most general stylistic distinction must be taken from the fact that "the former are horizontal planes the latter are vertical" (130). As he further explains, floor carpets "do not have 'up and down' treatment found in wall dressing . . . but rather—following quite contrary principles—an 'allover' treatment: a concentric or radial arrangement or a mixture of the two" (131).

17 A classical discussion of the relation between the pictorial painting and the gallery space can be found in O'Doherty's *Inside the White Cube* (1986).
18 Even though the museum of Islamic Art in Doha is located in a Muslim country, it is closer in principle to the exhibition of Islamic art in Western museums. Most significantly, while museums in Muslim countries such as Turkey, Egypt and Iran frame Islamic objects as part of their narratives of national histories, the museum in Doha recreates a "Muslim world."
19 The interior design of the galleries of Islamic art has employed almost no common technique for creating an *Islamic* context. However, in an apparent contradiction, the building that houses these galleries is designed in respect to "the essence of Islamic architecture," as its prominent architect, I. M. Pei, explains (in Jodidio 2008: 44). One may argue that the immersive interior space provides a context to the generalized notion of Islam suggested by the building and the institution itself.
20 For the difference between the appealing design of the "white-wall" trend and "contextualization," see Stefan Weber (2012).

Acknowledgements

I wish to thank Amir Ameri, John Potvin and Hans Morgenthaler for their helpful comments on this chapter.

References

Ameri, A. (2007), "On the Artifice of Art," *Form: The Journal of Architecture, Design, and Material Culture*, 7: 10–27.
Avcioglu, N. (2007), "Identity-as-Form: The Mosque in the West," *Cultural Analysis*, 6: 91–109.
Baker, M. (1996), "Bode and Museum Display: The Arrangement of the Kaiser-Friedrich-Museum and the South Kensington Response," *Jahrbuch der Berliner Museen*, 38: 143–153.
Benjamin, W. (2002), *The Arcades Project*. Cambridge, MA: Harvard University Press.
Blair, S. S. and J. M. Bloom (2003), "The Mirage of Islamic Art: Reflections on the Study of an Unwieldy Field," *The Art Bulletin*, 85: 152–184.
Bode, W. (1891), "The Berlin Renaissance Museum," *The Fortnightly Review*, 56: 506–515.
Canetti, C. (2011), *A "Flying Carpet" for Islamic art at the Louvre* [Online]. London: Embassy of France in London. Available: http://www.ambafrance-uk.org/Culture-A-Flying-Carpet-for [Accessed 13 July 2014].
Çelik, Z. (1992), *Displaying the Orient: Architecture of Islam at Nineteenth-Century World's Fairs*, Berkeley: University of California Press.
Department of Islamic Art (2001), "The Nature of Islamic Art" [Online]. New York: The Metropolitan Museum of Art. http://www.metmuseum.org/toah/hd/orna/hd_orna.htm [Accessed May 5, 2014].

Edwards, H. (2000), *Noble Dreams, Wicked Pleasures: Orientalism in America, 1870–1930*, Princeton, NJ: Princeton University Press, in association with the Sterling and Francine Clark Art Institute.

Goldin, A. (2011), "Islamic Art: The Met's Generous Embrace," in R. Kushner (ed.), *Amy Goldin: Art in a Hairshirt: Art Criticism, 1964–1978*, Stockbridge, MA: Hard Press Editions, 184–196.

Grabar, O. (2005), "An Art of the Object," in *Constructing the Study of Islamic Art*, Aldershot, Hampshire: Ashgate, 13–29.

Howard, D. (1999), "Ruskin and the East," *Architectural Heritage*, 10: 37–53.

Iqbal, R. (2012), "Louvre opens Islamic art wing amid cartoon row," *BBC News*, (September 21), http://www.bbc.com/news/entertainment-arts-19672951 [Accessed April 18, 2015].

Jodidio, P. L. L. (2008), *Museum of Islamic Art: Doha, Qatar*, Munich and London: Prestel.

Jones, O. (1854), *The Alhambra Court in the Crystal Palace*, London: Crystal Palace Library.

Jones, O. (1910), *The Grammar of Ornament,* London: Bernard Quartich.

Klonk, C. (2009), *Spaces of Experience: Art Gallery Interiors from 1800 to 2000*, New Haven: Yale University Press.

Komaroff, L. (1992), *Islamic Art in the Metropolitan Museum of Art: The Historical Context,* New York: The Metropolitan Museum.

Kroger, J. (2010), "The 1910 Exhibition 'Meisterwerke muhammedanischer Kunst'," in A. Shalem and A. Lermer (eds.), *After One Hundred Years*, Leiden: Brill, 173–82.

Kroger, J. (2012), "Early Islamic Art History in Germany, and Concepts of Objects and Exhibiton," in B. Junod, G. Khalil and S. Weber (eds.), *Islamic Art and the Museum*, London: Saqi.

Mackenzie, J. M. (1995), *Orientalism: History, Theory, and the Arts,* New York: Manchester University Press.

McWilliams, M. (2012), "Subthemes and Overpaint: Exhibiting Islamic Art in American Art Museums," in B. Junod, G. Khalil and S. Weber (eds.), *Islamic Art and the Museum*, London: Saqi: 151–172.

Mitchell, T. (1992), "Orientalism and the Exhibitionary Order," in N. B. Dirks (ed.), *Colonialism and Culture*, Ann Arbor: University of Michigan Press, 289–317.

Necipoğlu, G. (2012), "The Concept of Islamic Art: Inherited Discourses and New Approaches," *Journal of Art Historiography*, 6: 1–26.

O'Doherty, B. (1986), *Inside the White Cube: The Ideology of the Gallery Space*, Santa Monica, CA: Lapis Press.

Preziosi, D. (1998), "The Art of Art History," in D. Preziosi (ed.), *The Art of Art History: A Critical Anthology*, Oxford and New York: Oxford University Press, 507–525.

Roxburgh, D. J. (2000), "Au Bonheur des Amateurs: Collecting and Exhibiting Islamic Art, ca. 1880–1910," *Ars Orientalis*, 30: 9–38.

Roxburgh, D. J. (2010), "After Munich: Reflections on Recent Exhibitions," in A. Shalem and A. Lermer (eds.), *After One Hundred Years: The 1910 Exhibition "Meisterwerke Muhammedanischer Kunst Reconsidered,"* Leiden and Boston: Brill: 359–386.

Salway, O. (2006), "The Design of the Jameel Gallery," in R. Crill and T. Stanley (eds.), *The Making of the Jameel Gallery of Islamic Art*, London and New York: V&A Publications: 76–101.

Semper, G. (2004), *Style in the Technical and Tectonic Arts, or, Practical Aesthetics* (translated from the German), Los Angeles: Getty Research Institute.

Shalem, A. (2012), "What Do We Mean When We Say Islamic Art? A Plea for a Critical Rewriting of the History of the Arts of Islam," *Journal of Art Historiography*: 1–18.

Shaw, W. M. K. (2012), "The Islam in Islamic Art History: Secularism and Public Discourse," *Journal of Art Historiography*, 85: 1–15.

Stanley, T. (2006), "Islamic Art at the V&A," in R. Crill and T. Stanley (eds.), *The Making of the Jameel Gallery of Islamic Art*, London and New York: V&A Publications: 1–25.

Tallis, J. (1852), *Tallis's History and Description of the Crystal Palace, and the Exhibition of the World's Industry in 1851*, London and New York: J. Tallis and Co.

Tillinghast, R. (2007), "Art Islamic Art at the V&A," *Hudson Review*, 60: 293–298.

Troelenberg, E.-M. (2012), "Regarding the Exhibition: The Munich Exhibition Masterpieces of Muhammadan Art (1910) and Its Scholarly Position," *Journal of Art Historiography*, 6: 1–34.

Warner, M. (2011), *Stranger Magic: Charmed States and the Arabian Nights*, London: Chatto & Windus.

Weber, S. (2012), "A Concept of Things: Thoughts on Objects of Islamic Art in the Museum Context," in B. Junod, G. Khalil and S. Weber (eds.), *Islamic Art and the Museum*, London: Saqi: 28–56.

Whitehead, C. (2005), *The Public Art Museum in Nineteenth Century Britain: The Development of the National Gallery*, Aldershot, Hants, and Burlington, VT: Ashgate.

Wood, B. D. (2000), "'A Great Symphony of Pure Form': The 1931 International Exhibition of Persian Art and Its Influence," *Ars Orientalis*, 30: 113–130.

Ziter, E. (2003), *The Orient on the Victorian Stage*, Cambridge and New York: Cambridge University Press.

4

Orientalism and David Hockney's Male-positive Imaginative Geographies

Dennis S. Gouws

> *Though it was probably never [Edward] Said's intention, the unfortunate grammatical intersection of the discourse he called Orientalism with the genre of Orientalist painting, or those European paintings of foreign—especially now Middle Eastern— subjects, lead to an immediate and shared understanding that the two must be conceptual equivalents as well. . . . Art history has been singularly reluctant to work through the faults of Said's Orientalism and develop more nuanced lenses through which to view the Orientalist paintings that are still, by the unfortunate coincidence of terminology, believed to reflect its tenets.*
> (Weeks 2008: 24–25)

> *Orientalist painting invited viewers to fantasize about the* volupté *of distant places, but not all visitors to picture galleries (or all artists) focused their gaze on the women.*
> (Aldrich 2006: 155)

David Hockney imagines the Orient as a place of masculine erotic possibilities. In his works, he frequently peoples his Orient with attractive men, some from his own past, and in doing so, he consequently allies himself with British and European artists who have traditionally depicted the Orient according to their own fantasies and nostalgia, exhibiting a sense of entitlement that has troubled some twenty-first-century critics.[1] Hockney's Middle and Far East etchings, paintings and photographs provoke questions about the nature of their authority. This provocation arises because examining them as Orientalist works now customarily involves political and aesthetic inquiry: both methodologies are necessarily yoked because of the "unfortunate grammatical intersection" of Said's notion of Orientalism with Western Orientalist art, that "unfortunate coincidence of terminology" which Emily M. Weeks describes as complicating one's understanding of Orientalist art today. Said defines Orientalism as "a western style for dominating, restructuring, and having authority over the Orient" (1979: 3)—a discourse informed by Occidental impressions imposed on the Orient rather than by a clear understanding of its realities. Said argues that Orientalism has traditionally involved deductive myth-making in the service of imposed beliefs. It produced:

> not only a fair amount of exact positive knowledge about the Orient, but also a kind of second-order knowledge—lurking in such places as the "Oriental" tale, the mythology of the mysterious East, notions of Asian inscrutability—with a life of its own, what V. G. Kiernan has aptly called "Europe's collective day-dream of the Orient".
>
> (1979: 52)

This "second-order knowledge" is also evident in Western ideas of Eastern exterior and interior spaces. Said notes that this knowledge contributes to the creation of an imaginative geography, an invented understanding of place that is imposed on the Orient which he argues "legitimates a vocabulary, a universe of representative discourse" because "underlying all the different units of Orientalist discourse . . . is a set of figures, or tropes" which "are to the actual Orient . . . as stylized costumes are to characters in a play" (1979: 71).

In the visual arts, elements of this "representative discourse" are most clearly evident in the treatment of exterior spaces in landscape painting and in the interior spaces that frame portraiture. The extent to which some Oriental art might be classified as genre painting is for a discussion beyond the scope of this chapter. Through a combination of what Nicholas Tromans calls its "apparent intimacy and objectivity" (2008: 105), British Oriental landscape painting might be understood as exemplifying Said's notion of "the Westerner's privilege" which was available to him "because his was the stronger culture, he could penetrate, he could wrestle with, he could give shape and meaning to the great Asiatic mystery" (1979: 44). Tromans argues that British landscape artists used Western perspective and easily identifiable landmarks to "communicate a sense of place," thereby making the geography familiar and accessible to the Western viewer (2008: 107).[2] Depictions of interior spaces in

Orientalist portraiture reference similar imaginary geographies informed by second-order knowledge. Christine Riding has noted, for example, similarities between the visual luxury of the "Grand Tour portrait" and the fantastical fancy-dress portrait, originating from the popularity of Oriental dress at British masquerades, those "public events" whose "attraction was the undoubted frisson of adopting a variety of costumes and identities" (2008: 52)—an example of different classes of Britons picturing and performing second-order knowledge about the Orient. Terry Castle describes period costume catalogs that offered a British masquerader "hoping to pass for an Arab sultana or a Turkish janissary" not only "necessary visual information" but also "a measure of pseudo-anthropological detail suggesting ways to act one's unfamiliar part to perfection" (1986: 60).[3]

According to Said's notion of Orientalism, subsequently developed by these and other scholars, British Orientalist painting represented popular but inaccurate impressions of the Orient depicted in tropes that were easily understood and easily imitated. Rana Kabbani, for example, criticizes British Orientalist works that "significantly fail to meet the sterner challenge of uncovering the spirit of the people and the meaning of the place" (2008: 41). Some consensus has been reached among scholars that Orientalist art authorized imaginative geographies that deliberately misrepresent and often caricature their subject matter.

Eroticism in imaginative geographies, a common theme of Oriental portraiture, acknowledge possible sexual exploration for, and perhaps exploitation by, tourists; Oriental travel often involved sexual encounters whose politics have notably been discussed by Joseph A. Boone, Marjorie Garber and Robert Aldrich. Boone rightly criticizes Said for ignoring the fact that, "the sexual promise (and threat)" (1979: 188) that Said attributes to the Orient is for countless Western travelers inextricably tied to their exposure abroad to "... male homosexual practice" (1995: 90). Although Said acknowledged "the experience of feminist or women's studies" in his later reconsideration of Orientalism, he did not acknowledge desire among men in his work (1985: 91). Boone argues that "Said's analyses of colonialist erotics remain ensconced in conspicuously heterosexual interpretive frameworks" (1995: 90). Moreover, Boone argues that understanding colonialist male–male eroticism also requires careful discursive attention: examining the discourse of power that informs sexual encounters between Western travelers and locals, "where the Occidental traveller, by virtue of his homosexuality is already the other, the presumed *equivalence* of Eastern homosexuality and Occidental personal liberation may disguise the specter of colonial privilege and exploitation encoded in the hierarchy white man/brown boy" (1995: 4). Although Boone's recent work accepts that encountering the Orient "is not simply a case of establishing unidirectional domination over or a penetration of some monolithic Middle East" (2014: xxxiv), he suggests that sex with Oriental persons potentially serves the colonial hierarchy.

Like Boone, Marjorie Garber understands Western male sexual interest in the Orient as potentially appropriative, stemming from "the European fascination with the sexual and social ambiguities of the East"; however, she interprets this "[looking] East for role models and for deliberate cultural masquerade" as enabling marginalized Occidental identities to express and fulfill themselves (1997: 330, 352). She frames this quest within a gynocentric understanding of "the specter and spectacle of transvestism," that familiar Orientalist trope of posing and masquerading, in a place that accommodates a display of "the Western fantasy of the transvestic, pan-sexualized Middle East, a place of liminality and change" (1997: 346, 337).[4]

Although recognizing its exploratory potential, Garber misses the less meretricious discreet spaces within which male–male intimacy occurs—an imaginative geography recognized by Aldrich in Orientalist paintings of men. He describes these works' allusive representations of "underlined stereotypes of native sexual potency, as well as the homosocial camaraderie enjoyed by both natives and colonials" (2006: 155). This is closer to the psychic, somatic and spatial interiority of male eroticism that is central to the imaginative geographies in Hockney's male-positive Orientalism, spaces where the male body and masculine pleasures are celebrated rather than ridiculed, pathologized or shamed, as is evident in the otherwise astute criticism of Norman Bryson (1994: 228–259) and Ernst van Alphen (Bryson et al. 1994: 260–271; 1998 *passim*).[5] Adrian Searle (2009) rightly describes Hockney's early work as "full of pleasure," as "joyous, furtively funny, artistically inventive and responsive to all kinds of art being made at the time, as well as up front and celebratory about his sexuality."

Hockney's works offer more than a neo-colonial authorization of his Mediterranean and Asian Orient: they subvert generic Western depictions of the Orient—as well as some of the local customs—in order to create a homoerotic-specific commune informed by an ethos that presents an affirmative, unconventional view of the masculine sexual politics of Orientalism. They explore those "geographies ... beyond the thresholds of [current] scholarly imagination" about which Boone speculates (2014: xxxiv). The illustrated works accompanying this chapter—*Tea Painting in an Illusionistic Style [Typhoo Tea]* (1961), *In the Dull Village* from the series of Cavafy Etchings (1966), *Mark, Suginoi Hotel, Beppu* (1971) and *Gregory Watching the Snow Fall, Kyoto, Feb 21, 1983* (1983)—are not all from the early period of Hockney's career and are in various mediums. They do, however, depict instances of intimate masculine pleasure located in Oriental interiors that challenge the viewers' heteronormative gaze and invite a frank appreciation of male beauty. In addition, the implied eroticism between men in these images unsettle established conventions of the sexualized feminine intimate space in Oriental art and invite the viewer to experience that imaginative geography of opportunistic male–male desire evident in the homoerotic politics of Orientalist art. The male-positive imaginative geography they depict is one in which Oriental interiors foster intimacy among men and invite the reader to appreciate masculine beauty. The political and aesthetic characteristics of Hockney's Oriental interiors will be examined by investigating three topics: first, whether they exemplify Said's understanding of Orientalism; second, how they subvert the conventions of British Orientalist art; and finally, what kind of a male-positive imaginative geography they depict.

Second-order knowledge of the Orient in Hockney's early work

Whilst a student at the Royal Academy, Hockney recalls starting his day with a cup of Typhoo Tea, a popular brand which was his mother's favorite (Stangos 1977: 64). The brand name approximates the Chinese word for doctor and was established by the son of a Victorian tea trader in Birmingham; it signals popular second-order knowledge about the Orient through its association of tea with China. The packaging and product connote the availability of produce from the East for Western consumption, and arguably confirm Said's theory of Western domination and restructuring of the Orient; this commercial product produced in the Orient for sale in the UK symbolizes a form of economic domination. The brand name also renders the orient familiar—as does the commonly recognized architecture of the packaging. *Tea Painting in an Illusionistic Style [Typhoo Tea]* exemplifies second-order knowledge of the Orient not only in the cypher and branding, but also because it projects onto the Orient a fantasy of an intimate interior space where the body is available for scrutiny and, *pace* Boone, possible sale [Figure 4.1]. However, this work subverts the traditional connotation of Oriental art by inviting erotic inspection of a male body; consequently, the viewer assumes a gaze that differs from the heteronormative gaze that pervades Orientalist art.[6] The oculus in the figure's crotch area insists that the reader acknowledge this male body erotically. Painted at a time when male homosexual acts were illegal in the UK, this depiction of what is tantamount to a full-frontal male nude was a brave male-affirmative gesture. The box's interior is dominated by red, a color that combines Western associations of sex for sale with Asian associations of good luck. The figure's slope-shouldered posture and averted gaze, however, suggests diffidence and modesty. Rather than coming out (or more appropriate to the period, being found out), this male is drawing us in to an interior that may be commercial and confining but is potentially emancipatory in its frank embodied maleness (without resorting to transvestism and cultural masquerade); the fact that the box is open ensures that the spectator shares this intimate interior with this naked man. Unlike the other works discussed in this paper, the male body in *Tea Painting in an Illusionistic Style [Typhoo Tea]* remains self-consciously naked rather than assuredly nude; however, the painting makes a bold statement about the possibility of an Oriental interior in which the male body can be appraised and celebrated.[7]

FIGURE 4.1 David Hockney, *Tea Painting in an Illusionistic Style*, 1961. Oil on Canvas. 78 × 30″ © David Hockney. Collection Tate, London. Photo Credit: © Tate, London 2014.

The masculine Mediterranean interior in Hockney's Cavafy Etchings

"What happens when a boy from Bradford meets a world-weary Alexandrian?" asked Edward Lucie-Smith (1966: 20) in his review of David Hockney's *Illustrations for Fourteen Poems from C. P. Cavafy*. Unlike his Victorian predecessors who scrupulously depicted Middle-Eastern locales, Hockney relied on his general impressions of the region for his illustrations of Constantine P. Cavafy's homosexual-themed poems about Alexandria.[8] Instead of journeying to Egypt, Hockney scouted Beirut for suitable locations, arguing that the latter city seemed to be "the contemporary equivalent of Alexandria, in that it had now replaced Alexandria as the most cosmopolitan city of the Middle East" (Livingstone 1981: 85).[9] Although the etchings give a sense of local exteriors and interiors informed by Western representational conventions, they also comment on Middle-Eastern notions of gendered geography.

Traditional Orientalist art acknowledges customary, sex-separate spaces by depicting men and women at home in their appropriate discrete locations. Different permissions are afforded viewers of men and women. Tromans, for example, observes in J. F. Lewis's *The Mid-day Meal* (1875) a "bonhomie" that not only "embraces both the wealthy diners and their servants, who join in the jokes as part of the same masculine circle, undivided by social class," but also invites the viewer to participate in the festivities (a gesture evident in the partly eaten meal in the foreground) (2008: 82). Travelers might also experience this kind of harmonious masculine otiose: J. F. Lewis's extraordinary *A Frank Encampment in the Desert of Mount Sinai, 1842* (1856) shows a relaxed British gentleman in Arabic dress hosting a local Sheik. Tromans argues that this painting, "a riposte to the disorientation and placelessness threatened by the desert," depicts this gentleman as composed "and comfortable with 'every conceivable convenience, both Western and Eastern, ... at hand' in his masculine domestic space" (2008: 107).

The Cavafy Etchings depict the private world of male–male desire in a way that subverts Orientalist art's depiction of gendered domestic spaces. Six of Hockney's etchings depict male intimacy in the bedroom. These images unsettle conventional depictions of the sexualized intimate interior space in Oriental art and invite the viewer to experience that imaginative geography of opportunistic male–male sex evident in the homoerotic politics of Orientalism. The harem was the conventional sexualized domestic space in Orientalist art, and as Tromans suggests, a place in "the work of most British artists" where they "most obviously superimposed their own image" (2008: 17). The male artist projected his heteronormative desire onto artistic depictions of this secluded gynocentric space. The intimate life of the harem was shielded from public inspection; it was a circumscribed space but one that offered a locus of relative autonomy for its women occupants. The presence of a female guest in the harem, "forbade even the husband's entrance into the harem" (Tromans 2008: 135). Citing the marginality of the male viewer in J. F. Lewis's *Hareem Life, Constantinople* (1857), Tromans argues that harem women's lives often "seemed free of fear or constraint;" moreover, because they are veiled when outside of the harem, their identities particularly intrigued men because male "lust seems to be increased through the frustration of the gaze"—a frustration also evident in Hunt's *Lantern-Maker's Courtship* (2008: 135, 136). Lewis imagined the potential subversiveness of harem women in his *A Lady Receiving Visitors (The Reception)* (1873), a power noted by both Weeks and Fatema Mernissi. Mernissi's interpretation of the concept of *fitna* as women-embodied sexual disruptiveness is cited by Weeks in her praising of this painting for its evident acknowledgement of women's power to subvert male space through their occupation of the *mandarah*, traditionally the male domestic space and their breaking with tradition by not wearing their veils in that space (2008: 30, 27). Mernissi considers the harem a locus whose ambivalent connotations to Westerners—and particularly Western men—suggests a refusal to come to terms with *samar*, which she translates as "nights and dreams as sources of creativity and delights" as well as "the sense of 'dark color' with the pleasure you get from opening up to the mysterious 'other,' all the while being stimulated by the moonlight" (2008: 33–34). She also notes that the conditions of *samar* can be created "artificially by retreating to an inner cocoon-like space, of which the archetype is the harem" (Mernissi 2008: 34).

Hockney subverts these expectations of the harem by changing its gender dynamic. In the Cavafy Etchings, we have a male-only sexualized space occupied by nude men with comfortable and confident bodies, who seem unconcerned by the viewer's gaze. The men in *According to the Prescriptions of Ancient Magicians* openly display their mutual masculine desire whose pending consummation is implied by the movement of the male on the left getting into bed and the receptive pose of the figure reclining on the right. Both *In the Dull Village* and *Two Boys Aged 23 or 24* frankly depict male intimacy, and the pairs of male subjects seem totally engrossed with each other and not to care at all about the spectator. Hockney here represents what is forbidden in Orientalist discourse: we have figural embodiment and same-sex desire being openly represented and alluding, moreover, to a kind of darkness that is recreational rather than procreative, a touching of the dark, hidden inner-self of the male body; indeed, a pleasure resulting from opening oneself up to male–male sexual intercourse. This is the masculine *samar* of the male body unveiled, experienced and represented as positive. Male interiority enabled by an imaginative geography set in an Oriental interior. Tromans notes that "one meaning of *harim*, denoting what is restricted or forbidden, refers to those people who may not be looked at" (2008: 128). Hockney's subjects enact what is traditionally forbidden (this masculine s*amar*) and represent figural, embodied people who customarily should not be looked at in most Muslim-dominated Oriental culture (by virtue of their nudity and their unveiled attraction to men).

Four of the nude male figures in the Cavafy Etchings coolly address the viewer. In the aptly titled *One Night*—which could be understood as referencing this homoerotic *samar*—one of the men approaching the bed directly looks at the spectator, suggesting that even though he represents one of these *harim*, he will insist that the viewer acknowledge his presence, that he is being looked at. Both *The Beginning* and *In Despair* have all the male subjects looking at the viewer from bed; they challenge the spectator to acknowledge his/her relationship with them, to share in their depicted same-sex intimacy. This access to a male-exclusive interior space demands the spectator's frank acknowledgement of Orientalist male–male desire in both traditionally aesthetic and political contexts.

Rather than assume that the homoerotics of Orientalism were essentially hierarchical or gynocentric, Hockney's Cavafy Etchings imagine them as confident, celebratory and challenging. These aspects are most pointedly exemplified by *In an Old Book* [Figure 4.2]. Boone (2014: 313–314) notes that Middle-Eastern homoerotic literature was traditionally disseminated in albums in which illustrations were tipped or pasted, and the discovery of one such illustration seems to have occasioned Cavafy's poem. Rather than frustrating the gaze, the full-frontal figure challenges the viewer to imagine what participating in an intimate homoerotic relationship would be like. Like the unsettling gaze of the reclining nude courtesan who frankly appraises the viewer in Édouard Manet's *Olympia* (1863), Hockney's nude challenges conventional heteronormative scrutiny. The spectator becomes the celebratory collaborator. The sensuous line etching, without ground, presents a naked young man who frankly addresses the spectator. He wears no gender- or culturally specific clothing but sports a necklace that dignifies him with an internal life, a public manifestation of his private thoughts, an indication of his aesthetic appreciation of this jewelry and perhaps a person who might have given it to him. His display of pubic hair, his fleshy penis is unmarked by circumcision, that imposed Middle-Eastern patriarchal mark; its flaccidity and foreskin veil its masculine pleasure potential which he may choose to share with a partner whom he finds attractive. This presentation of a full but not erect penis undermines Ernst van Alphen's observation that the exposed penis reveals the limitations of patriarchal power, representing instead a "shrivelled shrimp" (1998: 179). On the contrary, this is a proud penis whose state suggests this empowered male's right to choose a partner. Boone reminds us of the traditional "Ottoman predilection for Greek youths" (2014: 350) and paintings such as Louis Dupré's *Voyage à Athènes et à Constantinople* (1824) suggest the painter registered the discreet power the socially subordinate boy holds over his master. The nude in *In an Old Book* frankly, and with dignity, presents his body for appreciation, yet his eyes engage the spectator, appraising his fitness to participate in what could be a mutually male-positive sexual experience—confident, embodied and full of pleasure—in an Oriental imaginative geography.

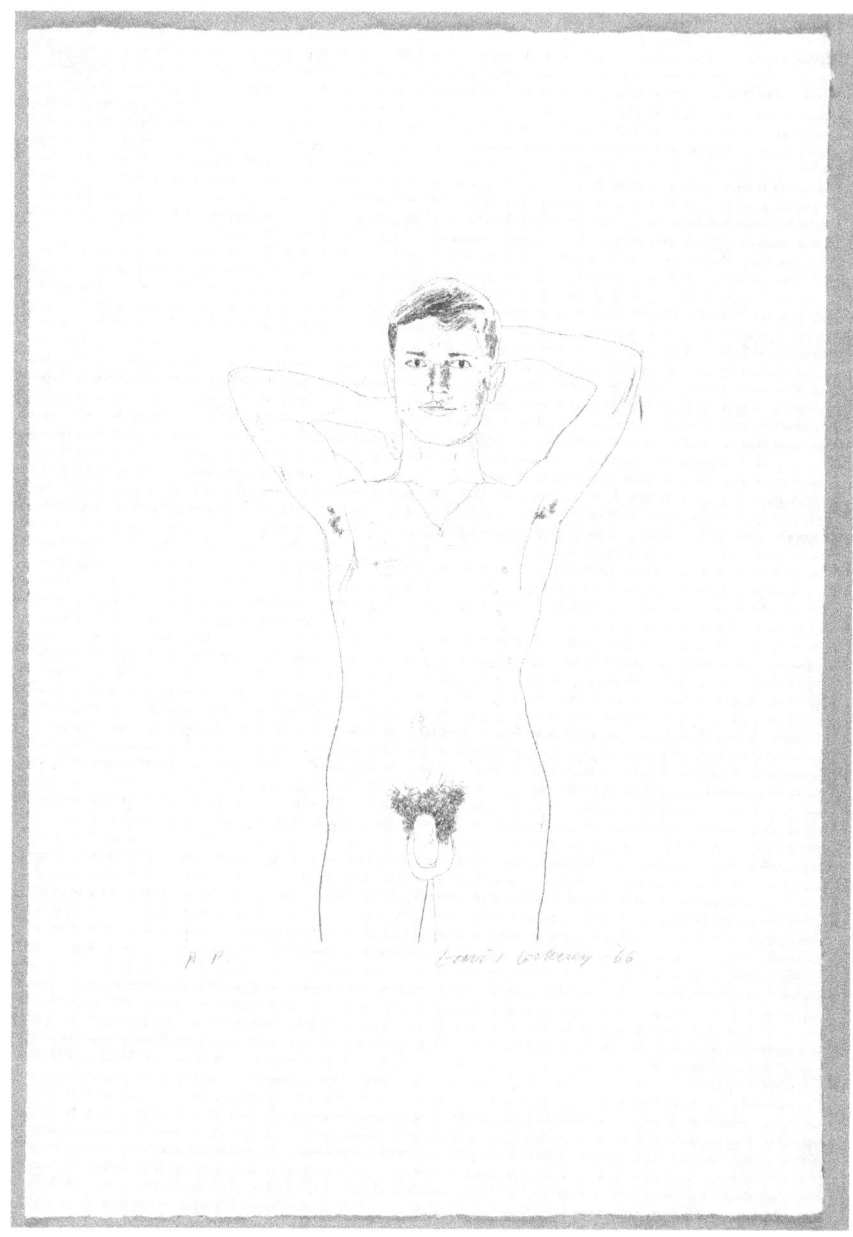

FIGURE 4.2 David Hockney, *In an Old Book from Illustrations for Fourteen Poems from C. P. Cavafy*, 1966–1967. Etching. 22½ × 15½″. Editioned. © David Hockney.

Japanese Oriental interiors: Enabling of dignified masculine desire

Japan's experience of the Occident before and after the Second World War were remarkably different. From the mid-nineteenth century, reciprocal trading and cultural relationships occurred; succinctly described as "two-way traffic; the island nation was as voraciously interested in the West as the West was desirous of Japanese styles" (Martin and Koda 1994: 71). Richard Minear reminds us that Japan never became a colony of Europe. Moreover, he notes that "nor did the abiding cultural ties which bound the West to the Orient exist between Japan and the West. . . . It held no special religious appeal and posed no special religious threat" (1980: 514). Although in the Orient and often mystified, pre-Second World War Japan was never subjected to the dominating, restructuring and subjugating central to Said's notion of Orientalism; Martin and Koda describe the attitude of *fin-de-siècle* Europeans as evincing "fanatical enthusiasm and a peculiar naïveté" (1994: 77). After this war, under American occupation, Japan experienced what John Mackintosh argues was a combination of sexual subordination and sexual emancipation: the Japanese male body was deemed effeminate compared to the masculine American male body, but Western classicism modeled dignified male-positive same-sex relationships; popular Japanese literature in this period depicts a "fetishized desire for the foreign" often consummated in hotel rooms, the primary locus homosexual acts with Americans (2010: 95, 103, 106, 122).

Robert Hughes once remarked that Francis Bacon's work depicts "perhaps the extreme voice of the *misère des hotels*, the sense of being trapped within the city by unassuageable and once almost unnamable appetites." That "in his work, the image of the classical nude body is simply dismissed; it becomes, instead, a two-legged animal with various addictions: to sex, the needle, security, or power" (Hughes 1981: 296). Hockney, on the other hand, depicts the *plaisirs des hotels*, the sense of possible pleasures among men enabled by contingent catered-for spaces. Hockney's *Mark, Suginoi Hotel, Beppu* (1971) and *Gregory Watching the Snow Fall, Kyoto, Feb 21, 1983* do not partake of the exploitative tourism suggested by Boone, nor do they exemplify the masquerade transvestitism theorized by Garber [Figures 4.3 and 4.4]. The dressing up is respectful, not a condescending masquerade of the kind described by Weeks. Both in its execution and representation, *Mark, Suginoi Hotel, Beppu* respectfully pays tribute to Japanese art conventions, as was the case in nineteenth-century European *japonisme*. Livingstone notes this work on paper's resemblance to Kuniyoshi's prints "in which a single figure is often framed by the thrusting diagonals of a simplified architectural setting and in which mood is frequently evoked through gesture and facial emotion" (1981: 153). The stylized interior offers *tatami* mats and a figure in a *yukata*, a cotton kimono. The work subverts conventional Oriental art because, rather than relying on Western techniques, the male subject is the object of the gaze, and the gender-ambiguous kimono undermines any suggestion of American hyper-masculinity. It also suggests the interior is one that comfortably accommodates male intimacy. The work does not parody or pretend to be Japanese erotic art—but the figure's bare leg hints at the tradition of partially clothed figures in Japanese eroticism (Mark's right ankle and foot are exposed). The dignity of the depiction of Mark is evident: his body language and averted gaze differ from that of the figure in *Typhoo Tea*; Mark seems composed and complete.

FIGURE 4.3 David Hockney, *Mark, Suginoi Hotel, Beppu, 1971*. Colored Crayon on Paper. 17 × 14". © David Hockney.

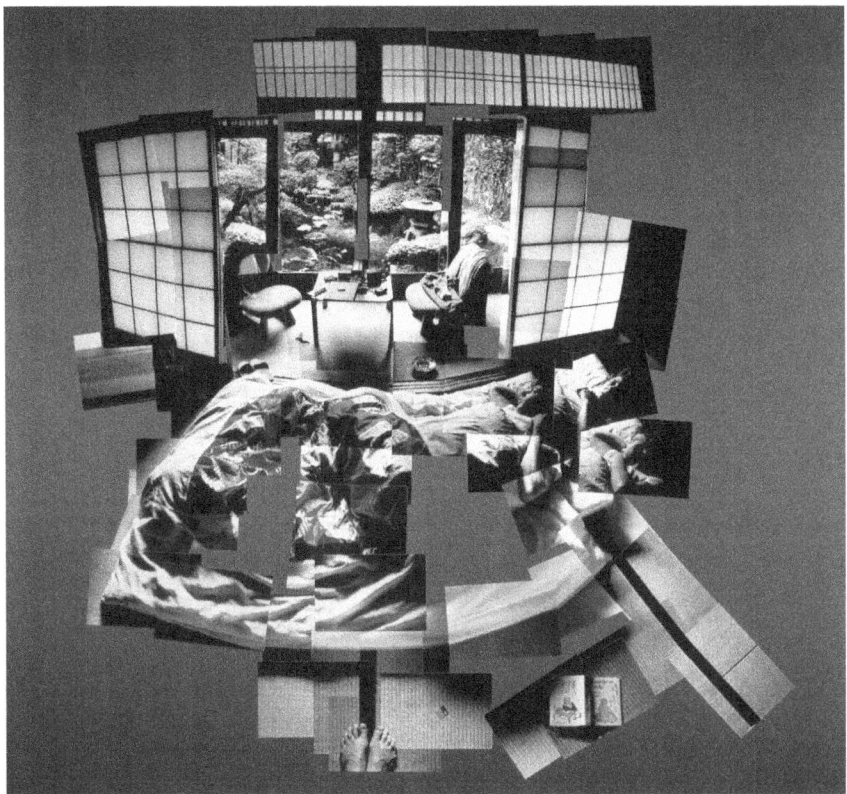

FIGURE 4.4 David Hockney, *Gregory Watching the Snow Fall, Kyoto, Feb 21, 1983*. Photographic Collage. $40\frac{1}{4} \times 50\frac{3}{8}''$. Edition of 20. © David Hockney.

In *Gregory Watching the Snow Fall, Kyoto, Feb 21, 1983* (1983), Hockney certainly dominates and restructures his depiction of this Oriental interior; however, his intervention is candid and respectful rather than authoritarian. The rejection of Western perspective means that the details of the interior are not hierarchized; all are presented for our inspection and with loving detail. Composed of a series of photographs encapsulating Hockney's feet, Gregory Evans reclining in bed, and a book on the floor is about *haiku*, a probable indicator of one of the men's interest in Japanese literature, the familiar is rendered unfamiliar because of the absence of conventional Western perspective. Moreover, the intimacy of the interior is masculine; a lived-in space occupied by two men who are close. Not only is the spectator's relationship with the space acknowledged (through Gregory's direct outward gaze), but Hockney's bare feet register the relaxed relationship between the two men. This imaginative geography makes visible and poignant the dignity between men who are aware of their Oriental surroundings but express no wish to dominate them. Webb observes that, "the image demonstrates that these collages can be touchingly intimate" (1988: 213). This observation registers Hockney's success at depicting male-positive *plaisirs des hotels*.

Conclusion

Christine Peltre shrewdly observes that: "The Orient of the Orientalist painters... is the mythic site of all possibilities" (1998: 275). These possibilities might certainly offer covert spaces for the kind of homoerotic exploitation that concerns Boone. However, these interiors also imagine a real reciprocity. Aldrich speculates: "Perhaps unbeknownst to the creators of these images themselves, the signals they sent out could be felt by a receptive audience, creating a homoerotic artistic tradition of the seduction of the exotic foreigner" (2006: 180). Whilst Hockney's works exemplify Said's Orientalism by projecting an erotic fantasy onto a Middle-Eastern context, their imaginative geography more importantly dignifies male–male desire and consequently offers new possibilities for understanding the homoerotics of Orientalism.

Notes

1 See E. M. Weeks (2014), J. M. MacKenzie (1995: 43–67), and J. Jones (2008) for concise, informative examinations of current debates about Western depictions of the Orient. Disagreeing with most scholars who share Edward Said's assumptions, MacKenzie notably offers this assessment: "Far from offering an artistic programme for imperialism, [the "nineteenth-century Orientalists"] were finding in the East ancient verities lost in their own civilization. Many of them set out not to condemn the East, but to discover echoes of a world they had lost" (67). Jones succinctly offers a similar criticism of Said's *Orientalism*: "The real story here, that Said reveals against his intentions, is the remarkable fact that Europeans and Americans in the nineteenth century knew more about the cultures of the Middle East than we do now. They read the Tales of the 1001 Nights and dreamt of the Alhambra. Was this just a complacent Imperialist celebration of power, based on the contrast between nostalgia for the great Oriental past and contempt for the Arab present? No, I think there was real curiosity and admiration." This paper includes materials covered in my paper on Hockney's Cavafy Etchings (2012).

2 Several of Hockney's works associated with those discussed in this paper can be read as conventional Orientalist landscapes. The early stylized Egyptian works use cyphers; the Cavafy Etchings use international symbols; the Japanese prints use clichéd motives.

3 Castle (1986: 60) observes of eighteenth-century Britain that the "spirit of Orientalism suffused masquerade representation: Persians, Chinese, and Turks remained exemplary subjects for sumptuous reconstruction throughout the century"; the first chapter of her book (1986: 1–51) usefully contextualizes the cultural origins and protocols of eighteenth-century British masquerades. G.-G.

Lemaire (2000: 48–65) describes the centrality of Oriental fantasy to European masquerades.

4 The *OED* defines *gynocentric* as, "Centred on, dominated by, or concerned exclusively with women; taking a female or a feminist point of view." Garber's essay is gynocentric because it assumes that the feminine and female are central to male desire (see, for example, her treatment of T. E. Lawrence (1997: 305–307)); moreover, it depicts male transvestism as pathological but female transvestism as clever and strategic (compare her treatment of the man "*en femme berbère*" (1997: 330–336), with that of the "*bon garçon*" (1997: 324–329). Her discussion of Oscar Wilde relies on similarly gynocentric assumptions (1997: 339–340).

5 Bryson, for example, remarks on "the fears, anxieties, and strains of producing the masculine" (1994: 231); van Alphen notoriously coined the phrase "shrivelled shrimp" to describe the actual male penis rather than its patriarchal ideal (1994: 26; 1998: 179).

6 Boone (2014) succinctly surveys the homoerotic counter-tradition in Orientalist European art in chapters seven and eight.

7 Kenneth Clarke concisely distinguishes between *naked* and *nude* in *The Nude: A Study in Ideal Form*: "to be naked is to be deprived of our clothes, and the word implies some of the embarrassment most of us feel in that condition. The word 'nude,' on the other hand, carries, in educated usage, no uncomfortable overtone. The vague image it projects into the mind is not of a huddled and defenseless body, but of a balanced, prosperous, and confident body: the body re-formed" (1972: 3).

8 See Tromans, "The Orient in Perspective" and "The Holy City" for a discussion of British artists' attempts at faithfully depicting Oriental places. Peter Webb notes that Hockney's Cavafy Etchings, "were made with no particular poems in mind. At first Hockney wanted to include a variety of Cavafy poems, but finally it was decided to concentrate on the homosexual ones" (1988: 74).

9 Marco Livingstone suggests that Hockney's trip to Beirut, "provided [him] with architectural settings of suitably Arabian character for three of the prints, but what he most wanted was simply to get the flavor of the place and its way of life. The poems, however, have a far more general application as reveries on human relationships, and Hockney thus felt free to take inspiration from his own experience and environment" (1981: 85). Webb reports that Nikos Stangos, whose translations were used in the book edition of the etchings, "chose which poems would go with the chosen prints," that "the prints are not literal illustrations of the poems but visualizations of their nostalgia for fleeting but memorable sexual encounters; the feeling of authenticity generated by the images is due to Hockney's own personal experiences" (1988: 74).

References

Aldrich, R. (1993), *The Seduction of the Mediterranean: Writing, Art and Homosexual Fantasy*, London and New York: Routledge.

Aldrich, R. (2006), *Colonialism and Homosexuality*, London and New York: Routledge.

Boone, J. A. (1995), "Vacation Cruises; or, the Homoerotics of Orientalism," *Publications of the Modern Language Association*, 110(1): 89–107.
Boone, J. A. (2014), *The Homoerotics of Orientalism*, New York: Columbia University Press.
Bryson, N., M. A. Holly, and K. Moxley (eds.) (1994), *Visual Culture: Images and Interpretations*, Middletown, CT: Wesley University Press.
Castle, T. (1986), *Masquerade and Civilization: The Carnivalesque in Eighteenth-Century English Culture and Fiction*, Stanford, CA: Stanford University Press.
Clarke, K. (1972), *The Nude: A Study in Ideal Form*, Princeton, NJ: Princeton University Press.
Dupré, L. (1824), *Voyage à Athènes et à Constantinople*.
Garber, M. (1997), *Vested Interests: Cross-Dressing and Cultural Anxiety*, New York: Routledge.
Glazebrook, M. (1982), *Hockney and Poetry*, London: John Roberts Press.
Gouws, D. S. (2012), "Orientalism and David Hockney's Cavafy Etchings: Exploring a Male-Positive Imaginative Geography," *The Journal of the Arts in Society*, 6(6): 181–188.
Hughes, R. (1980), *The Shock of the New: Art and the Century of Change*, London: BBC.
Kabbani, R., "Regarding Orientalist Painting Today," *Lure* (London): 40–45.
Jones, J. (2008), "Orientalism Is Not Racism," *Guardian*, May 22: http://www.theguardian.com/artanddesign/jonathanjonesblog/2008/may/22/orientalismisnotracism [Accessed May 15, 2014].
Lemaire, G. (2000), *The Orient in Western Art*, Cologne: Könemann.
Livingstone, M. (1981), *David Hockney*, London: Thames and Hudson, 1983.
Lucie-Smith, E. (1966), "When the Paths of Painter and the Writer Meet," *The Times*, May 3: 20.
MacKenzie, J. M. (1995), *Orientalism: History, Theory and the Arts*, Manchester and New York: Manchester University Press.
Mackintosh, J. D. (2010), *Homosexuality and Manliness in Postwar Japan*, London and New York: Routledge.
Manet, E. (1863), *Olympia*. Oil on canvas. Musée d'Orsay, Paris.
Martin, R. and H. Koda (1994), *Orientalism: Visions of the East in Western Dress*, New York: Harry N. Abrams.
Mernissi, F. (2008), "Seduced by 'Samar', or; How British Orientalist Painters Learned to Stop Worrying and Love the Darkness," Tromans *Lure* (London): 33–39.
Minear, R. H. (1980), "Orientalism and the Study of Japan," *Journal of Asian Studies*, 39(3): 507–517.
Peltre, C. (1998), *Orientalism in Art*, John Goodman (trans.), New York, London and Paris: Abbeville Press Publishers.
Riding, C. (2008), "Travellers and Sitters: The Orientalist Portrait," *Lure* (London): 48–61.
Said, E. (1979), *Orientalism*, New York: Vintage-Random.
Said, E. (1984), "The Mind of Winter—Reflection on Life in Exile," *Harpers*, 269/1612 (September): 49–55.
Said, E. (1985), "Orientalism Reconsidered," *Cultural Critique*, 1 (Autumn): 89–107.
Searle, A. (2009), "The Pleasure Principle: David Hockney at Nottingham Contemporary," *Guardian*, November 11. http://www.theguardian.com/

artanddesign/2009/nov/11/david-hockney-nottingham-contemporary [Accessed December 20, 2014].
Stangos, N. (ed.) (1977), *David Hockney by David Hockney*, London: Harry N. Abrams.
Tromans, N. (ed.) (2008a), *The Lure of the East: British Orientalist Painting*, London: Tate Publishing.
Tromans, N. (ed.) (2008b), *The Lure of the East: British Orientalist Painting: 1830–1845*, New Haven: Yale Center for British Art.
Van Alphen, E. (1998), *Francis Bacon and the Loss of Self*, London: Reaktion Books.
Webb, P. (1988), *Portrait of David Hockney*, New York: Penguin-E. P. Dutton.
Weeks, E. M. (2014), *Cultures Crossed: John Frederick Lewis and the Art of Orientalism*, New Haven: Yale University Press.

5

The Excessive *Trompe l'Oeil*: The Saturated Interior in *Tears of the Black Tiger*

Mark Taylor and Michael J. Ostwald

Written and directed by Wisit Sasanatieng, the Thai film *Tears of the Black Tiger/Fa Thalai Jone* (Sasanatieng, dir., 2000) occupies a contested position in the history of the cinema. Critically acclaimed and awarded at both European and Asian film festivals, it was first heavily edited and then supressed by its American distributors as being unsuitable for Western audiences (Fellion 2013). Despite its lack of international release, it has since gone on to achieve cult status, being especially celebrated for its exuberant art direction and set design. Combining a visual palette of bold, rich hues with costumes that often appear as an extension of their painted backdrops, *Tears of the Black Tiger* sets out to celebrate and challenge the cinematic traditions of the American western and the European romance by re-imagining them through the lens of a distinctly Asian genre; the overwrought comedy-action-melodrama. While both the characters and the actions they undertake in the film are used to advance Sasanatieng's critical homage to the West, it is in the film's *mise-en-scène* in general, and in its set design in particular, that he brings into question the very notion of the Oriental interior as "other."

In the structuralist and modernist theories of the late nineteenth and early twentieth centuries, continental philosophers often positioned their own cultural, political and social values in juxtaposition to those of an ill-defined "other." While poststructuralist and postmodern theorists have since uncovered a myriad of these constituted others, probably the most famous was identified in Edward Said's (1978) *Orientalism*. In that work, Said argued that Western depictions of Asian and Arabic cultures emphasized various imagined qualities in such a way as to construct an artificial "other" against which the values of the West could be positively contrasted. Thus, European works of art and literature used depictions of the indolence, decadence and immorality of the East to foreground the purpose, integrity and industriousness of the West. While Said's argument was largely constructed using literary cases, European paintings of imagined Asian and Arabic interiors were amongst his most evocative examples. In such instances, Said proposes that the Oriental interior is not represented for the purpose of recording the character of a real space, but rather as a type of self-affirmation of the innately civilized or superior nature of the Western interior. Thus, Said's *Orientalism* highlights the inherently patronizing appropriation of the Eastern interior by the West. But what of the reverse case, when the Western interior is appropriated and represented in, for example, Asian cinema?

In *Tears of the Black Tiger*, Wisit Sasanatieng presents an intensely artificial reimagining of two of Western cinema's most famous "interior" types: the frontier soundstage and the European villa. The first of these became well known through its role in the classic American westerns of the 1940s and 1950s, where flat painted backdrops on soundstages were used in place of real exterior locations. The second type, the foyer of the grand house, with its sweeping symmetrical staircase and high ceilings, was similarly celebrated in European and American cinema of the era. The reinvention of these interiors in *Tears of the Black Tiger* is the subject of the present chapter. However, rather than reviewing these spaces through the lens of Orientalism or postcolonial theory, this chapter's reading of two interior scenes from the film is informed by Jean Baudrillard's writings on the appropriation and simulation of spatial signs. Baudrillard's work is especially relevant in this context because it recognizes the existence of a special type of constitutive other, the simulacra.

A simulacrum is an artificial or constructed reflection of a space, practice or event. In postmodern theory, the simulacra, like any sign or signifier, is conceptually neutral, however its signified or meaning can be used to interpret its purpose and affect. For example, at one extreme, a sign that is either too abstract or too perfect can be regarded as "empty" and is therefore so open to interpretation as to be meaningless (Barthes 1983). In contrast, a sign that has a deliberately rich representational content might communicate multiple additional, coherent meanings (Barthes 1981). An appropriation and reconstruction of a cultural spatial type, for example an Arabic interior in a Western painting, is an example of a simulacrum which requires careful analysis before any conclusion can be reached about its purpose or affects. Thus, Said (1978) may be right when he argues that the Arabic appropriation of Western depictions of the Orient represents both a willing subjugation of cultural richness and a loss of veracity. However, we cannot assume that the

Orient is always the submissive "other," and this is especially the case when examining Eastern appropriations from the West. This is why Baudrillard's perspective is valuable in the present context, because it suggests that any simulacra must be interpreted in its own right. Baudrillard (1994) even defines three types of simulation and suggests clues for reading their intent, including paying close attention to their imperfections. Because a simulation is never perfect, it must accommodate its lack of authenticity in some way. It could, for example, attempt to hide its flaws, potentially resulting in the production of a facile or repressed sign, or it could seek to celebrate them, a possible sign of dissidence, resistance or even revolution.

One example Baudrillard (1983; 1994) uses to conceptualize different types of simulacra and how they function is the *trompe l'oeil*. A *trompe l'oeil* is a type of spatial illusion produced by painting, modeling or covering a wall in such a way as to suggest artificial depth. The Western tradition of *trompe l'oeil* has a history that stretches back to the decorative paintings of Roman times, the illusory surface of baroque painted surfaces and eighteenth-century panoramic landscapes that dematerialized the domestic interior. While examples of realistic illusions were produced in the seventeenth century (*quodlibet*), and were criticized by John Ruskin in *Modern Painters* (1843), the *trompe l'oeil* was mostly celebrated for creating intensely vivid optical illusions which delighted the eye. It is this aspect that Baudrillard evokes to define the *trompe l'oeil* as a type of "enhanced simulation," the ultimate artificial space of seduction which can, in its most perfect form, serve through its falsification of experience, to negate the object of it representation. Baudrillard (1989) describes the *trompe l'oeil* as an example of the "excess of reality" which can function to either question or reinforce traditional binary opposites, like East and West. Baudrillard is critical of the degree to which the production of apparent perfection, what he calls "hyper-reality," can undermine the efficacy of both the original and its reflection. However, he observes that, in some cases, the *trompe l'oeil* extends or attenuates its reflection, taking on a life of its own which adds value both to the original *and* to the simulation. It is this last quality, associated with the moment when the *tromp l'oeil* transcends its spatial inspiration, that is most valuable for considering the interiors in *Tears of the Black Tiger*.

Background

In order to appreciate the role played by the two chosen interiors (the soundstage and the villa) in the *mise-en-scène* of *Tears of the Black Tiger*, it is important to present an overview of the film. However, even this task is not without its challenges, as the film merges multiple genres in such a way as to resist simple classification or description. For example, one critic described it as "an old-fashioned cowboy melodrama with frenetic shoot-outs and mad romantic yearning" (Bradshaw 2001: 1), whereas it was also promoted as "a 50s swashbuckler, as re-imagined for the Hong Kong-style action crowd" (Seattle Film Festival 2000). Olivia Khoo describes the opening sequence as a "parody of 1940s and 50s melodramas" (Khoo 2013: 89), while *The Wall Street Journal* dubbed it a "Rice Noodle-Western," a none-too-subtle reference to director Sergio Leone's famous Italian-made films of the 1960s and early 1970s which were known as "spaghetti westerns." As Fellion (2013) notes, the Rice Noodle-Western moniker effectively marginalizes the film as being just another "international reappropriation of the US West" (52), but this time from Asia.

Despite drawing its narrative elements and setting from a diverse range of sources, at its heart *Tears of the Black Tiger* is a love story about two people from different social backgrounds, Dum (Chartchai Ngamsan), a young man who is from a poor rural community, and Rumpoey (Stella Malucchi), the daughter of a wealthy governor. The story is set in the Thai province of Suphan Buri in the 1950s, and revolves around Dum's failure to meet Rumpoey at a designated time and place (the *sala* on the lake). Dum is a member of an outlaw cowboy gang and, complicating their relationship, Rumpoey's father has arranged her engagement to Kumjorn, an ambitious police captain. Through flashbacks, Sasanatieng shows how, as children, Dum and Rumpoey spent time together during the Second World War, when Rumpoey and her father left the city to stay on Dum's father's rural farm. However, due to an incident when Rumpoey nearly drowned, they became separated for almost ten years, before accidentally meeting outside a Bangkok college where they were both studying. At this meeting, they agreed to seek each other out, and rendezvous at the *sala* on the lake in one year's time to elope. But, following a fight to save Rumpoey from being attacked by a gang of boys, Dum is expelled and returns home.

Dum arrives at the family's rural farm only to find his father and brothers have been shot, and in their dying moments he learns who has committed the atrocity. Taking his father's rifle, he attacks the perpetrators, killing several before escaping to the forest where he prepares to kill himself. At this moment, he is saved by Fei, the leader of an outlaw cowboy gang, who recognizes the rifle as belonging to Dum's father and agrees to make amends. Dum joins the gang, wherein he is known as the Black Tiger, and soon becomes the bandit leader's second-in-command, a rank that causes some tension with Fei's deputy, Mahesuan, leading to the duel scene [Figure 5.1]. Meanwhile, Captain Kumjorn obtains the provincial governor's approval to hunt down Fei's gang, but before leaving, he meets Rumpoey in the hallway to say goodbye. Having tracked the bandits to their hideout, there follows a spectacular gunfight, in which he almost succeeds in his mission until Dum and Mahesuan arrive with hand-held rocket launchers, decimating everyone except Kumjorn.

Dum follows Kumjorn, intent on his execution, and in this process discovers a photograph that leads him to realize that Kumjorn is engaged to

FIGURE 5.1 *Tears of the Black Tiger* "duel" scene between hero gunfighter Dum and gang member Mahesuan. Credit: *Tears of the Black Tiger* (written and directed by Wisit Sasanatieng, 2000; distributed by Five Star Production and Magnolia Pictures).

Rumpoey. This revelation causes Dum to let Kumjorn escape, even though the outlaws' leader Fei vows to attack the governor's mansion and disrupt the wedding. Dum betrays his leader and tries to warn Kumjorn, but the attack takes place and Dum is caught up in the conflict, killing his rival Mahesuan, who was attempting to carry away the unconscious Rumpoey. After rescuing her, Dum helps Rumpoey to her feet, and is then confronted by her betrothed Kumjorn, who, in the heavy rain, sees Dum reaching for something, and assuming it is a gun, shoots and kills him. The film ends with Rumpoey crying over the dying Dum, the latter having not been reaching for a weapon, only a photograph of Rumpoey.

What this description of the narrative elements of *Tears of the Black Tiger* cannot adequately convey is the impact of the cast's deliberately stilted performances and the film's exuberant visual style. Bradshaw describes the film's key elements as being its "brash overacting and oversaturated Day-Glo colours, cheekily obvious sets and back projections" (Bradshaw 2001: 1). The Seattle Film Festival described the "sumptuous, at times almost hallucinatory, richness of the imagery" in the film (quoted in Harrison 2007: 199). Edward Buscombe observes that Sasanatieng "saturates the screen with rich hues of turquoise, pink and lime green," a palette which Buscombe equates with the stencil-colored stills of B-Westerns rather than the black-and-white films themselves (Buscombe 2001: 1). Rachel Harrison (2007) notes that every shot seems to have some digital enhancement, whether it is through altering the color grading or applying an effect to create flashbacks that are "authentic" to both timeline and plot direction. This effect was achieved by Oxide Pang, Sasanatieng's *telecene* colorist on the production, who filmed certain scenes on 35mm black-and-white film before transferring them onto Betacam tape and then digitally recoloring the footage. In this way, several scenes in the film evoke 1950s Thai cinema and, at the same time, the re-colored film posters released to promote American westerns in Thailand. In large part because of this inventiveness, *Tears of the Black Tiger* has been a rare Thai film that has received a critical academic response from the West.

While some research has been undertaken into the history of Thai cinema, including early screenings and buildings (Barmé 1999), Lewis argues that the relationship between Thai cinema and the country's cultural identity has been largely overlooked (Lewis 2003). However, *Tears of the Black Tiger* is an exception to this, being analyzed in literary and cinema studies as well as through Asian studies. For example, Buscombe suggests the Thai western is another example of "cross-cultural fertilization" that includes the transposition of stories and characters from one location to another (Buscombe 2001: 34). However, to place the film in this category and argue that its postmodern agenda has no content and/or is all parody is, as Damian Sutton (2012) argues, mistaken. References to Thai culture and history include the historical period when bandits and lawlessness took hold in the province of Sephan Buri, the way the bandit Mahesuan spits Betel nut juice (a traditional Thai male custom), and the original title *Fa Thalai Jone* which is derived from a traditional herbal remedy that literally translates as "bandits attacked from the skies" (Sutton 2012: 40). While the first example might be mistaken for a general parody of American cowboy films, and the second a reference to Clint Eastwood's character in *The Outlaw Josey Wales* (Eastwood, dir., 1976), the third example has no such Western interpretation and grounds the film firmly in Thai culture.

Khoo's critical examination of Asian cinema argues that the "Asian western" is notable for not being a copy or parody of an American "original," but rather it represents the desire for a new cinematic trajectory (Khoo 2013: 84). To conceptualize the place of the Asian western in cinema studies, Khoo draws upon Jeffrey Sconce's term "bad" cinema, noting that this descriptor enables audiences to "approach a film with a fresh and slightly defamiliarized perspective," thereby providing the possibility for a critique of dominant film methodologies (Sconce 2008: 17). Sconce's terminology offers the possibility to question not only "taste," relative to the super-saturated architectural color field, but also the spatial uncertainty induced by *trompe l'oeil*. Moreover, Western audiences tend to seek imagery of the undeveloped world as "nostalgia for primitivism" evidenced not only through constructed histories, but in mainstream media and television travel and cooking shows that promote local color over engagement with modernity. To this extent, this chapter examines the interiors of new Thai cinema and how they might contest existing representations of architectural space.

The Western interior as "Other"

Caught between his rural family farm, the governor's house and the bandit camp, Dum's world is set within three spaces reflecting, respectively, his peasant traditions, political aspirations and revolutionary intentions. The rural home with its thatched roof is presented in muted colors, the governor's neoclassical house with a brightly colored yellow exterior and pink and blue interior, and the anarchic bandit camp with its brown hues reminiscent of cowboy forts and stockades. With this in mind, two scenes emerge that suggest the potential of *Tears of the Black Tiger* to affect an understanding of the Oriental interior, or at least an interior that is recast through Baudrillard's notion of the seductive and potentially subversive *trompe l'oeil*. The first is the excess of reality in the "duel" scene, the second is the strangely colored, but otherwise statically framed, blue and pink interior of the governor's house.

The duel scene commences with Dum reclining on a tree trunk, playing the harmonica, and being confronted by Mahesuan. In the foreground is a field of knee-high grass, the tree is angled to the right of the viewer and behind the tree is a line of low hills and a sun-filled sky. Yet none of these elements even aspire to realism. The grass is unnaturally golden and consistent, seeming to glow from below. The tree is patently artificial, with plastic shiny leaves, and the sky is a dramatic painted backdrop, positioned barely behind the actors and with no illusion of depth. The rays of the sun, angled gold and orange bands against a bright blue sky, are echoed in the design on the back of Mahesuan's shirt, so that when he faces into the "view" he partially merges with the scenery. This densely colored and layered sequence is largely filmed from one frontal angle, which is interspersed with close-ups of the actors' faces. As if to exaggerate the already overwhelming sense of unreality, in one sequence Mahesuan even slides sideways through the grass without moving his legs or body, as if floating along a perfectly smooth, sound stage floor.

Much like its 1940s American western counterpart, the duel scene was filmed entirely in a studio. In the DVD Special Feature "Making of *Tears of the Black Tiger*" (2000), Sasanatieng describes this as a moment when "everything needs to be unreal," "like a stage set" with a "wealth of surreal beauty" and where the setting represents an important moment in time, even if it is nothing more than a painted backdrop with a few minimal props [Figure 5.2]. This scene, with the two gunfighters facing each other, is superficially reminiscent of a museum diorama or a traveling nineteenth-century panorama with the players—often animals, native people or historic

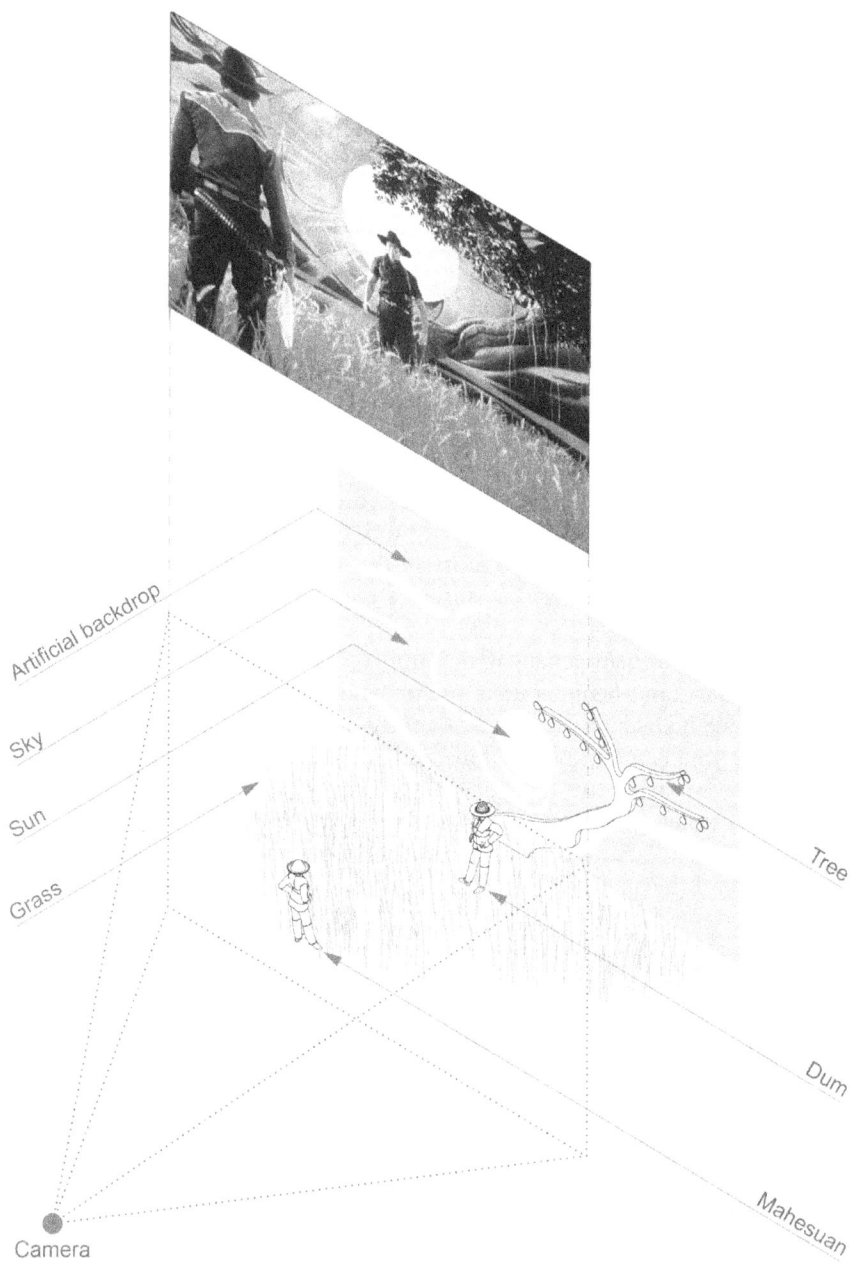

FIGURE 5.2 Digital reconstruction of *Tears of the Black Tiger* "duel" scene showing camera position, character placement, and stage set. Drawn by Jasmine Richardson.

events—neatly presented for visual consumption. In the original Hollywood films of the 1930s and 1940s, the painted "backing" with its artificial scenography was meant to give the illusion that the event was occurring in both a real place and in a wider context (Ramírez 2004). Yet, large sections of Sasanatieng's film are actually photographed in real locations, with expansive views of the countryside. Furthermore, some sequences that are filmed in real locations have also been modified during post-production to bring out their colors or control the levels of saturation. Yet, even with these techniques available, Sasanatieng still chose to depict a key scene in the film using a version of the classic western backdrop.

Sasanatieng's *trompe l'oeil* in the duel is a curious simulacrum as it is neither hyper-real (an almost-perfect replica which through its verisimilitude challenges the status of the original), nor an empty sign (a lifeless but accurate representation, divorced of its content and meaning). Instead, this setting exposes its interiority, making a statement about a distinct characteristic of the Hollywood studio system of the 1940s that the original westerns tried so hard to hide. Where the original backdrops commissioned in Hollywood by the likes of Cecil B. DeMille and John Ford oscillated, respectively, between hyper-real and lifeless, Sasanatieng celebrates the forgotten interiority of the western sound stage using a local tradition as inspiration. As Sutton notes, the painted backdrops used by Sasanatieng are strongly reminiscent of those found in "Thai *likay* folk theatre" (2012: 40).

Several further factors that are both noteworthy and closely related to the *likay* tradition include the way Mahesuan and Dum are clothed, positioned and then moved around this interior, as if no more than stage props themselves, and typically with their feet hidden from view. While the filming, with its alternating close-ups of faces and eyes, juxtaposed with long shots of the two protagonists, is reminiscent of the famous "stand-off" in *The Good, the Bad and the Ugly* (Leone, dir., 1966), Sasanatieng's costumes and staging are static and artificial like those of the *likay* theater. Thus, on one level, they are still "cowboy" clothes and postures (although more in the manner of Gene Autry than John Wayne), but in most other ways they recall a distinct Thai presentation. *Likay* was a popular form of entertainment in Thailand in the 1920s and 1930s, where it was celebrated for its stilted, pantomime performances, lack of props and its flamboyant costumes that often covered the legs and feet of performers, allowing them to seem to glide across the stage (Brandon 1967). When seen in this way, Sasanatieng's duel sequence is not just an appropriation of a Western motif, but a celebration of its themes and limitations using the values of traditional Thai theater.

The governor's house is seemingly a very different type of space. Despite its vividly colored exterior, the house has a symmetrical composition following the classical tradition, and is sufficiently articulated for the viewer to recognize that it is not a painted backdrop. However, the way the house is presented, from its decoration to its color pallet and inhabitation, shows a similar set of concerns to the way Sasanatieng constructed his duel interior. The primary space in the governor's house considered in this chapter is the hallway where Kumjorn meets Rumpoey and then declares he is going to hunt down the outlaw gang [Figure 5.3]. This space is dominated by a grand staircase, reminiscent of that used by Scarlett O'Hara (Vivian Leigh) in the motion picture version of *Gone with the Wind* (Fleming, dir., 1939). In a key scene, Rumpoey, leaving her maid behind on the half-landing, slowly descends down the center of the red-carpeted stairway into the foyer of the governor's house. She is wearing a turquoise dress fitted across the shoulders and tight in the waist, which drops into a folded full skirt. This costume seems to be based on original post-Second World War clothing, or derived from period films and film posters. Waiting at the base of the stairs and half-turned towards the camera is Kumjorn, wearing a khaki military uniform, with peaked hat, brown leather boots, belt and sash. He stands to the side, allowing the viewer an uninterrupted view of Rumpoey. This neoclassical interior is split into two striking colors, teal blue for the ground floor and pink on the first floor, with door frames and window reveals in white, and stairs and balustrades in gray and brown. The heavily pattered tiled floor provides a textured backdrop for the actors' movements and accentuates the brightly colored setting. In the center and directly above Rumpoey, the pink wall is divided by a white cruciform frame on which hangs a coat-of-arms.

What is most striking about this interior, and the people arrayed in it, is its curiously rich, yet visually static, presentation. Much like the interior presented in the duel and in traditional *likay* theater, this space is sumptuous yet strangely formal. People are either static or, like Rumpoey as she descends the stair, moving as if in a choreographed and controlled way. In the European cinematic tradition, classic romantic dramas of the 1940s frequently portrayed women progressing slowly down a long staircase of this type. Alison McKee argues that this cinematic framing authorized a "heteronormative masculine-identified point of view" (2014: 139). Mary Ann Doane proposes that in 1940s cinema, the "staircase is traditionally the locus of the specularization of a woman" (1987: 136). Whether such a reading is reasonable or not, these views emphasize the glamor of the setting, the clothing and the leading lady. In the case of *Tears of the Black Tiger*, the camera's objectification transforms the staircase and the interior into an extension of Rumpoey's dress, while simultaneously suggesting her social passage from being a private member of her father's household (signified by the upper level of the hallway, which is lined with bedrooms) to her suitor waiting in the more public space of the foyer below. This shift is reinforced by the use of pink for the more private space and blue for the public, dramatizing the separation between levels.

Ultimately, the exaggeration present in the interior of the governor's villa is not a result of a staged painted backdrop, this is not a literal *trompe l'oeil*, but

EXCESSIVE *TROMPE L'OEIL* IN *TEARS OF THE BLACK TIGER* 87

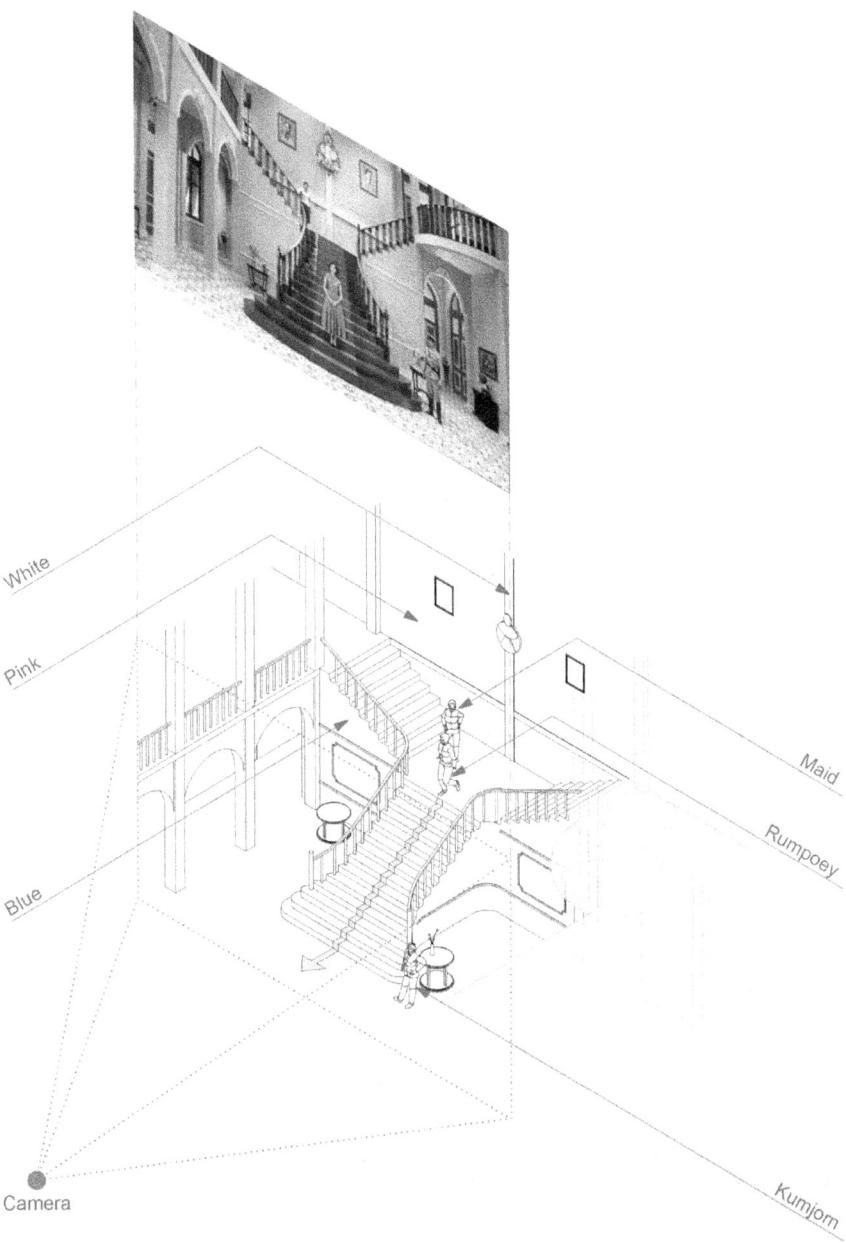

FIGURE 5.3 Digital reconstruction of *Tears of the Black Tiger* "hallway" scene showing camera position, character placement, and stage set. Drawn by Jasmine Richardson.

of its use of flat, saturated colors across entire surfaces. This affect suggests a defamiliarized reality where the expression of the European neoclassical interior is questioned. For example, where a real neoclassical interior might feature muted pink, patterned walls, or a pale blue freeze and even white timber detailing, none of these features would draw the eye in such a way. Sasanatieng's interior takes colors and motifs that might be present in a European romance, and then exaggerates them, a move that gives the interior a flattened appearance. Rather than drawing an artificial reality on a flat backdrop, the three-dimensional properties of the governor's villa are repressed.

The *trompe l'oeil*

In both scenes from *Tears of the Black Tiger*, the interior is brought into focus not only by the décor and coloration, but by the inclusion of actors or participants who add a further cultural construction such that body and space are intertwined. Whereas the nineteenth-century European notion of gendered spaces proposed that the body and interior space were interchangeable, and affirmed women as an important ornamental factor in decorating a room, this conflatory metaphor is evident, but not central, to the scenes described. In this Eastern or Oriental retelling, the clothing of the gunfighter Mahesuan replicates the painted backdrop to create a spatial tension, rather than a submissive appropriation of the cinematic genre. Rumpoey, in her turquoise gown, remains the exquisite centerpiece of the room. However, by merging her into the interior, the masculinizing eye of the camera, and of the Western cinema's objectification of her body, is challenged.

Far from Said's reading of patronizing appropriations of the Eastern interior by the West, Sasanatieng's interiors are transformed from their conceptually sterile Western equivalents into color-saturated, preternaturally delineated constructions; hybrid spaces of Western origin which have become Easternized in their design, decoration, inhabitation and construction. These interiors have been wrenched from the annals of Western cinema, seemingly reversing the traditional readings of cultural appropriation promulgated by early postcolonial theorists. In Baudrillard's terms, the *trompe l'oeil* leaves the viewer "bewitched by the spell of the missing dimension" (1990: 67), its "uncanniness" (64) resists its potential to be dismissed as a lifeless copy, giving it a new life, and a new seductive potential.

References

Barmé, S. (1999), "Early Thai Cinema and Filmmaking: 1897–1922," *Film History*, 11(3): 308–318.
Barthes, R. (1981), *Camera Lucida: Reflections on Photography*, New York: Hill and Wang.

Barthes, R. (1983), *Empire of Signs*, New York: Hill and Wang.
Baudrillard, J. (1983), *Simulations*, New York: Semiotext(e).
Baudrillard, J. (1989), "The Trompe-l'Oeil," in Norman Bryson (ed.), *Calligram: Essays in New Art History from France*, Cambridge: Cambridge University Press: 53–62.
Baudrillard, J. (1990), *Seduction*, New York: St Martins Press.
Baudrillard, J. (1994), *Simulacra and Simulation*, Ann Arbor: University of Michigan Press.
Bradshaw, P. (2001), "The Lurid and the Lovely," *The Guardian*, May 14, http://www.guardian.co.uk/Archive/Article/0,4273,4185983,00.html [Accessed April 20, 2015].
Brandon, J. R. (1967), *Theatre in Southeast Asia*, Cambridge, MA: Harvard University Press.
Buscombe, E. (2001), "Way Out East," *Sight and Sound*, 11(9): 34–35.
Doane, M. A. (1987), *The Desire to Desire: The Woman's Film of the 1940s*, Bloomington: Indiana University Press.
Fellion, C. (2013), "Third Cinema Goes West: Common Ground for Film and Literary Theory in Postregional Discourse," *Western American Literature*, 48 (1): 41–55.
Harrison, R. (2007), " 'Somewhere Over the Rainbow': Global Projections/Local Allusions in *Tears of the Black Tiger/Fa thalai jone*," *Inter-Asia Cultural Studies*, 8 (2): 194–210.
Khoo, O. (2013), "Bad Jokes, Bad English, Good Copy: Sukiyaki Western Django, or How the West Was Won," *Asian Studies Review*, 37(1): 80–95.
Lewis, G. (2003), "The Thai Movie Revival and Thai National Identity," *Continuum: Journal of Media and Cultural Studies*, 17(1): 69–78.
McKee, A. L. (2014), *The Woman's Film of the 1940s: Gender, Narrative, and History*, New York: Routledge.
Ramírez, J. A. (2004), *Architecture for the Screen: A Critical Study of Set Design in Hollywood's Golden Age*, Jefferson, NC: McFarland.
Ruskin, J. (1843), *Modern Painters*, London: Smith, Elder and Co.
Said, E. W. (1978), *Orientalism*, London: Penguin Books.
Sconce, J. (2008), "'Trashing' the Academy: Taste, Excess and an Emerging Politics of Cinematic Style," in E. Mathijs and X. Mendik (eds.), *The Cult Film Reader*, Maidenhead: McGraw-Hill: 100–118.
Sutton, D. (2012), "Philosophy, Politics and Homage in *Tears of the Black Tiger*," in D. Martin-Jones and W. Brown (eds.), *Deleuze and Film*, Edinburgh: Edinburgh University Press: 37–53.
Tears of the Black Tiger/Fa Thalai Jone (2000), motion picture, Dir. Wisit Sasanatieng, Film Bangkok, DVD distributed by Magnolia Home Entertainment.

PART TWO

Gender and Sexual Identities

Introduction

John Potvin

Oriental interiors mark highly contested terrains and fraught spaces for the perceptions, conceptions and lived performances of gender and sexuality. The gendering of interior space in the East, differently though it is understood in the West, has long activated Orientalist responses to and perceptions of the Orient, largely expressed as a feminine site to be dominated, penetrated and protected precisely because of its fragility and vulnerability. The unbalanced gendered association with Oriental interiors is also a result of different modes of representation, which have affected who or what is depicted. In the case of Turkish baths, for example, manuals on the subject largely tended toward a discussion of men's use of the hygienic system, while academic paintings, such as those by Jean-Dominique Ingres and Jean-Léon Gérôme would have us believe these were spaces exclusive to women. Yet, imported to the West, Turkish baths usually serviced as an alternative all-male space; an interior design that facilitated homosocial communities, exoticism and sensualities to unfold (Potvin 2005).

Madeleine Dobie has shown how tenacious gendered representations are, especially of Oriental women. For her, stock portrayals of Oriental women "constitute a key dimension of what Edward Said has described as the 'citational' repertory of Orientalism: the practice of intertextual borrowing and repetition from which Western representations of the Orient derive their authority" (Dobie 2001: 3). Reina Lewis's enquiry into women's representations of Oriental women has largely been responsible for instigating the study of gender and sexuality beyond the trope of male fantasy "thereby transforming the harem from a sexual to a social space" (Beaulieu and Roberts 2002: 15). As Lewis claims: "Orientalism establishes a set of polarities in which the Orient is characterized as irrational, exotic, erotic, despotic, and heathen, thereby securing the West in contrast as rational, familiar, moral, just and Christian" (1996: 16).

Much of the scholarly work in the area of gender, sexuality and Orientalism has largely, while not exclusively, been confined to women. Yet, a crucial aspect of the typological constructions that helped fashion the Orient/Occident binary is the way in which despotism, religious fanaticism, barbarism and violence have been grafted onto the bodies of Eastern men (Potvin 2003). The concern for masculinity, the interior and Orientalism remains, nevertheless, an undermined field of enquiry. Three of this Part's four chapters respond to the need for more attention to be paid to masculine experiences of Oriental interiors by calling attention to different forms of expression well beyond traditional confines and social expectations. In his recent, impressive and richly documented exploration of Orientalism and homoeroticism, Joseph Allen Boone attempts to chart the "ghostly presence of something 'like' male homoeroticism that haunts many Western male's fantasies and fears of Middle Eastern sexuality" (2014: xx). Boone argues that such a methodology would "bring Western and Middle Eastern discourses into proximity" and as a result provides a way to "dislodge the Eurocentric biases and Eurocentric biases and historicist logic that have traditionally organized the binary relation of Orient and Occident in an unequal hierarchy" (2014: xxii). Likewise, the four chapters that comprise this Part explore how the Oriental interior becomes a site of gender play and sexual dissidence, celebrating while circumnavigating, the implications and steadfast associations of the East–West axis as much as male–female binaries.

Inspired by the English translation of Antoine Galland's *Arabian Nights' Entertainment* (1706), women writers from the eighteenth century set out to fashion their own rewritings. In "Oriental Interiors in Eighteenth-Century British Women Writers' Novels," Marianna D'Ezio shows how some women writers deployed the luxuriant and licentious scenes in Eastern interiors as a means to call attention to patriarchal culture, providing a space in which readers could set out to question and challenge Western sexual mores and cultural ideals. Constantly teetering on the edges between Christian virtue and Oriental temptation, tyrannical masculinity and feminine piety, the scenes and spaces these British women writers describe even help to construct entire cities like Venice as a hybrid and liminal space precariously at the threshold between East and West.

Notions, values and theories of collecting have played a significant role, not only in the histories of the interior, but also factor into the interpolation of gender and sexuality into the expressions and experiences of the Oriental interior. Collections are integral to identity formation, the production of the self and the material culture of subjectivity. As Boone beautifully evokes:

> the physical or imaginative impulse to cross borders and enter the realms of the foreign and unknown is not simply a case of establishing unidirectional domination over or penetration of some monolithic ...

'Orient'. The act of crossing—whether traveling, writing, or reading—also tacitly signifies one's willingness to offer oneself up to unsuspected, multiple ways of being.

(2014: xxxiv)

Both the interior and the various collections they contain help to construct an imaginary landscape for the subject, as it speaks to the identity of the collector, the subjective value placed in the objects and the whole impression they help to fashion. As Christopher Reed shows, Oriental homosociality takes different forms. In "Bachelor Quarters: Spaces of *Japonisme* in Nineteenth-Century Paris," Reed discusses how French *japonisme* in the latter half of the nineteenth century gave rise to the construction of homosocial space as a form of private retreat. Inspired by fantasies of Japan, elaborate bachelor quarters designed by the Goncourt brothers, Henri Cernuschi and Hugues Krafft were direct responses to the increasing feminization of the public face of *japonisme*. East/West, feminine/masculine, private/private come together in Reed's exploration of *fin-de-siècle* bachelorhood, interior design and collecting.

Until more recently, Lord Leighton's Orientalism was seen to be confined to or localized in the form of the Arab Hall of his Holland Park home. However, as Anne Anderson shows in "Coming Out of the China Closet?: Performance, Identity and Sexuality in the House Beautiful," extant photographs of Leighton's collections of ceramics and textiles reveal a much more elaborate and sophisticated decorative program at play throughout the entire house. Japanese, Chinese, European and Islamic ceramics vied equally in Leighton's London studio-house, and, as Anderson evokes, Leighton's own identity and interior design program soon stood as being at odds with normative, gendered associations emblematized by the "china closet." Through various collections of different ceramic types, each displayed in its own room in the house, Leighton's domestic landscape blurred and troubled the traditional gendered attributions given to different interior spaces.

In my own chapter, Orientalism, dissident sexuality and aesthetic modernism overlap in the homophobic panic and cultural anxiety that ensued around impresario Rolfe De Maré's Villa Park (Hildesborg) in 1910s Stockholm. In "At the Edge of Propriety: Rolf de Maré and Nils Dardel at the Hildesborg Estate," I explore the clashing subjective expressions and social perceptions of male sexuality and the interiors that housed de Maré's collection of Oriental objects, furniture, rugs and skins as well as his collection of expressionist paintings by former lover Nils Dardel. These two men, along with ballet dancer Jean Börlin, expressed their sexual dissidence as much as their modernism in opposition to Swedish conversativism through an Orientalism that only served to further distance them from within Swedish society. As a result, the hybrid interiors of Villa Park offered both liberation and confinement for the men who dwelt in them.

References

Boone, J. A. (2014), *The Homoerotics of Orientalism*, New York: Columbia University Press.

Dobie, M. (2001), *Foreign Bodies: Gender, Language, and Culture in French Orientalism*, Stanford: Stanford University Press.

Lewis, R. (1996), *Gendering Orientalism: Race, Femininity, and Representation*, London and New York: Routledge.

Potvin, J. (2003), "Warriors, Slave Traders, and Religious Fanatics: Reporting the Spectacle of Islamic Male Bodies in the *Illustrated London News*, 1890–1900," in I. Boer (ed.), *After Orientalism*, Amsterdam and New York: Rodopi: 81–103.

Potvin, J. (2005), "Vapour and Steam: The Victorian Bath, Homosocial Health and Male Bodies on Display," *Journal of Design History*, 18(4) (Winter): 319–333.

6

Oriental Interiors in Eighteenth-century British Women Writers' Novels

Marianna D'Ezio

Following the publication of the English translation of Antoine Galland's French version of *Arabian Nights' Entertainments* (1706), in which the literary replica of the Oriental interiors of palaces and seraglios belonging to sultans and emperors were tainted with overt sensuality, a new trend in eighteenth-century British literature was set in motion, witnessing the production of numerous adaptations of the *Arabian Nights*. Women writers also attempted their own re-writings: their interest focused on the alluring connotations of Oriental interiors, where authors such as Penelope Aubin, Eliza Haywood, Frances Sheridan and Charlotte Dacre[1] would stage the actions of sultans and *jinns*—good and/or evil supernatural creatures (El-Zein 2009)—at the expense of innocent European women who, after a series of unfortunate events at sea, inevitably end up in a harem. Such luxuriant and aestheticized Oriental sceneries, harems, palaces, bedchambers, gardens, at first informed what Ros Ballaster identifies as European "mental maps" (2005a: 8) of the East that eighteenth-century readers were construing in their imagination, spaces where objects, scents, colors and flavors contributed to the creation and establishment of motifs and myths which will then typify the genre of the Western Oriental tale.

However, Oriental interiors and sultans' gardens also represented tangible examples of the European' (dangerous) fascination with "the unknown and the forbidden" (Yeazell 2000: 8) and were seen as both a *locus* where to reinterpret (and contest) misconceived notions of female submission to male power, and a space which could elicit an indirect reconsideration, and more often a confirmation, of women's role in what was viewed at the time as a patriarchal society. Eventually, Oriental houses and palaces were also idealized spaces through which Western readers could start questioning their own identity from social, gendered, national and cultural perspectives. Assuming that, by the end of the eighteenth century, representations of Oriental interiors had been codified as signifiers of Eastern ominous characteristics and, by analogy, as threatening symbols of Oriental degradation and inferiority, to become a synecdoche of Oriental territories and cultural practices as a whole, this chapter analyzes the ways in which Oriental spaces were gradually canonized for Western readers in a selection of popular eighteenth- and early nineteenth-century British women writers' novels.

In particular, I will first look at Penelope Aubin's novels, in which imaginary Oriental interiors, houses, bedchambers, gardens, turn into stereotyped spaces of lust and desire, fabricated to be perceived by British readers as a tantalizing yet dangerous "other" space. European women's resistance to the temptations of desire in such spaces through edifying symbolic actions embodied the notion of European "superior" courage and Christian virtue in opposition to the sanguine temper of Eastern "tyrants." At the other end of the scale, Charlotte Dacre's *Zofloya, or The Moor* (1806) enacts the transmigration of Oriental spaces into a European setting: Venice and Gothic Italian landscapes thus become a hybrid space, suspended between East and West, and provide a peculiar stage onto which Dacre could project, and eventually dispel, (European) fantasies of illicit eroticism. In Dacre's case, the attraction that the heroine of her novel feels for the Oriental "other" will be punished as Victoria di Loredani's failure to control her sensuality and resist the captivation of the Oriental atmospheres of Venetian bedchambers and orientalized gardens will lead her to inevitable perdition: her exposure to and experience of "Eastern" locations will thus become tantamount to embracing the debauchery of Eastern morals.

European versions of Oriental interiors: The legacy of Montagu's *Turkish Letters*

In 1711, the Earl of Shaftesbury's peremptory "Advice to an Author"[2] had already fully predicted, and also stigmatized, the influence that the appearance of the first English translation of Galland's *Livre des Mille et une Nuit* would have on its readers' taste and imagination as well as on the numerous translations, adaptations and imitations of *Arabian Nights* throughout the century.[3] The Earl, as Khalid Bekkaoui points out (2008: 156), insistently directed his reproof on *female* readership, and specifically on the "perversion" that the "monstrous Tales" of the *Arabian Nights* instilled in "the Fair Sex of this Island," persuasively transforming "their natural Inclination for fair, candid, and courteous Knights, into a Passion for a mysterious Race of Black Enchanters: such as of old were said to creep into Houses, and lead captive silly Women" (Cooper 1711: 1,348). The success of *Arabian Nights* contributed to the further spread of literary images of fascinating Oriental sultans and emperors tainted with despotism, violence, and overt sensuality and sexuality, besides fueling the "transmigration" (Ballaster 2005b) of its literary genre into Europe, shaping the trend of Oriental narratives, particularly in France and Britain.

About seventy years after the publication of *Arabian Nights* in English, Clara Reeve systematically discussed the passion for, and the fashion of, Oriental tales, concluding that the readers' attraction towards exotic landscapes and interiors and virile Moors, the settings and antagonists of Oriental narratives, could blur the boundaries between Orient and Occident to become universally acknowledged "in all the Countries beyond the Levant" (1785b: 1, 23–24). However, Reeve also echoed the Earl's censure of *Arabian Nights*, recognizing that Eastern tales "do more than catch the attention, for they retain it. There is a kind of fascination in them, when once we begin a volume, we cannot lay it aside ... and yet upon reflection we despise and reject them" (1785b: 2, 5, 8–9). In short, Reeve noted, Oriental tales "are certainly *dangerous* books for youth, they create and encourage the wildest excursions of imaginations," thus sympathizing with the Earl's definition of "monstrous Tales" that seduced and debauched female readership: Reeve's and the Earl's language of rejection and condemnation patently drew its lexicon from a paradigm of traditional, clear-cut oppositions that already (and still) ideologically distinguished the West from the East, such as Christian *vs.* non-Christian, civic liberties *vs.* despotism, political order *vs.* anarchy, modern conquest *vs.* classical heredity, and enlightened thought *vs.* violent behavior. Similar oppositions informed eighteenth-century Grand Tour narratives and descriptions of the "warm South," especially Italy and the Mediterranean, which, particularly towards the end of the century, rivaled with Oriental narratives as the favorite setting of an obscure "Otherness," as happened, for example, in the interiors of Gothic novels, such as ruined castles, dark monasteries, secret trap-doors and vaults (Pfister 1996: 5).

The majority of adaptations and imitations of *Arabian Nights* confirmed and insisted upon such oppositions. Representations of Oriental interiors that emerged from the *Arabian Nights* were particularly captivating, providing readers with a taste of Oriental life and customs; the result was a literary medium that categorized differences between cultures, employing eighteenth-century European projections of imagined gardens and interiors to support contrasts between East and West.

The few descriptions of "real" Oriental interiors, not the luxurious gardens and the sumptuous yet oppressive harems of novels and translations, were penned by women travelers who had the uncommon opportunity to observe Eastern interiors as ambassadors' and diplomats' wives, and produced authentic accounts of their first-hand experience. At the beginning of the eighteenth century, Lady Mary Wortley Montagu provided the archetypal description of a Turkish house, a model on which successive writers based their invented descriptions charged with the troubling presence of clichéd Oriental ravishers, as "required" for European imagination. Montagu reversed the stereotype the recipients of her letters had in mind, to offer an unbiased version of the "magnificence" of the interiors she was invited to explore while in Adrianople in 1717:

> I suppose you have read, in most of our accounts of Turkey, that their houses are the most miserable pieces of building in the world. I can speak very learnedly on that subject, having been in so many of them; and, I assure you, 'tis no such thing . . . Every house, great and small, is divided into two distinct parts, which only join together by a narrow passage. The first house has a large court before it, and open galleries all round it . . . This gallery leads to all the chambers, which are commonly large, and with two rows of windows . . . [T]he adjoining one is called the "haram," that is, the ladies apartment, (for the name of "seraglio" is peculiar to the grand signior;) it has also a gallery running round it towards the garden, to which all the windows are turned, and the same number of chambers as the other, but more gay and splendid, both in painting and furniture. The second row of windows is very low, with grates like those of convents; the rooms are all spread with Persian carpets, and raised at one end of them . . . about two feet. This is the sofa, which is laid with a richer sort of carpet, and all round it a sort of couch, raised half a foot, covered with rich silk, according to the fancy or magnificence of the owner. Mine is of scarlet cloth, with a gold fringe; round about this are placed, standing against the wall, two rows of cushions . . . and here the Turks display their greatest magnificence. They are generally brocade, or embroidery of gold wire upon white sattin [sic]. Nothing can look more gay and splendid . . . The rooms are low, which I think no fault, and the ceiling is always of wood, generally inlaid or painted with flowers. They open in many places, with folding doors, and serve for cabinets, I think, more conveniently than ours. Between the windows are little arches to set pots of perfume, or baskets of flowers. But what pleases me best, is the fashion of having marble fountains in the lower part of the room, which throw up several spouts of water, giving, at the same time, an agreeable coolness, and a pleasant dashing sound, falling from one basin to another . . . Each house has a bagnio, which consists generally in two or three little rooms, leaded on the top, paved with marble, with basins, cocks of water, and all conveniences for either hot or cold baths.
>
> (1965: 1,234–1,235)

Montagu's description contains all the items that will become customary in subsequent narratives set in the East, as well as those sharing with

Oriental settings their fictional display of luxuriousness and extravagance, as opposed to European rationalized and efficient spaces of houses and gardens. In Montagu, however, Persian carpets, sofas, couches, cushions, sophisticated fabrics, brocades, embroidery and rich perfumes contribute to define Oriental spaces as fascinating, not tantalizing; magnificent, not provocative. Her plethora of charming details, in the houses as well as in the well-known episode at the Turkish *hammam*, bestows on the women she meets a strong effect over the spaces they preside as mistresses in charge of power, rather than slaves anxiously waiting for their master. Montagu's ground-breaking account, an exception in its own right, was construed on the basis of a shared notion of the private spaces of the house that Western and Eastern women alike knew very well. The "ladies apartment" that Montagu portrays undoubtedly resembles that liminal space suspended between public and private that constituted eighteenth-century European women's opportunity to lead their own coterie, the salon. Condemned by Rousseau as "dangerously frivolous female establishments" (1967: 204), networks of exclusively female gatherings, such as the Bluestockings in Britain, resisted the masculinized nature of public spaces and represented a comfortable option for women who were not allowed to frequent clubs and coffee-houses of London. The seraglio that Galland turned into a salon where "*précieuse* women orchestrate and regulate polite speech" (Ballaster 2005a: 12) could be threatening not because of its mesmerizing features, rather for its innuendo about a *locus* for potential subversion of the established gender hierarchy.

In their passage from East to West, the Oriental interiors that Montagu had accurately and rightfully described unavoidably mingled with and contributed to the accepted conventional version of *Arabian Nights*,[4] and from that moment on were manipulated, transformed and eventually distorted into a "hybrid commodity" (Ballaster 2005a: 4) for the amusement of middle- and upper-class readers who could thus only gather a "manufactured" (Said 1978: 46) version of the Orient and its interiors.

"Needless to tell you the Beauty and Magnificence of the Place": Aubin's "Oriental" interiors

The chronotope of opulent, lavish interior spaces of Oriental palaces that featured in British Oriental narratives required that the physical territories of European heroines characterized by well-regulated spaces and strong morality be confronted with the lasciviousness and depravity of her attractive Eastern male counterparts and tempted by the dangerous, excessive beauty of luxurious Oriental houses and gardens, rich costumes, and the sensual atmosphere of sumptuous palaces controlled by treacherous yet intriguing and attractive masters. The latent temptation of enjoying the pleasures linked to such places and intersecting with their possessors challenges Christian European heroines who therefore have to struggle in order to bridle their instinctive desires. If European women eventually surrender to the seductions of Oriental lasciviousness and sensuality, their attractiveness as female protagonists is consequently encoded into Eastern patterns of beauty, characterized in turn by excessive fierce passions, and leading to uncontrolled violence and destruction. Narratives of *women* exposed to and jeopardized by the lust of Oriental interiors and gardens were particularly effective, since their resistance to the temptations of desire, represented by Eastern fascination, could help establish pious examples of European superior courage and models of Christian virtue.

Novels and tales inspired by *Arabian Nights* skillfully portrayed Oriental interiors to depict imagined details of unknown places which endlessly repeated the same pattern. The typical setting for an Oriental "scene" would aim at displaying grandeur in furniture and details, and charm in perfumes and flavors, to foster the stereotype of the beautiful captive who audaciously resists the seductive menace of Eastern tyrants, triumphantly shrinks from the encounter with Oriental "others" and, back to her country, juxtaposes her untainted virtue in the West with the violence of sexual subjugation in the East. Unlike Montagu's, fictionalized representations of Oriental interiors purposely insisted on descriptions of houses and interiors "with every thing that could charm the senses, or captivate the fancy" such as "costly furniture, magnificent habits, sumptuous equipage, and a grand retinue" (Sheridan 1767: 38–39). Interiors are now conceived as spaces where "time stands still" (Grosrichards 1998: 169), "senses [are] ravished with delight" and their inhabitants grow "lazy and effeminate," surrounded by the stillness of a magnificence that makes leaving the house unnecessary (Sheridan 1767: 41).

Aubin's novels contained the stereotypical interiors which characterized eighteenth-century Oriental narratives and established the fictional archetype for the genre. Her adventurous, almost picaresque novels, written and published on the wave of the success of *Arabian Nights*, featured a series of intricate plots that invariably surround the main storyline of a beautiful young and motherless heroine who, owing to improbable events, is forced to leave Europe and is taken captive by lewd sultans, or more generally Oriental "Barbarians," whose only objective seems to be her submission "to their libidinous Desires" (Aubin 1722a: 85).

In *The Strange Adventures of the Count de Vinevil* (1721), for the first time Aubin channels a sketched "Oriental interior" into a standard strategic description which will later characterize the setting of all her novels and feature in her readers' imagination. The "Apartments" in which the heroine Ardelisa is confined are initially described as rooms "where Painting, Downy Beds, and Habits fit for to cover that soft Frame, Gardens to walk in, and Food delicious, with faithful Slaves to wait upon you, invite your Stay; where I will feast each Sense, and make you happy as Mortality can be" (Aubin

1722a: 64–65). Such a "Stay," which Ardelisa seems to irresistibly enjoy, is further enhanced by delicious food and wardrobes full of wonderful clothes, and represents an interlude in the hectic narrative of her adventures, a delay in the development of the typical Western narrative of advance and progress, as opposed to "Oriental histories, endlessly circulating stories which only serve to confirm an unchanging state of subjection" (Grosrichards 1998: 169). Such fictional space is "a beautiful Apartment [with] a lovely Room [where] two Eunuchs enter'd ... with Sherbets of delicate Taste, preserv'd and cold Meats ... showing a rich Bedchamber, with Closets full of Womens Clothes" (Aubin 1722a: 65–66), where Ardelisa and her maid Nannetta linger, sip chocolate and even fantasize about exercising their control on the space that surrounds them. Illusory and manufactured as it is, however, this space is also identified by contrasts, such as deformed men (eunuchs and mutes) who "serve to magnify [the] complete masculinity of the sultan's power" (Ballaster 2005a: 82; Grosrichards 1998: 128). In Aubin's much-generalized East, ranging from Algiers to Constantinople, "the Monarch gives a loose to his Passions, and thinks it no Crime to keep as many Women for his Use, as his lustful Appetite excites him to like" (Aubin 1722b: x). The "Bedchamber" and "beautiful Apartment" thus function as places of expectation for the bursting on the scene of the real antagonist of the novels; the lustful, cruel sultan as the epitome of the entire East.

Aubin's novels support and further standardize the beautiful Western heroine/violent Eastern male pattern that insisted on "our beautiful Heroines" called to "suffer such Trials," since "the *Turks* and *Moors* have been ever famous for these Cruelties" (1722b: x). Ardelisa's morality, mirrored in her virtue since she married the Count de Vinevil, but did not consummate the marriage, is challenged by the absence of her lover and the temptations that the charm of Eastern locations suggest: the luxurious atmospheres of the Orient address European vulnerability and aim at its corruption, inflaming the protagonists' sexual desire, still unfulfilled. Eve-like, Ardelisa is thus tempted by the beauty of the garden in Osmin's seraglio, which stands for the ideal place for her seduction:

Ardelisa and *Nannetta* ventur'd into the Garden ... one of the most delightful Places Eyes ever saw: Fountains, and Groves, and Grottoes, where the Sun could never enter; long Walks of Orange and Myrtles, with Banks, where Flowers of the most lovely Kinds, and fragrant Scents stood crowded, with Pleasure-Houses built of *Parian* Marble, and within so wrought and painted, that it appear'd an earthly Paradise.

(1721: 69)

Ardelisa's fascination with the Turk's garden and her seclusion in the "beautiful Apartment" do not succeed in enthralling her as she resolves to resist Osmin's charming enticement. She rejects the enchantment of her own sexual desires and chooses to preserve her chastity, thus becoming "a warrior in the ideological crusade against the heathen, ignorant, and immoral East" (Gollapudi 2005: 678). Her resistance, deservedly rewarded with her safe return home and the consummation of her marriage, is sanctioned and even glorified when compared to her Eastern suitors' innate violence, that is in fact overtly *sexual* violence. Ardelisa's Christian morality triumphs over her Oriental ravishers, and she staunchly reifies her beauty as an object of unattainable desire, turning it into a powerful weapon for the defeat of the licentious Oriental potentates who attempt to exploit her femininity within the spaces of Oriental palaces and gardens. Ardelisa's extreme act of disobedience to Eastern power is, however, a violent one that aims at shattering the illusory reality of the Oriental spaces and dissolving her dangerously bewitching dream: as soon as she finds a way to escape Osmin's palace, "the Seraglio [was] being fired ... by *Ardelisa*, who left it burning" (87). Ardelisa's moral integrity surpasses temptations and boastfully defies the sensual attraction towards the "corrupted" pleasures represented by the supposed immorality of Eastern locations.

Zofloya, or Oriental interiors crossing the boundaries of Europe

If Aubin's popular novels had portrayed and perpetuated Oriental interiors as places *par excellence* to condemn Eastern dangerous excess while celebrating European virtue, in Dacre's *Zofloya* readers witnessed the transmigration of Oriental stereotyped interiors, sensual beauty and violence into Europe itself, with the fatal consequences of undomesticated desire, nourished by the decline of the Oriental narrative genre and the emergence, by contrast, of a literature of national celebration. Notwithstanding the changing attitude towards Oriental cultural practices that had emerged in Britain during the period of the Hastings trial (1787–1795), prompted by a persistent ambivalence between colonial anxiety and imperial guilt, the "East," now including not only the "fictionalized and fantastic exoticism" of that "pseudo-Arabia" and "pseudo-Islam" (Makdisi et al. 2008: 16) of the *Arabian Nights*, but also the south of Asia and especially India, continued to be depicted and perceived as dangerous and depraved.

Conventional representations of Oriental interiors became more conspicuous, capitalizing on Aubin's descriptions which had become customary in the last wave of publications devoted to the trend of the Oriental tale. "Neat" and "well-furnish'd Houses" with "Carpets, Porcelane, Quilts, Painting, Screens, and such Furniture as the *Persians* of Distinction use; with three well-drest Slaves, who brought Wine, Sherbet, and Fowl, and boil'd Rice," "Sweet-meats, Cold-meats, and the most delicious things that please the Taste" (1722b: 26, 105), and their occupants, as, for example, the Turkish Admiral in Aubin's last novel *Count Albertus*, "seated on a *Persian* carpet, with a Banquet before him; every thing ... magnificent, his dress and Turbant shone with Diamonds and precious Jewels" (1728: 86) will continue to distinguish Western descriptions, either directly or indirectly, of Oriental interiors and characters (see, for example, Jane Eyre's perturbing portrayal of Rochester, or more recently, Frank Miller and Lynn Varley's representation of Xerxes in their 1998 graphic novel *300*). Despite the uproar and indignation that Hastings raised in public opinion, native despotism would still remain the lens through which Europeans viewed the Orient, at least officially. The stage on which Aubin displayed the opposition between providential Christian chastity *versus* perverse lasciviousness found new vigor: Oriental captivity narratives, with their harems, palaces and gardens full of appealing flowers and fruits, turned into undisputed expressions of some of the most pervasive myths of Western culture and mirrored Europeans' psychosexual needs to provide a peculiar space onto which to project illicit erotic fantasies.[5]

Dacre's *Zofloya* easily fits in such literary milieu. "Of an implacable, revengeful, and cruel nature" (4), Victoria di Loredani's immoral personality emerges in her propensity for spaces that are unmistakably styled after the Oriental interiors capitalized by Aubin. Her deficiency in redeeming her impetuous nature follows a path that is the opposite of Aubin's female characters, because hers is governed by sexual desire. She is not capable of nurturing any sentiment of love, and her frantic attachment to Berenza, her first lover and then husband whom she will poison to pursue his brother Henriquez, is but an early proof of her "unabashedly libidinous imagination" (Dunn 1998: 307). Borrowing the allegory of the beautiful heroine imprisoned in the exotic garden of the seraglio, where female virtue is tempted, Dacre describes the garden of the villa where Victoria's mother Laurina and her lover Ardolph confine her as a place of an allusively erotic freedom "yet unknown to Victoria":

> It so happened, that one evening they perambulated to a part of the garden which was yet unknown to Victoria: it was a beautiful close avenue, the sides and roof of which were interwoven branches of vine and honeysuckle; the entrance was almost concealed by a thick shrubbery, which it required no slight ingenuity to penetrate; and, from the serpentine direction of the path, it appeared wholly impossible to ascertain its extent.
> (53)

Rather than resisting the lure of temptation, as happened to Aubin's female protagonists, Victoria rebelliously abandons herself to her desires, and when she finally slips away from her confinement, it is to satisfy her sexual attraction for Berenza that "she darted, like a wild bird newly escaped from its wiry tenement, into the beautiful and romantic wood that presented itself to her ravished view" (56). Victoria's depravation articulates through the spaces she experiences in her symbolic descent from heaven to the abyss of hell. When she flees from her family and moves in with her suitor Berenza, Victoria finds herself in "a sumptuous an brilliantly illuminated chamber [where] the walls were covered with large resplendant [sic] mirrors, that variously reflected her simply attired but graceful figure" (66). Reminiscent of Montagu's descriptions of the "haram," Victoria's "elegant bed . . . rose in the form of a dome, bordered with deep gold fringe . . . and was surmounted by a superb canopy, the curtains . . . drawn on each side, but remained opened at the foot" (69, 81), like a stage altar on which she could perform the offering of her body, first to Berenza, then to the Moor Zofloya.

However, it is in a scented Oriental garden that her fatal encounter with her brother-in-law's servant Zofloya occurs, definitively sanctioning Victoria's passage from coveted desire to overt sensuality which will develop into cruelty as the presence of Zofloya in gardens and bedchambers becomes more and more persistent. Zofloya's allure draws entirely on descriptions of Oriental masters: he is of "a noble and majestic form" (136), "polished and superior appearance" (137), and "his form and attitude . . . was majestic, and solemnly beautiful, not the beauty which may be freely admired, but acknowledged with sensations awful and indescribable" (151). Dacre's "hyper-masculinization" of Zofloya (Gentile 2009: 17) mirrors the de-femininization of Victoria, who eventually turns into "horrible Victoria" (260) and not only subverts gender stereotypes, but also engages in an interracial intercourse with Zofloya that is culturally unacceptable, and therefore diabolical, notwithstanding the Moor's noble origins.[6] Zofloya's presence is in fact increasingly sexualized, especially when he appears in Victoria's dreams, in her bedchamber:

> Scarcely had her head reclined upon her pillow, ere the image of Zofloya swam in her sight; she slumbered, and he haunted her dreams; sometimes she wandered with him over beds of flowers, sometimes over craggy rocks, sometimes in fields of the brightest verdure, sometimes over burning sands, tottering on the ridge of some huge precipice, while the angry waters waved in the abyss below.
>
> (143)

"Wretched" Victoria's fall into the abyss, her fate at the end of the novel, with Zofloya revealing himself as Satan dragging her to Hell, also occurs because of her frustration with respect to the paradigms of femininity imposed on her. She reacts to Berenza and his brother Henriquez's demanding stereotype of female beauty, which requires "not the perfection of the *body* only . . . but the perfection also of the *mind*" (70), and resolves to destroy such a paradigm by killing Henriquez's fiancée Lilla. Victoria's violent fierceness on Lilla's body is indeed a symbol of her obstinate rejection of the ideal of "fairy-like beauty" and "angelic countenance" (133) that Lilla represents and that Aubin had idealized through her virtuous heroines. In the bloody scene where Victoria repeatedly stabs Lilla, "virtually enact[ing] male penetration" (Dunn 1998: 314), Victoria finally turns into "Barbarous Victoria," and the scenery changes from the luxuriant gardens of her desire to "a stunted shrub," "huge precipices" and "surrounding solitude" (225) that reflect her defeat, since she has not been able to domesticate her desire to dwell instead on the "gloomy anarchy" (182) represented by the Moor. At the end of the novel, those "[c]ommon objects" which had characterized Victoria's safe spaces before the Moor "penetrated her thoughts" eventually "shrink in his presence" (233) to transmute the slave Zofloya into Victoria's "equal" (242): though Dacre's novel, on one hand, tried to reassess the targets of women's desires, on the other hand fully restrained such desires by ultimately punishing the libidinous attractiveness of Oriental interiors and Eastern characters.

Visions and revisions of the Orient *could* offer women writers a new possibility to analyze and question their position in their own society, and indeed provided a fictional space onto which they could project their ambitions and aspirations in keeping with a much more desirable physical space where learned women wanted to be accepted as social and cultural agents in their own right. The prospects offered by the hybrid space of the Oriental interiors, as Montagu had posited, could be a starting point to reconsider gendered spaces in Western societies—the public clubs, coffeehouses, and assemblies on one side, and the private salons and conversations on the other—from a more malleable perspective, allowing more mature opportunities for learning from women's agency, rather than "domesticating" it to relegate them in clear-cut, easily identifiable spaces, as happened for Oriental characters. Yet a conscious stance in favor of the liberation of female desire within the spaces of Oriental interiors reinforced the tacit acceptance of European gendered and politicized norms of femininity which had safely guaranteed Aubin's novels the popularity they enjoyed at the time, rather than carving out a significant space for an alternative female voice that persuasively challenged political misrepresentations of the East. Aubin's "beautiful Ardelisa[s]" and Dacre's twofold female ego Victoria/Lilla were both expressions of an idealized, culturally constructed version of femininity which viewed exposure to Oriental settings and characters as a constant threat to the establishment, and as such regarded them as dangerously linked to the corruption of Western notions of propriety of female behavior and women's position within the appropriate spaces of eighteenth-century society.

Notes

1 Numerous British women writers, after the success of *Arabian Nights*, utilized the frame and narrative topoi of Galland's version and produced countless adaptations and pseudotranslations. Besides Aubin's and Dacre's novels, which will be discussed in more detail, it is worth mentioning Eliza Haywood's *Philidore and Placentia* (1727) and *Unfortunate Princess* (1741), Frances

Sheridan's *History of Nourjahad* (1767), Clara Reeve's *History of Charoba* (1785), Ellis Cornelia Knight's *Dinarbas* (1790), Mary Pilkington's *Asiatic Princess* (1800), and Maria Edgeworth's *Murad the Unlucky* (1804), among the most representative. For a more comprehensive list, see Conant (1908), Caracciolo (1968), Oueijan (1996), Makdisi and Nussbaum (2008).

2 "The love of strange narrations, and the ardent appetite towards unnatural objects, has a near alliance with the like appetite towards the supernatural kind . . . The tender virgins, losing their natural softness, assume this tragic passion, of which they are highly susceptible . . . A thousand Desdemonas are then ready to present themselves, and would frankly resign fathers, relations, countrymen, and country itself, to follow the fortunes of a hero of the black tribe. But whatever monstrous zeal, or superstitious passion, the poet might foretel, either in the gentlemen, ladies, or common people of an after-age; it is certain that as to books, the same Moorish fancy, in its plain and literal sense, prevails strongly at this present time" (Cooper 1711: 1,348–1,349).

3 The first "European" version of *Arabian Nights* is based on Antoine Galland's *Livre des Mille et une Nuit*, published in Paris between 1704 and 1717 in twelve volumes. As soon as the first seven volumes appeared in French (1706), they were translated into English, and by the end of 1712 a second English translation began to be published in Britain. All the editions of *Arabian Nights* that appeared during the century were translations from Galland's version. Among the numerous modern editions, I recommend *Arabian Nights' Entertainments* edited by Robert L. Mack (1995), based on Galland's edition, and *The Thousand and One Nights*, edited by Musin Mahdi (1984–1994).

4 Galland's version followed the original "but when modesty obliged us to [vary] it" (Mack 1995: 2). Galland's "version," with all its edulcorations, was a European text, designed for a European readership, and as such constituted a handbook of Eastern cultural practices, comprised by a series of tales that Galland often created "out of a slender outline" (Knipp 1974: 49).

5 This type of narrative continued to be very popular in nineteenth-century British literature, as in *The Lustful Turk* (1828), *The Seducing Cardinal's Amours* (1830), and *Scenes in the Seraglio* (1820–1830). See Romanets (2010).

6 Zofloya's past nobility, as Craciun notes, "disturb[s] the myth of European racial superiority" (2008: xx). On this, see also Mellor (2002), and Michasiw (1997: xxiii). Zofloya's origins, "though a Moor, and by a combination of events, and the chance of war . . . reduced to a menial situation, was yet of noble birth, of the race of the Abdoulrahmans" (Dacre 1997: 141), also inform Schotland's interesting reading of Zofloya in relation to abolitionist uprisings and contemporary debates on slavery (2009).

References

Aubin, P. (1721), *The Strange Adventures of the Count de Vinevil and His Family . . .*, London: Printed for E. Bell.
Aubin, P. (1722a), *The Life and Amorous Adventures of Lucinda, an English Lady . . .*, London: Printed for E. Bell.

Aubin, P. (1722b), *The Noble Slaves*, London: Printed for E. Bell.
Aubin, P. (1728), *The Life and Adventures of the Young Count Albertus* ..., London: Printed for J. Darby.
Ballaster, R. (2005a), *Fabulous Orients: Fictions of the East in England 1662–1785*, Oxford: Oxford University Press.
Ballaster, R. (2005b), "Narrative Transmigrations: The Oriental Tale and the Novel in the Eighteenth Century," in P. R. Backscheider and C. Ingrassia (eds.), *Eighteenth-Century Novel and Culture*, Oxford: Blackwell.
Bekkaoui, K. (2008), "White Women and Moorish Fancy in Eighteenth-Century Literature," in S. Maksidi and F. Nussbaum (eds.), *The Arabian Nights in Historical Context Between East and West*, Oxford: Oxford University Press.
Caracciolo, P. L. (1968), *The Arabian Nights in English Literature: Studies in the Reception of The Thousand and One Nights into British Culture*, London: St Martin's Press.
Conant, M. P. (1908), *The Oriental Tale in England in the Eighteenth Century*, New York: Columbia University Press.
Cooper, A. A., Earl of Shaftesbury (1711), *Characteristics of Men, Manners, Opinions, Times, With a Collection of Letters*, 3 vols, London [n.s.].
Craciun, A. (2008), "Introduction," in C. Dacre, *Zofloya, or The Moor*, Oxford: Oxford University Press.
Dacre, C. (1997), *Zofloya, or The Moor*, ed. K. I. Michasiw, Oxford: Oxford University Press.
Dunn, J. A. (1998), "Charlotte Dacre and the Feminization of Violence," *Nineteenth-Century Literature*, 53(3): 307–327.
El-Zein, A. (2009), *Islam, Arabs, and the Intelligent World of the Jinn*, Syracuse: Syracuse University Press.
Galland, A. (1712–1722), *Arabian Nights Entertainments: Consisting of One Thousand and One Stories, told by the Sultaness of the Indies, to divert the Sultan from the Execution of a Bloody Vow he had made to Marry a Lady every Day, and have her cut off next Morning, to avenge himself for the Disloyalty of his first Sultaness* ... London: Printed for Andrew Bell.
Gentile, K. J. (2009), "Sublime Drag: Supernatural Masculinity in Gothic Fiction," *Gothic Studies*, 11(1): 16–31.
Gollapudi, A. (2005), "Virtuous Voyages in Penelope Aubin's Fiction," *Studies in English Literature 1500–1900*, 45(3): 669–690.
Grosrichards, A. (1998), *The Sultan's Court: European Fantasies of the East*, trans. L. Heron, London: Verso.
Knipp, C. (1974), "*The Arabian Nights* in England: Galland's Translation and His Successors," *Journal of Arabic Literature*, 5: 44–54.
Mack, R. L. (ed.) (1995), *Arabian Nights' Entertainments*, New York: Oxford University Press.
Mahdi, M. (ed.) (1984–1994), *The Thousand and One Night*, 3 vols, Leiden: E. J. Brill.
Makdisi, S. and F. Nussbaum (eds.) (2008), *The Arabian Nights in Historical Context Between East and West*, Oxford: Oxford University Press.
Mellor, A. K. (2002), "Interracial Sexual Desire in Charlotte Dacre's *Zofloya*," *European Romantic Review*, 13: 169–173.
Michasiw, K. I. (1997), "Introduction," In C. Dacre, *Zofloya, or The Moor*, ed. K. I. Michasiw, Oxford: Oxford University Press: vii–xxx.

Montagu, M. W. (1965), *The Complete Letters of Lady Mary Wortley Montagu*, 3 vols, ed. R. Halsband, Oxford: Oxford University Press.
Oueijan, N. B. (1996), *The Progress of an Image: The East in English Literature*, New York: Peter Lang.
Pfister, M. (1996), *The Fatal Gift of Beauty: The Italies of British Travellers, An Annotated Anthology*, Amsterdam and Atlanta: Rodopi.
Reeve, C. (1785), *The Progress of Romance*, 2 vols, London: Printed for G. G. J. and J. Robinson.
Romanets, M. (2010), "Roxolana's Memoirs as a Garden of Intertextual Delight," in G. I. Yermolenko (ed.), *Roxolana in European Literature, History and Culture*, Burlington: Ashgate.
Rousseau, J. J. (1967), *Lettre à d'Alembert sur son article Genève* (1758), Paris: [n.d.].
Said, E. (1978), *Orientalism*. New York: Pantheon Books.
Schotland, S. D. (2009), "The Slave's Revenge: The Terror in Charlotte Dacre's *Zofloya*," *Western Journal of Black Studies*, 33(2): 121–131.
Sheridan, F. (1767), *The History of Nourjahad*, London: Printed for J. Dodsley.
Yeazell, R. B. (2000), *Harems of the Mind: Passages of Western Art and Literature*, New Haven and London: Yale University Press.

7

Bachelor Quarters: Spaces of *Japonisme* in Nineteenth-century Paris

Christopher Reed

Japonisme occupies two very different places in the history of art. On one hand, it is the original primitivism. More than just the repertoire of exotic settings and motifs offered by earlier forms of Orientalism, Japanese art challenged Western ideas of "correct" perspective, figure-ground relationships and chiaroscuro—compositional principles enmeshed in Western notions of truth and reality. From Impressionism through the various Post-Impressionisms (until, that is, the Cubists turned to Africa as the locus of the primitive), *japonisme* is central to standard accounts of the development of the avant-garde. On the other hand, *japonisme* is also characterized as a "fashion," a "vogue," or a "craze," vocabulary that belittles it through association with middlebrow culture and female consumers. This duality perpetuates nineteenth-century rhetorics, in which arguments over *japonisme*—and modernism in general—played out in highly gendered terms. To return to these sources, however, is to discover visual and verbal discourses far more complex and interesting than art history's schematization of a critical avant-garde *versus* frivolous home decorators. Contests over gender and *japonisme* were, among other things, also debates about the meaning of masculinity, in which the destabilizing effect of Japanese aesthetics on Western notions of what is right and real allowed the look of Japan to signify alternatives to bourgeois domestic norms centered on the family. It is significant that the pioneering spaces of *japonisme* in nineteenth-century Paris were the houses of bachelors.

Japonisme was associated with bachelors from the beginning. From the fictional studio where male artists pored over albums of Japanese prints in the Goncourt brothers' 1867 popular novel *Manette Salomon* to the real-life drinking club of artists and writers who came together around 1868 as the "Société japonaise du Jinglar" (*Jinglar*, word-play on the cheap, sharp wine called *ginglard*, referred to *sake*), the social structures of *japonisme* were originally male and homosocial. The *japonistes* later reacted with dismay to the feminization of *japonisme*. An 1882 article by the jeweler Lucien Falize—who professed "that intimate satisfaction of being among the first to understand" Japanese art—complained that, after "Japan opened itself to us" and "a small group of artists thrilled and rejoiced at the fresh scents of that virgin art," then "fashion, that ever-alert panderer, seized the new idea, turned it over to commerce, prostituted it in the boutique, rolled it in the mud of the lowest craftwork, stripped it, dirtied it, and the poor girl, ashamed, sprawled across our discount shops" (330). For Falize, the feminization of *japonisme* is personified as a washed-up prostitute, violated not by her affairs with artists but by her recent commerce with the women's world of "fashion," "boutiques," and "discount shops."

Responses among the *japonistes* varied. Falize reacted by assuming the blasé tone of a worldly bachelor. Comparing the situation of *japonistes* in the 1880s to a man when the "fever of possession has calmed and one sees in broad daylight one's mistress of the night before: she is still beautiful, smiling and full of grace, but one hesitates to take her as a wife," he asks:

> [H]aven't we, all of us artists, cohabited to some degree with the Japanese fairy? Hasn't each of us had children born of that love? The little ones so resemble their mother that it would be criminal to repudiate her, but, before giving them our name, making her French through marriage, let us check to make sure she is not already too demanding a mistress, and if in this household we would know how to dominate her enough to remain masters at home.
>
> (330)

If Falize was willing to abandon his passion for Japan and move on to other exotic lovers in accordance with tastes that changed "every four or five years," others refused to leave *japonisme* to the ladies. Toulouse-Lautrec's *japoniste* imagery of the 1890s, set in brothels and nightclubs, embraced an idea of *japonisme* so racy as to repel women of the bourgeoisie. Such metaphorical refusals to allow *japonisme* to marry into the French family were literalized in the spaces that authoritatively—albeit differently—represented Japan: the Paris houses of Henri Cernuschi (1821–1896) and Edmond de Goncourt (1822–1896), and the country estate, near Versailles, of Cernuschi's Paris neighbor, Hugues Krafft (1853–1935). All of these *japoniste* spaces, created between the mid-1870s and the mid-1880s, were private houses that could boast a very public presence. Destinations for connoisseurs and celebrities, they were also known through a wide variety of books and periodicals. And all three were bachelor residences at a time when bachelorhood among bourgeois Frenchmen was a source of increasing social stigma (Borie 1976).

The house-museum of Henri Cernuschi

Henri Cernuschi's *japonisme* originated in an act of mourning among men. In 1871, this economist, banker, and republican revolutionary made Japan his first stop on a journey to Asia following the traumatic collapse of the Paris Commune, during which, while attempting to rescue the journalist Gustave Chaudey from prison, he and Théodore Duret were themselves arrested and sentenced to death. Although Cernuschi and Duret escaped, they learned that Chaudey had been executed the night before. In distress, they set out for the opposite side of the globe. "The atrocious loss I suffered of Chaudey decided me on this absence," Cernushi wrote to explain his departure for Asia (Leti 1936: 181). Duret told the painter Camille Pisarro that having "lost a great friend. . . . I have only one wish, to leave, to flee Paris for a few months" (Chang 2006: 67). By the time they returned in October 1872, Duret bragged to Edouard Manet, "Cernuschi is bringing from Japan and China a collection of bronzes the like of which has never been seen anywhere. There are pieces that will bowl you over; that is all I am telling you!" (Inaga 1998: 89). Cernuschi's purchases—over 900 crates containing approximately 1,500 bronzes followed by an equal number of ceramics—constituted a collection critics hailed as "more than in all the museums of Europe put together" (Chang 2010: 49).

Cernuschi's large collection was clearly intended for display. Rather than place it in a museum, however, he built a house for it on the fashionable Avenue Vélasquez. The unusual house was organized around a huge central room—twenty meters long and twelve meters high—where a monumental bronze Buddha on a high plinth presided over tiers of shelves filled with metalwork [Figure 7.1]. If the layout evoked the form of a Japanese temple, this was a temple devoted to the ideals and sensibility of the collector. The exterior also drew attention to its owner. Amid its mansard-roofed neighbors, the house's severe neoclassical lines and roof "*à l'italienne*" evoked for nineteenth-century commentators Cernuschi's national origins (Demaison 1897: 252). Two polychrome mosaics depicted Aristotle and Leonardo da Vinci, avatars of Cernuschi's energetic rationalism [Figure 7.2]. Above them, sculpted herms at the roofline resembled no one more than Cernuschi himself, who was recalled as "a wiry great devil, long-haired and bearded with laughing eyes sparkling with good humor" (Maurel 1925: 139). Cernuschi's republican ideals found expression on the bronze double doors at the entry,

FIGURE 7.1 Photographer unknown, Great Buddha Hall at the Musée Cernuschi around 1900. Photograph from Pierre Despatys, Les Musées de la Ville de Paris, Paris: G. Boudet, n.d.

which were inscribed with the words "Février" and "Septembre," the months of the revolutions that brought republican government to France (in 1848 and 1870). Period descriptions of the building read the façade as an expression of Cernuschi's identity as explicit as the plaques that "attested to the immutable tenacity of his ardent convictions" (Demaison 1897: 252). Inside, the central hall recalled the *portego* of a Venetian palace and was flooded with light from a massive neo-Palladian window. Over the "Great Buddha," neoclassical ceiling coffers displayed escutcheons bearing the phrase "LIBERTAS ET VIRTUS" above a frieze of plaques with the names of Asian cities Cernuschi had visited. Painted decorations around the ceiling of the staircase center on the names of continents—Asia, Europa, America—crossed with palms of peace. Japanese art was thus organized within architectural rhetorics in which the grandeur of Italian history and cosmopolitan Enlightenment ideals extended to the four corners of the earth.

Also central to Cernuschi's identity was his bachelor status. He was famous for consorting with women of the stage, and the costume parties he hosted at the foot of his giant Buddha were the talk of Paris. Louis Gonse, whose pioneering survey of Japanese art illustrated items from Cernuschi's collection, recalled attending one such event costumed as a Japanese nobleman in a Noh mask and elaborate eighteenth-century kimono, accompanied by Tadamasa Hayashi, a leading dealer in Japanese art,

FIGURE 7.2 William Bouwens der Boijen, architect, detail of the façade of the Musée Cernuschi in 2012. Photograph: Christopher Reed.

"disguised as an old beggar with a wrinkled head and quivering jaw. The effect was irresistible" (Gonse 1992: 85). Reporting on a visit to Cernuschi in 1883, the American Japanist Edward Morse described him as "an old bachelor," and observed: "Breakfast for fifteen or twenty is served at 12; certain of his friends have a standing invitation to come in any Sunday" (Wayman 1942: 298). Readers of Alphonse Daudet's 1884 novel *Sapho*, a tale of men and their mistresses subtitled *The Mores of Paris*, recognized Cernuschi as the bearded bachelor playboy with a "taste for art" and "contempt for public opinion" that "result from a life of travel and bachelorhood." The novel opens at a masked ball at this man's house, characterized by "the Oriental hangings, the gilded Buddhas, the bronze chimeras, the exotic luxuriousness of that vast hall where the light fell from a high window" (6, 165).

Today, this house is the Musée Cernuschi, the Asian art museum of the City of Paris. The architecture and preserved decorative scheme of the ceilings evoke its original owner's contextualization of Asian art within structures of Enlightenment rationality. But while a makeover some years ago involving a lot of Lucite and shiny black plastic arguably continues to rebuff associations of *japonisme* with femininity, the bachelor extravagance of this pioneering *japoniste* environment has largely given way to institutional authority.

Edmond de Goncourt predicted it. After seeing Cernuschi's new house in 1875, he observed, "these objects from the Far East seem unhappy" where "the rich collector has given his collection a setting at once imposing and cold as a Louvre" (1956 v. 2: 211). Reflecting later on his own collection, Goncourt wrote, "I do not want for the objects I have possessed, after me, burial in a museum, that place where people pass by bored without looking at what is before them. I want each of my objects to bring to its owner, a very distinct being, the little burst of joy I had in buying it" (1956 v. 3: 27). This personal, emotional relationship to collecting, distinguished from edifying display for an indifferent crowd, offered an alternative paradigm of bachelor *japonisme*.

The *Maison des Goncourt*

Although the Goncourt brothers' fiction associated Japanese prints with artists in the mid-1860s, it was not until the early 1870s—just when Cernuschi opened his house-museum—that they began to think of themselves as collectors of a wider range of Japanese art. This shift coincided with another, as the Goncourts' move from a shared apartment in central Paris to a house in suburban Auteuil in 1868 located these pseudo-aristocrats in a setting so explicitly upper-middle-class that the conditions of sale specified that houses in the district "may only be occupied bourgeoisly [*bourgeoisement*]" (Periton 2004: 148). The Goncourts' journal—an expression of a male homosociality so complete that it was written by both brothers in the first person singular—energetically rejected these connotations, however. Here, the purchase of the house and the acquisition of Japanese art were cast as forms of anti-bourgeois recklessness:

> Exhausted and feverish tonight as if after a mad night of gaming. After the purchase of that house for almost one hundred thousand francs, so unreasonable to bourgeois reason in the face of our small fortune, we offer 2000 francs, a price beyond the whim of an emperor or a Rothschild, for a Japanese monster, a mesmerizing bronze I don't know what told us we had to possess.
>
> (1956 v. 2: 175)

A week later, the journal records, "The first quill sharpened in our house" signed the receipt for this "*vasque au monstre japonais*" (1956 v. 2: 176).

Edmond leans companionably on this "pot-bellied vase"—his words—in an 1888 painting, where, echoing the pairing of the brothers in the small double portrait on the wall behind, it seems to stand in for Jules, who died in 1870 [Figure 7.3]. If the big Buddha installed at the center of Cernuschi's house-museum used Japan to construct a cosmopolitan republican identity, this large *vasque-monstre* deployed an idea of Japan as the realm of

FIGURE 7.3 Jean-François Raffaëlli, *Portrait of Edmond de Goncourt*, 1888, oil on canvas, 260 × 170 cm (102 × 67 in.), Musée Historique Lorrain, Nancy. Photograph: DeAgostini/Getty Images.

the irrational, intoxicating beauty of the grotesque. In their first book of extracts from their journal, the brothers asserted: "Over there the monster is everywhere. It's the decoration and almost the furnishing of the house. It's the *jardinière* and the incense burner. . . . In the world of pale women with painted eyelids, the monster is a daily, familial, beloved image" (Goncourt 1866: 16–17).

Although the Goncourt collection was auctioned off in accordance with Edmond's directions after his death in 1896, it was carefully preserved in the form of a book. His two-volume *La maison d'un artiste,* published in 1881, is an original if unstable fusion of literary genres—part autobiography, part art history, part ekphrastic exercise, part collection catalog—that stands at the origin of the genre of the celebrity house-tour. At its worst, it is an unreadable inventory. At its best, however, *La maison d'un artiste* offers a pioneering exploration of the domestic interior as significant of psychological interiority. From this perspective, the Goncourt house is a monument to the mourning of one bachelor for another.

Goncourt begins by invoking death. He asks, "why not write the memoirs of things among which a human existence has run its course" (1881: n.p.). More than seven hundred pages later, in a text organized as a visit to the house, we mount a staircase on which eighteenth-century French drawings alternate with Japanese *kakemonos*, ascend to the attic, go past frames in need of gilding and broken Japanese bric-à-brac, to arrive at "the student garret where my brother liked to work, the room chosen by him to die in" with the furnishings preserved just as he left them. There, "On certain anniversaries and sad days, when the long unforgettable past of our life as two returns to my heart, I go up to that room, I sit in the big armchair near the empty bed . . ., I give myself the sad pleasure of remembering." In these rituals of remembering, Edmond first sees Jules as "my good and handsome brother," but this vision is followed by memories of Jules' slow, delirious death. As Jules dies, he becomes "no longer my brother" but an androgynous work of art: "the indefinable smile on his violet lips gave him a troubling resemblance to a mysterious inhuman face by da Vinci that I saw in some dark corner in Italy in I don't know what picture or Museum" (369–371). This rehearsal of Jules' death, which reviewers cited as the quintessence of the book, completes the tour.

Edmond's narration of his acts of remembrance and mourning emphasizes his house's status as both the site and the expression of *notre vie à deux*. This deviance from bourgeois familial norms was signaled by the décor, as commentators were quick to observe. The entrance hall set the tone. Zola explained, "It is not the bare and banal vestibule of bourgeois houses. It is cheered, almost seems to be heated, by the porcelains, the bronzes, and above all by the *foukousas*" (1882: 207). Gustave Geffroy likewise contrasted the "bourgeois and discreet" façade with "[a]n artistic impression [that] lets loose with an extraordinary intensity from everything that surrounds the visitor." Here, against a striking leather wall-covering of "parrots on a sea-green background, . . . are hung *foukousas*, those squares of embroidered silk, softly nuanced, on which the Japanese artists have placed their strong and emphatic design" (1891–1892: 147). But these evocative accounts pale before Goncourt's own description of this space, which draws attention to the "fantastic gilded parrots" on the green wall-covering, before going on to list, "[a]gainst this leather, in a calculated disorder . . . all sorts of striking, eye catching things, brilliant copper cut-outs, gilded pottery, Japanese embroideries, and still more bizarre, unexpected objects, astonishing in their originality, their exoticism." These things, says Goncourt, remind him of the eighteenth-century Jesuit philosopher who wrote: "Here are things I do not know, I must write a book about them" (1881 v. 1: 4).

A century later, Roland Barthes followed Goncourt in making Japan an occasion for writing. Linking the "fundamental absence of monotheism" in Japan to what he saw as the free play of Japanese signifiers, Barthes credited Japan with turning him toward a mode of "novelistic" writing antagonistic to conventions of authoritative truth-telling he associated with Western religion (1985: 84). Between Edmond de Goncourt and Roland Barthes runs a chain of aesthetes, including the fictional Jean des Esseintes in Joris-Karl Huysmans' *A rebours* and the real Comte de Montesquiou. Citing "the volumes of *La maison d'un artiste* leafed through a hundred times," Montesquiou recalled that, after making his first purchases of Japanese art at the Paris Exposition of 1878, "there hardly passed a day that did not see me bring back to my own 'house of an artist' one of these captivatingly attractive objects" (1923 v. 2: 102). When Huysmans' *A rebours* appeared in 1884, Goncourt claimed the novel as his progeny, exalting, "it seems like the book of my much-loved son," but then complaining that readers who fell into "admiring stupefaction over Huysmans' discovery of des Esseintes' *oranged* interior" underestimated how hard he had worked in his own house to harmonize his pink *foukousa*, yellow Kutaniware decorated with mauve chrysanthemums, and *kakemono* with the crane on the bluish background with the golden leaves, all surrounded by Chinese porcelains and Japanese bronzes. In contrast to this complexity of objects, "This *oranged* . . . is, in the end, a color of a painting, not a room," Goncourt groused (1956 v. 2: 1,074).

Des Esseintes is invoked in Susan Sontag's "Notes on Camp" to help explicate this concept, which could be used to trace Edmond de Goncourt's bachelor aesthetic up through Andy Warhol, with whom he shared a penchant for performing in the public eye a scintillating combination of ambiguous asexuality, constant gossip, and compulsive collecting. Although the Japanese objects that filled the *maison des Goncourt* were dispersed without record, this campy legacy of bachelor *japonisme* rivals the longevity of Cernuschi's museum aesthetic. My third bachelor *japoniste* is not so well remembered. But his Japanese environment was in its day a must-see for Parisians with a taste for Japan. Combining elements of Cernuschi's cosmopolitanism and Goncourt's campy extravagance, Hugues Krafft's house proposed something neither of its forerunners did: to recreate Japan.

Hugues Krafft's *Midori-no-sato*

Krafft grew up in the shadow of Cernuschi's house-museum. Or vice versa. In the late 1860s, when "Hugo" was a teenager, his parents—wealthy German immigrants—built one of the large family mansions on the exclusive block-long Avenue Vélasquez where Cernuschi located his museum in 1873. The scion of two prosperous champagne dynasties (his mum was a Mumm), Krafft refused to marry and turned his back on the family business. In 1881, he set off on a global tour he defined by its homosociality: "I did not undertake a voyage for purposes of scientific discovery; I did not accomplish any special mission; I simply went around the world in good company, with my brother and two close friends" (Esmein 2003: 163).

Like Duret and Cernuschi, Krafft claimed no interest or expertise in Japan before he set off. But Japan exerted a mysterious—and mystified—fascination. Krafft's published memoir of his *tour du monde* describes the group's five-month stay in Japan; in reality, he sent his companions on for big-game hunting in America and remained an extra two months without them. Announcing this to his sister, Krafft wrote: "While our 'party' will be in the grips of the progressive and electrified Yankees, I will still be enjoying curious and singular sights; I will be buying bibelots; I will be taking photographs and I will be sketching in order to preserve a maximum of memories form this little paradise of nature" (Beaulieu 2008: 164).

This catalog of activities offers only a partial account of Krafft's doings in Japan. He joined the "thousands of male spectators, to the exclusion of all women" in admiring the "parade of torsos"—"very fat or else truly superb men, built like so many Hercules" —showing off their "*avantages musculaire*s" at a *sumo* competition (Krafft 1885: 325–327). His photograph of sumo wrestlers in the privately published *Souvenirs de notre tour du monde* is among the first in any Western publication. Krafft was also taken with *kabuki*, which for him "enlightened the foreigner about the philosophy and extraordinary force of resistance" that characterize the Japanese, more particularly "the coldness and exterior impermeability one notes in daily relations, where affections and friendships are hidden beneath manners imprinted with the most formal politeness" (Krafft 1885: 336–337). Krafft's accounts of the formality of Japanese life are unusual. Virtually every other Western visitor commented on the affection shown between Japanese parents and children, but Krafft insists they neither hug nor kiss. Perceptions of Krafft's "coldness" by other Europeans suggest that he sought, and therefore found, in Japan endorsement for his own dissimulation of "affections and friendships." This may explain his identification—unique among Frenchmen at the time—with the look of Japanese domestic life.

Krafft commissioned his Japanese house in February 1883, a month after his French companions headed off to America. The disassembled structure was shipped to France and rebuilt. When it was officially opened in 1886 at a ceremony that included the Japanese ambassador, Krafft renamed his country estate *Midori-no-sato*, which he over-elaborately translated as *Colline de la fraiche verdure* [Hill of Fresh Greenery] (the relatively common Japanese name more literally means "green place"). Inside, Krafft's house was furnished with the trappings of Japanese domestic life, including futons, mosquito nets, a bath, and a closet discreetly described as furnished with "a basket in blue porcelain" with a nearby washbasin on an ivy-covered, sawn-off tree trunk. A servant's bedroom was embellished with a Shinto shrine (Régamey 1893: 226–228). Outside, Krafft literally moved mountains (or at least large hills), dug ponds, and imported hundreds of Japanese trees and shrubs in order to create the first—and for decades the largest—Japanese garden in France, complete with a symbolic *tori* gateway, lantern, basin, and gray stone Buddha [Figure 7.4].

This promise of the illusion of Japan made *Midori-no-sato* a pilgrimage point for Japanese and *japonistes*. Both Cernuschi and Goncourt signed the guestbook. Robert de Montesquiou met Krafft through the Japanese gardener they shared, and brought Marcel Proust to visit in 1895 (Suzuki 2011: 107–108). Krafft's guestbook filled with comments affirming the authenticity of his accomplishment. An article by Louis Gonse effused: "When one finds oneself in the middle of this garden or in this house with the shutters open on a beautiful spring or fall day, one feels exactly the

FIGURE 7.4 Hugues Krafft, *"Zashiki" et "toro,"* photograph on cardboard, c.1885, Japan Society [UK]. Photograph: Christopher Reed.

sensations the Japanese have for nature" (1898: 101–102). Félix Régamey, illustrator of several books about Japan, said that, standing on "a bridge of red lacquer" above a little waterfall, looking up at the little Japanese house, "all that is wanting to the balcony, standing out from the white background of the papered frames, are some little *mousmés* in dazzling robes, to render the illusion complete" (1893: 218–219).

If there were no girlish *mousmés* in Krafft's Japan, still less was there room for French women. Although Régamey published an account of the house presented as a visit by a countess enthusiastic about Japanese décor (1893: 66), Krafft responded frostily to one of the Japanese art dealers who attended the opening of *Midori-no-sato* when he forwarded such a request: "in my view, Madam the Baroness Durieux will not find in my little Japanese 'zashiki' . . . the sort of things that will give her ideas for furnishing a modern salon '*à la japonaise*' " (Institut de Tokyo 2001: 197). Here, Krafft reiterated a point he made in a lecture to a scholarly society, where he stressed the "simplicity" of Japanese houses: "I want to insist particularly on this essential point, because I found, contrary to my expectations when I arrived in Japan, the Japanese arrangement of interiors was completely different from what I had erroneously imagined from a perspective shared by everyone whose knowledge of Japan comes from reputation alone." In Japan, Krafft found "in dwellings of all types, neither grand decorated porcelains nor multicolored embroideries used as curtains or ornament, no extraordinary furniture of lacquer or wood, no bibelots of bronze or ivory, in short, none of those luxurious or exotic objects with which we decorate our rooms '*à la japonaise*.' " In contrast, he described simple wooden houses with sliding doors, no furniture, ornamented with a single hanging scroll and vase of seasonal blossoms (Esmein 2003: 105–106).

This now-familiar idea of minimalist Japanese domesticity was new to Paris, where *japonisme* had played out through the adoption of Japanese objects and motifs in Western rooms, Western paintings, and Western objects of décor. Challenging Parisian ideas of Japanese aesthetics, however, Krafft did not contest the adaptation of Japanese elements by the avant-garde or such bachelor compatriots as Cernuschi and Goncourt. His attribution of misunderstanding and excess to the feminized realm of décor *à la japonaise* was cast so as to preserve his invocation of Japan in France as a reproduction of the homosocial world of adventuring expatriates he had experienced abroad.

This idea of Japan as a world of men was documented in the hundreds of photographs Krafft made in Japan and circulated on his return in exhibitions and donations to scholarly institutions. When Krafft donated his photographs, he grouped them in numbered series mounted and labeled to suggest voyages. A series of eighty-two numbered photographs (many now missing) that he gave to the Japan-London Society starts at a house in Yokohama, proceeds to just outside the gate of this community, then goes to Tokyo and on to sites in Kyoto, before offering informal views of two routes between Tokyo and Kyoto, the coastal Tokaido road and the more mountainous inland Nakasendo. These pictures capture Krafft's enthusiasm.

"Japan is decidedly the country for excursions," his memoir announces. "What a procession! Fourteen jin-riki-shas with two runners each, make, with Ito [the interpreter], a party of thirty-two men! A whole little battalion!" (1885: 254, 259). Krafft urges readers to "admire with us our untiring and cheerful runners" as they wash their "admirably muscled naked limbs" in the fountains they pass. He reports that, though they wear vests in the presence of policemen, they prefer to run attired just in their *fundoshi* [loin cloth], and he highlights the two tattooed runners in his group: "The designs in flat tones of blue and red blend admirably with their suntanned skins, which are remarkably soft and supple" (1885: 260, 267, 292).

Krafft's Japanese photographs document not only his runners but other men in outfits appropriate to their work, including (in addition to the *sumo* wrestlers), priests, carpenters and fishermen. This personification of Japan by its men is unusual for a European, and extends through Krafft's documentation of *Midori-no-sato* in another numbered set of photographs and also donated to educational institutions. In this series, sequenced as a visit from the "Great entrance gate" to the house and through the garden, the only human figure is a Japanese man in a carpenter's uniform, who is shown tending the gardens, both full-sized and *bonsai* [Figure 7.5].

FIGURE 7.5 Hugues Krafft, *Jardin miniature*, photograph on cardboard, c.1885, Japan Society [UK]. Photograph: Christopher Reed.

Conclusions on the origins of *japonisme*

That *japonisme* was associated with bachelor culture might seem all too predictable. The broader art-world culture that structured itself around military terms like "avant-garde" and "movements" (taken from the movements of troops) positioned itself as an extended performance of masculinity guaranteed, as I have argued elsewhere, by repeated repudiations of femininity in general and of particular women (Reed 1996: 7–17). From this perspective, the efforts of *japonistes* to defend their ground against the incursion of middle-class women simply concentrate and exaggerate these tendencies. But at some point, this concentration and exaggeration become so extreme that any credibility they might have as defenses of patriarchy (as if patriarchy were really threatened by ladies caught up in a "Japan craze") is overshadowed by the overt artifice and unabashed eccentricity that rendered the bachelor residences discussed in this chapter bastions of a non-normativity justified in the name of Japan. From this perspective, it is significant that, in contrast to the *japonisme* of the painters, these bachelor houses have been written out of the histories of art and design—Cernuschi's drastically remodeled, the Goncourts' pathologized (Silverman 1989: 17–39), Krafft's lost and forgotten—as resolutely as the feminine "craze" for Japan.

All three of these houses were thriving in 1889, however, when Oscar Wilde famously noticed that "[t]he whole of Japan is a pure invention ... simply a mode of style, an exquisite fancy of art" (1905: 47). This association of Japan with an inventiveness that challenges accepted truths as we know them is echoed when Barthes, introducing the essays occasioned by his three trips to Japan in 1966–1967, asserts: "If I want to imagine a fictive nation, ... I can ... isolate somewhere in the world (*faraway*) a certain number of features ... and out of these features deliberately form a system. It is this system which I shall call: Japan" (1982: 3). This invented Japan, for Barthes, supported a project he described as "disconnecting myself from the ideological instance as signified, as the risk of the return of the signified, of theology, monologism, of law." For this purpose, he claims that Japan has "a partial but indisputable superiority over our Western societies, where the liberation of the signifier has been hampered for more than two thousand years by the development of monotheism and its hypostases ('Science,' 'Man,' Reason')" (Barthes 1985: 84).

For Cernuschi, the Goncourts and Krafft, too, Japan enabled a rejection of Western norms. *Japonisme* allowed their refusal of imperatives that bourgeois men perform the role of *paterfamilias* to play out as something other than absence or failure—and to do so at home, the site where such imperatives are most intense. These performances were not the same. Cernuschi's deployment of Japan within a system of display that manifests his cosmopolitan rationalism is very different from the Goncourts' delight in the emotive and grotesque, which, in turn, was at an opposite extreme from

Krafft's bid for authenticity. But these houses had crucial elements in common. All three were recognized as refusing domesticity. Cernuschi's study and bedroom adjacent to the Buddha hall amazed visitors by being, like it, lined with shelves of displays. Contemporaries marveled that "he lived there ... among these monstrous divinities, between furnishings that were primarily display cases. One hardly dared sit on a chair, so much did one have the impression it must be the guard's" (Fouquières 1954: 197). Edmond de Goncourt's loving descriptions in *La maison d'un artiste* of the items in "my bathroom ... literally covered with porcelains and watercolors" (189)—including, "amid all this pottery from Asia," an eighteenth-century German "statuette of a little Chinaman, with cheeks barely pink in his white face" and a head that bobbles on a gilded bronze mechanism, which was "the first bibelot purchased by my brother" (193)—lend credence to Daudet's claim that, with the bathroom, "like the whole house, invaded by kakemonos and display cases," its owner had to bathe in the kitchen (1896: 45). No one attempted to live in Krafft's *zashiki*. And for all three *japonistes*, the fascination with Japan manifest in their houses was grounded in recollections of bonds between men. Cernuschi's and Goncourt's houses originated in homosocial mourning; Krafft's evoked the community of men he enjoyed in Japan. To return to these well-known spaces of Japan in nineteenth-century Paris is to find *japonisme* deployed, variously and inventively, to articulate non-normative forms masculinity.

References

Barthes, R. (1970), *Empire of Signs*, Richard Howard (trans.), New York: Hill and Wang, 1982.
Barthes, R. (1981), *The Grain of the Voice: Interviews 1962–1980*, Linda Coverdale (trans.), New York: Hill and Wang, 1985.
Beaulieu, A. L. (2008), "Hugue Krafft's Midori no Sato," in P. ten-Doesschate Chu and L. S. Dixon (eds.), *Twentieth-Century Perspectives on Nineteenth-Century Art: Essays in Honor of Gabriel P. Weisberg*, Newark: University of Delaware Press: 162–170.
Borie, J. (1976), *Le célibataire français*, Paris: Le Sagittaire.
Bouillon, J.-P. (1978), " 'A gauche': Note sur la Société du Jing-Lar et la Signification," *Gazette des Beaux Arts*, 6(91) (March): 107–118.
Chang, T. (2006), "Disorienting Orient: Duret and Guimet, Anxious *Flâneurs* in Asia," in A. d'Souza and T. McDonough (eds.), *The Invisible Flâneuse: Gender, Public Space, and Visual Culture in Nineteenth-Century Paris*, Manchester: Manchester University Press: 65–78.
Chang, T. (2010), "Asia as a Fantasy of France in the Nineteenth Century," in M. North (ed.), *Artistic and Cultural Exchanges between Europe and Asia, 1400–1900*, Farnham, UK: Ashgate: 45–52.
Daudet, A. (1896), "Ultima," manuscript for an essay published in the *Revue de Paris*, August 15, 1896, in *Cahiers Edmond and Jules de Goncourt*, 4 (1995–1996): 30–51.

Daudet, A. (1899), *Sapho (Moeurs Parisien)*, 1884, translated as *Sappho to which is added Between the Flies and the Footlights*. Boston: Little, Brown.
Demaison, M. (1897), "Le Musée Cernuschi," *La Revue de l'art ancien et moderne*, 2(7) (October): 251–266.
Esmein, S. (2003), *Hugues Krafft au Japon de Meiji*. Paris: Hermann.
Falize, L. [writing as M. Josse] (1882–1883), "L'Art Japonais à propos de l'Exposition organizée par M. Gonse," *Revue des arts décoratifs*, 3: 329–338.
Fouquières, A. de (1954), *Mon Paris et mes Parisiens. Vol II: Le Quartier Monceau*, Paris: Pierre Horay.
Geffroy, G. (1891–1892), "La Maison des Goncourt," *Revue des art décoratifs,* 12: 146–151.
Goncourt, E. de (1881), *La Maison d'un Artiste*, 2 vols, Paris: Bibliothèque Charpentier.
Goncourt, E. and J. de (1866), *Idées et Sensations*, Paris: G. Charpentier.
Goncourt, E. and J. de (1956), *Journal: Mémoires de la vie littéraire*, Robert Ricatte (ed.), 3 vols, Paris: Fasquelle and Flammarion.
Gonse, F. (1992), "Louis Gonse (1846–1921) et le Japon," *Gazette des Beaux-Arts*, 6, 134(1477) (February): 81–88.
Gonse, L. (1898), "L'Art Japonais et son influence sur le goût européan," *Revue des arts décoratifs*, 18(1) (April): 97–116.
Inaga, S. (1998), "Théodore Duret et Henri Cernuschi: Journalisme politique, voyage en Asie et collection Japonaise," *Ebisu*, unnumbered special issue: 79–93.
Institut de Tokyo, Institution Administrative Indépendente, Centre National de Recherche pour les Propriétés Culturelles (2001), *Correspondance adressée à Hayaski Tadamasa*, np: Kokushokankôkai.
Krafft, H. (1885), *Souvenirs de notre tour de monde*, Paris: Hachette.
Leti, G. (1936), *Henri Cernuschi, sa vie, sa doctrine, ses oeuvres*, Paris: Presses Universitaires de France.
Maurel, A. (1925), *Souvenirs d'un écrivain, 1883–1914*, Paris: Hachette.
Montesquiou, R. de (1923), *Pas effacés*, 3 vols, Paris: Paul-Louis Couchoud.
Periton, D. (2004), "The Interior as Aesthetic Refuge: Edmond de Goncourt's *La maison d'un artiste*," in M. Hvattum and C. Hermansen (eds.), *Tracing Modernity: Manifestations of the Modern in Architecture and the City*, London: Routledge: 137–155.
Reed, C. (1996), "Introduction," in C. Reed (ed.), *Not at Home: The Suppression of Domesticity in Modern Art and Architecture*, London: Thames and Hudson.
Régamey, F. (1891), *Japan in Art and Industry*, M. French-Sheldon and E. Lemon Sheldon (trans.), New York: G. P. Putnam's Sons, 1893.
Silverman, D. L. (1989), *Art Nouveau in Fin-de-Siècle France: Politics, Psychology, and Style*, Berkeley: University of California Press.
Sontag, S. (1964), "Notes on Camp," *Against Interpretation*, New York: Noonday, 1966: 275–292.
Suzuki, J. (2011), "Le jardinier japonais de Robert de Montesquiou—ses evocations dans les milieux littéraires," *Cahiers Edmond et Jules de Goncourt*, 18: 103–112.
Wayman, D. G. (1942), *Edward Sylvester Morse: A Biography*, Cambridge, MA: Harvard University Press.
Wilde, O. (1905), *Intentions*, New York: Brentano's.
Zola, É. (1882), *Une campagne, 1880–81*, Paris: G. Charpentier.

8

Coming out of the China Closet?: Performance, Identity and Sexuality in the House Beautiful

Anne Anderson

Until *Closer to Home,* the re-opening exhibition at Leighton House Museum held in 2010, it was generally assumed that Lord Frederick Leighton's Orientalism was confined to the so-called Arab Hall, an architectural conceit constructed 1877–1881 to house his Islamic tiles and vessels. This misapprehension had been prompted by the dispersal of Leighton's collections following his death in 1896. Although the Arab Hall remained as a "fixture and fitting," his Oriental ceramics and textiles were sold. Photographs taken during his lifetime show the dining room laden with a surprising variety of ceramics including so-called Persian and Rhodian wares alongside Chinese porcelains; a sideboard, designed by architect George Aitchison, was decked out with an array of blue and white wares. Leighton's dining room betrays the hybridity that underpins the exoticism of the Aesthetic Movement, with Chinese, Japanese, Islamic and European ceramics freely mixed in a space firmly rooted in Western traditions. Leighton invested in a purpose-built studio-house that legitimized his claims to artistic superiority as both a painter and interior decorator. This was a site where artistic genius was performed; here, arresting *objets d'art* were artfully arranged to form a pleasing composition, a *tout ensemble*. As novelist Henry James observed, the true artist expressed his genius in the "arrangement and effect of everything" (1908: 249). The painter-sculptor repositioned himself as the *amateur de curiosité, décorateur* or *metteur-en-scène*, literally a "scene-setter" or inventor of interiors, cultivating the myth of expressing flair and originality through décor (Goncourt 2003: 25–26).

Leighton performed and spatialized his identity through the expression of idiosyncratic taste; as selector and arranger he transformed domestic interiors into a "third space" that transcends binary oppositions. He displaced the histories of his ceramics to create a particularized expression of gender and class. As literary theorist Bill Brown argues, Leighton was not just accumulating *bric-à-brac* but also "fashioning an object-based historiography and anthropology" (2003: 5). Leighton carefully constructed his persona through his "things;" he exemplifies the transformation of the artist into a refined, cosmopolitan "gentleman of the brush." Both Louise Campbell (1999) and Andrew Stephenson (1999) rightly argue that Leighton's studio-house was a public relations exercise, framing a respectable professional British artist, with an impressive intellectual pedigree and commanding institutional authority.

Yet, although assuming the persona of the connoisseur, Leighton's preference for displaying Eastern ceramics in a domestic setting immediately problematized his identity, as the "china closet" had been gendered feminine, "a metonymy for woman," since the eighteenth century (Alayrac-Fielding 2012: 1). Moreover, so-called Old Blue china (Lamb 1885: 148–149), the Chinese porcelain Leighton selected to enhance the ambience of his dining room, was prized firstly "as an undeniably exquisite decoration for the interior of our houses" (Hollingsworth 1891: 25); men were supposed to be serious collectors, forming academically rigorous assemblages, not decorators, a role previously ascribed to the "lady of the house." *Objet's d'art* were no longer to be segregated in purpose-built galleries but artfully arranged within the House Beautiful, being in effect utilized on a daily basis. By repositioning the home as a Work of Art that expressed not only individual but superior taste, Aestheticism collapsed traditional gender roles; women could no longer simply rely on their intuition, while men were now charged with demonstrating their advanced knowledge. The ornamental value of Old Blue shifted the emphasis from objective rule-governed possession to subjective idiosyncratic expression. However, by being no more than "a decorator's taste" (Reitlinger 1982: 202–203), prized for its color and form, Old Blue retains its commodity status, failing to sever the connection between domestic consumption and collecting.

In the 1890s, Max Nordau (1849–1923), Zionist leader, physician and social critic, linked aesthetic sensibility, especially the love of old china, to decadence, a perceived perversion in taste denoting effeminacy and homosexuality. Citing Leighton's flirtation with the "more effeminate, homoerotic and perverse varieties of Aestheticism" (Edwards 2006: 65), some have tried to "out" him (Stephenson 1999). I challenge the assumption that *Chinamania*, so dubbed by the *Punch* cartoonist George Du Maurier, connoted effeminacy by showing that male collectors repositioned Old Blue as masculine. I argue Old Blue was recuperated as "manly" by valorising its color as Sublime, a concept gendered masculine in Edmund Burke's *Treatise on the Beautiful and the Sublime* (1757). Moreover, while eighteenth-century chinoiserie was identified with femininity and the effeminate (Clunas 1994), in the nineteenth century the cult of Old Blue was situated in *japonisme*, which, as Christopher Reed argues in this volume, began as a "structure of male homosocial bonding." Despite the increasing demands of female consumers, the leading players in the market for Old Blue were men, reclaiming the Orient for the masculine sphere. I explore how blue and white wares claimed their position within the dining room, deemed a masculine domestic space since the eighteenth century: as architect Robert Kerr decreed "the whole appearance of the room ought to be that of masculine importance" (1865: 94). Here, both connoisseurship and artistry were demonstrated, through "discrimination and selection" (James 1908: v), preserving masculine identity within the feminine domestic realm. Leighton's modes of display offer a starting point for examining the practices of his fellow collectors; I review William Morris's dining room at Kelmscott House, Hammersmith; Frederick Leyland's spectacular Peacock Room; and Deming Jarvis's sensational mass of intense Blue.

The cult of Old Blue

Collectors of Old Blue china were chiefly interested in Asian specimens, notably Chinese K'ang Hsi (1662–1722), Yung Cheng (1723–1735) and Ch'ieu Lung (1736–1795) porcelains; these were often styled Nankeen, Nankin or Naking wares. The abolition of the East India Company's monopoly in 1858 had, according to dealer Frederick Litchfield, "a great effect upon the trade in foreign china, letting in quantities of Chinese porcelain, which had hitherto been rare and expensive" (1900: 338). Collectors also prized early English porcelains, especially First Period Worcester and Caughley, printed earthenware, notably Willow pattern, and all forms of tin-glazed Delft. Utilized as a "property" in their paintings, as well as a means to enhance the ambience of their studio-houses, Old Blue's artistic credentials were bestowed by James McNeill Whistler (1834–1903) and Dante Gabriel Rossetti (1828–1882), who were both enthralled by its color; "Sky blue after rain" (Hollingsworth 1891: 25). Whistler opted for K'ang Hsi porcelain, prized for its clear sapphire blue. Neither artist attempted to amass a typological or representative collection of Chinese porcelains; like connoisseur Alexander T. Hollingsworth, they cherished their Old Blue as "a fascinating style of decorating" (1891: 16). Old Blue was ultimately prized for its hue, both literally and metaphorically, demonstrating the superior visual cognition of the aesthete. Its aesthetic appeal centered on abstract or formal values; Roger B. Stein reads this formalism as liberating, as it stresses intrinsic visual qualities and compositional values over meaning (1986: 39). Repositioned in a Western context, Oriental Old Blue was not required to serve any other purpose than to please the eye. Hence, Old Blue embodied the "Art for Art's Sake" dictum, promising only a momentary pleasure (Pater 1990: 152). However, Old Blue went beyond simply satisfying the eye, as author Rosamund Marriott Watson claimed: "blue china will produce an effect not merely of exquisite decorative refinement but of decorative romance and colour entirely satisfying both to the eye and the imagination" (1897: 103). Campbell recognizes Leighton's penchant for Eastern ceramics as a means to "liberate his imagination and evoke an imaginary orient" (1999: 285).

By the 1870s, collecting Oriental ceramics offered a means of homosocial bonding [Figure 8.1]. As Stacey Pierson observes, Oriental blue-and-white was no longer the preserve of "delicate, refined aristocratic women but

FIGURE 8.1 George Du Maurier, "A Disenchantment," *Punch*, Vol. 71, July 29, 1876: 40, wood engraving. Swellington Spiff (who collects Blue China, because it's the thing to do) is invited to breakfast by a noble Duke (who also collects Blue China). He is much elated at the prospect of sitting down to table with possibly two or three cabinet ministers-At all events, with nothing under a viscount! Imagine his disgust, on entering the drawing room, at being presented by his Grace to Robinson, Smith, Jones, Brown, Perkins, Blenkinsop, and Parker, who all collect Blue China, and whom he has known ever since he began to collect Blue China himself. Credit: Anne Anderson.

rather prominent, wealthy men, usually, but not always businessmen" (2007: 69). The "fever spread from Whistler and Rossetti to the ordinary collector" (Pennell 1908, 1: 117); the leading aficionados were physician Sir Henry Thompson (1820–1894), shipping magnate Frederick Leyland (1832–1892), financier Louis Huth (1821–1905) and collector/dealer James Orrock (1829–1913), known as *Admiral of the Blue* and *Emperor of China*, who converted William Hesketh Lever, 1st Viscount Leverhulme. Noted dealers played their part in promoting Old Blue: Dutch-born Emmanuel Murray Marks (1840–1918) assisted Huth and Thompson, who were "speedily bitten with what their enemies called the mania for collecting Blue china" (Williamson 1919: 34). Brothers Joel Joseph Duveen (1843–1908) and Henry Joseph Duveen (1854–1919), also Dutch immigrants from a family with a long tradition of dealing in *objets d'art*, established their business in Hull. They capitalized on their proximity to the Low Countries, which offered a rich bounty of antique blue and white wares. The Duveens came to dominate the market, "Uncle Henry" snaring the American department-store king Benjamin Altman and New York financier John Pierpont Morgan. However, Lever favored Thomas Agnew and Sons of Bond Street, making his first recorded purchase in 1894; Agnew remained his major supplier until 1911, when he began negotiations with Edgar Ezekiel Gorer (1872–1915), who challenged Duveen's supremacy until his untimely death on the *Lusitania*. These dealers set themselves above common trade; they made buying easy, but their clients paid "top dollar" for the privilege. Conversely, their clients, who could afford any price, insisted on authenticity and quality and demanded expertise.

Old Blue's ascent can be tracked through the salerooms; blue-and white was classified and sold under the heading "Nankin" for the first time at the Henry Loftus Wigram sale in 1870 (Reitlinger 1982: 325). An upward trend was propelled by the Sir Henry Thompson sale on June 1, 1880: 377 lots realized a total of £4,328 7s 6d. Prices quickly escalated; Huth's famed K'ang Hsi so-called "Hawthorn" Ginger jar,[1] with its "vibrating ground of pellucid blue," broke all records selling at Christie's for £5,900 in 1905 (Reitlinger 1982: 206). Old Blue was now entrenched as a fetishized commodity [Figure 8.2]. By 1900, no self-respecting American Robber Baron could exist without a Hawthorn Ginger jar prized for its unearthly sapphire blue. The Pittsburgh coal magnate Henry Clay Frick acquired four Hawthorns that had previously belonged to Pierpont Morgan. Although Lever outdid his American rivals, securing a record nine specimens, Huth's "sapphire jewel" was won by the naturalized Lord Astor. As collector and expert on Asian art Gerald Reitlinger asserts "the whole point of the high prices of the blue hawthorns resided in the quality of the blue" (1982: 206).

Inevitably, Old Blue instigated intense male rivalry, with connoisseurs not only competing for the best and rarest pieces but also amassing stupendously large collections with the explicit intention of creating arresting displays.

FIGURE 8.2 "Trade Card designed for Mr Marks by, it is stated, Rossetti, Whistler and William Morris," coloured wood engraving, G. C. Williamson, Murray Marks and His Friends, A Tribute of Regard by Dr G. C. Williamson, London: John Lane, Bodley Head, 1919, facing 14. Credit: Anne Anderson.

Lever, founder of the soap manufacturing company Lever Brothers, was tempted to procure the entire collection of Bolton manufacturer Richard Bennett, amounting to some 500 pieces. Offered by Gorer, this would have incurred an outlay of £275,000, but after protracted negotiations, which dragged on until 1913, he acquired 51 pieces for £55,000. Lever realized the decorative potential of Old Blue at his two residences Thornton Manor, Cheshire, and The Hill in Hampstead. Nick Pearce observes: "More than the process of collecting itself, Lever seemed to obtain the greatest pleasure from conceiving and achieving the perfect display, whatever the material" (2014: 10). Apparently, Lever had at one time dreamed of becoming an architect; Gorer appealed to Lever by offering his services as interior decorator and cabinet-maker. While Duveen promoted Dutch and Flemish Renaissance styles that complimented the Old Masters they sold, Gorer offered a style seemingly more appropriate to the Oriental objects he offered, an "Aesthetic Movement-Chinese Chippendale hybrid" (Pearce 2014: 7). Lever certainly favored Chinese Chippendale, acquiring both authentic and reproduction pieces. With a decorator's eye, he sought garnitures of three or five coordinated vases, which were placed atop cabinets and side tables in scrupulously symmetrical arrangements; a cabinet situated in the Inner Hall of Thorton Manor was adorned with five perfectly matched Hawthorn Ginger jars, while the mantelpiece carried a garniture of three covered vases and two beakers. Lever appears to have been guided by *marchand-amateur* James Orrock (1829–1913), who meticulously filled his Georgian cabinets with the finest Oriental porcelains. Lever and Orrock considered K'ang Hsi and Qianlong porcelains to be an expression of eighteenth-century English taste; the Orient had been fully assimilated into our domestic décor according to Byron Webber, Orrock's biographer: "The decorative beauty of Blue China ... is beyond compare. Form and colour and pictorial design accord with the appointments of a room or hall exemplifying English Art in a manner that no other order of ceramics could provide" (1913: 187).

Complementing his furniture with appropriate *objets d'art*, Lever created "period rooms;" he preferred Jacobean Libraries, Georgian dining rooms and Adam drawing rooms, while the Music Room at Thorton Manor was conceived in an "Inigo Jones type of Renaissance" (Figueiredo 2001: 30). Here, Lever conceived his most spectacular display of Oriental ceramics; a set of five floor-to-ceiling mirror-backed cabinets filled with choice specimens, including an Old Blue wine ewer that had formerly belonged to Rossetti, created a sensational effect emulating a china closet or cabinet (*porzellankammer*) of the late seventeenth and early eighteenth centuries. Commenting on a pair of Powder-Blue vases, of true lapis-lazuli shade, Mrs Willoughby Hodgson enjoyed a "feast of colour rarely met with in any collection" (1911: 84); Old Blue lent itself to fabulous displays.

China closets

Old Blue provided a keynote in the "harmonious" House Beautiful as articulated by Clarence Cook (1828–1900) in the 1870s and Oscar Wilde (1854–1900) in the 1880s. Although Aestheticism embodied a complex set of discourses and modes of practice, devotees aspired to a home that was both individual and original (Neiswander 2008). William Watt, who manufactured the Anglo-Japanese furniture designs of architect E. W. Godwin, assured his readers that: "We have no set rules for furnishing the home, for every man's house should not only be to him a castle, but a field for the display of individual taste and through it of individual character" (1877: iv). Old Blue offered an original touch as the variety of blues and whites ensured there was "little danger of monotony in the effect" (Anon. 1881: 41). Hence, it was deemed perfectly acceptable to mix-and-match different types of pottery and porcelain; English Willow Pattern competed with Chinese Nankin on the sideboard or dresser.

Old Blue was fully assimilated into English culture with the advent of Blue Willow in the 1780s. Traditional motifs from imported wares were pieced together to create the famous design, which, although varied, is characterized by the bridge with three figures, the central willow tree, the boat, the two "love birds," the teahouse and the fence running across the foreground. By the 1870s, the "poor man's *blue and white*" (Hiller 1968: 214) appealed to the fashion-conscious, as these verses from *A China Wedding* (1877), an "original, mythical, fancy" in one act, illustrate:

> Coming along, I found myself
> In ev'ry window, case, and shelf,
> And when I said "the pattern's mine",
> Was answered "yes", in ev'ry chine,
> And here, the fashion of the time.
> It won't last long, some other delft
> Will push me from the rich man's shelf.
> But as the world goes round and round,
> The poor man's plate I'm always found.
>   (Digges 1877: 2)

This "fashion of the time" was instigated by the Pre-Raphaelite circle: Rossetti and his wife Lizzie Siddal (1829–1862) favored Willow in their marital home, 14 Chatham Place, Blackfriars; "the fireplace was surrounded by real old blue glazed Dutch tiles to match the traditional willow pattern chinaware" (Marsh 1999: 233). Lizzie concluded a note to Georgiana Burne-Jones with "a willow-pattern dish full of love to you and Ned" (1904: 221). Following the death of his wife, Rossetti maintained his affection for Blue Willow; a dish can be seen above Gabriel's head in Henry Treffry Dunn's *Dante Gabriel Rossetti and Theodore Watts—Dunton in the Dining Room (?) at 16 Cheyne Walk* (1882). However, falling under the influence of Whistler, Rossetti's imagination was captivated by the Hawthorn jar; he acquired two "sumptuous specimens," much to the amazement of his brother, for £120 in 1867 (Rossetti 1970: 233).

The dining room proved to be the forum where "manly" blue and white came into its own. It was a welcome anecdote to the Dresden Shepherdess and Rococo Sevrès vases that smothered the boudoir and drawing room. For Hollingsworth, a room "tastefully adorned with Blue China" invited repose and contemplation, fashioning "one nook in the world wherein you may find that true joy which a fancy, Bridecake [sic] style of decoration can never bring" (1891: 28–29). The Rev. William Loftie, editor of Macmillan's *Art at Home* series, opined that ceramic displays should reflect the function of the room: "China in the dining-room may consist of plates and dishes, ranged neatly on the Sideboard, but china in the drawing-room should only consist of purely ornamental objects and tea things" (1876: 82). This separation also reinforced the gender divide, perpetuating the eighteenth-century distinction between the masculine dining room and the feminine drawing room. Loftie, who conceded his own "taste in ceramics is warped, no doubt, by a strong admiration for the porcelain of China and Japan"

(1876: 7), declared for decorative purposes "Oriental . . . only is worth much . . . If you buy with a view to making your house look pretty you will avoid the European and cleave to the Oriental" (1876: 81).

Apparently, his wife, Mrs Martha Jane Loftie, who contributed *The Dining Room* (1878) to Macmillian's *Art at Home Series*, shared these views. She condemned modern manufactures: "It is like a bad dream to go into a modern china shop seeking for a nice dinner service. One cannot help wishing to be the proverbial bull and to toss all the shelves into the street" (Loftie 1878: 109). From convenience and "an art point of view," no shape could rival a small square willow pattern dish (Loftie 1876: 108). However, although fine old willow pattern was good enough for any use, even the "best design" was apt to be tiresome when too often repeated (Loftie 1876: 106). There was no reason why everything on the table should be of the same pattern, as blue and white lent itself to "variety with uniformity;" she commended three dozen old blue oriental plates "all different" and "above all superior in the lovely delicacy of the tinted ground" (Loftie 1876: 106). Mrs Loftie recalled a dinner party at which the soup and fish were served on "nankeen," the meat on "willow" and the pudding and dessert on "old oriental." Although the effect was not incongruous, it gave intense pain to the old family butler who bemoaned his master was "reduced to not having a *Christian dinner set*" (Loftie 1876: 111). A critic similarly paused to consider how Leyland's Peacock Room could serve its purpose as a dining room; *London* could not fathom a family saying grace in such a room (Merrill 1998: 254).

Following Rev. Loftie's precepts, Leighton opted for plates and dishes on the "big ebonized sideboard, designed by Mr Aitchison"; "The blackness of this latter is broken by a crowd of china on the shelves, blue Nankeen and old English, which tell pale" (Haweis 1882: 9) [Figure 8.3]. The nature of these blue and white wares can be deduced from the 1896 sale catalog (Christie, Manson and Woods 1896). They numbered a set of six fluted plates with "subjects from history" with a border of asters (Lot 353); a fluted bowl with flowering asters (Lot 337) and a pair of bowls and covers with eight flowering peonies (Lot 358). Agnew, apparently on behalf of Lever, acquired a pair of fluted plates with panels of flowering asters (Lot 355; LL6181 and LL6146), even though he purchased few plates and dishes as they did not fit easily into his decorative schemes. Here, provenance outweighed other considerations. Like the Hawthorn Ginger jar, the so-called Aster plate acquired iconic status;[2] Rosalind Marriott Watson was moved to verse: "My Aster plate hangs safe upon the wall, In rounded perfectness, not large, nor small . . . Thou art sun and moon and stars to me . . ." (1912: 91). Although appearing to reflect the poet's own ardor, the owner of "this dark, blue disc" is in fact male and willing to sacrifice his wife, children and friends, even his books and marquetry, providing Fortune "let[s] no evil chance befall My Aster plate" (1912: 91).

FIGURE 8.3 Artist unknown, "A Portion of the Dining Room," Wood engraving, W. Meynell (ed.), "The Homes of Our Artists," Sir Frederick Leighton's House in Holland Park Road, Cassell's *Magazine of Art*, 4, 1881, reprinted in The Modern School of Art, 1, Cassell, c.1885. Credit: Anne Anderson.

William Morris (1834–1896) shared this predilection for Aster plates. A photograph taken by his colleague Emery Walker of the south wall of the dining room at Kelmscott House, Hammersmith, his London residence from 1878, shows his Old Blue plates carefully arranged on purpose-built white shelves; three long shelves divided into twelve sections, with three equally sized plates displayed in each section. A row of Aster plates can be seen on the bottom shelf, while the top houses twelve Hawthorn or *prunus* plates. The shelving, which forms the superstructure of a buffet, is attributed to architect Philip Webb, who is also credited with designing the fixed shelves on turned columns for the "china closet'" at Kelmscott Manor, near Lechlade, Morris's summer retreat (Kelmscott 2013: 83). Morris, who made few structural changes to the Manor, is thought to have opened a small window to light the china closet off the Panelled Room in 1877: "The new window is made, and the little room looks much better for it" (Kelvin 1984, I: 420). We can only speculate what was displayed here in Morris's day, as no documentary evidence survives. Following his death, Janey gave up their London residence, removing the contents to the

Manor: apparently, the Hawthorn plates found a new home in the china closet. In a Memorandum attached to her will, dated 1926, May Morris itemized those family possessions she intended to bequeath to Oxford University: "CHINA ROOM out of Panelled room‖ The blue china except twelve blue Hawthorn plates: their place can be filled by some of my less rare blue china" (Dufty 1963: 108–109). A great deal of blue and white was sold at the Kelmscott Manor auction held in 1939, following the death of Miss Mary Lobb, May's principal beneficiary, including "12 oriental plates" (Lot 650):[3] the sale also included a "Blue oriental tureen with dish and cover and 2 large dishes" (Lot 645), "5 blue oriental teapots" (Lot 656) and "twenty-seven pieces blue oriental plates and saucers" (Lot 658; Hobbs and Chambers 1939). Much of this appears to have been of a type in daily use, including a Booth's blue Willow tea service numbering sixty-seven pieces.

Morris upheld the convention of decorating his dining room with functional pieces. Framed within a Georgian architectural setting, Morris utilized Old Blue's credentials as "English Art" in addition to harnessing its power to evoke an imaginary Orient. His Oriental fantasy was amplified by a vast Persian carpet suspended like a canopy over an Italian chest laden with "Eastern Riches": as May Morris observed, "That side of the room had more than a touch of the *Thousand and One Nights*" (1973: 367). Small wonder one contemporary visitor described this space as "a sumptuously furnished dining room" (Pinkney 2005: 45). Morris certainly exercised his connoisseurship in the selection of objects; he also proved his ability as a decorator in their compositional arrangement. Just like Leighton, Morris constructed his persona through his "things." Kelmscott House was another public relations exercise, framing a respectable professional British artist. Moreover, this show-house was intended to instruct his clients and solicit commissions.

Leyland's Peacock Room (1877), at 49 Princes Gate, can be read as a public relations exercise of a different sort; according to Theodore Childe, Leyland dreamed "that he might live the life of an old Venetian merchant in modern London" (1890: 81–82) [Figure 8.4]. His ascension from obscurity to notoriety illustrates the flexibility of Victorian social structures. With Old Blue transformed into a sign of distinction, marking social and financial success, its acquisition legitimized claims to cultural superiority and guaranteed acceptance into an elite coterie (Saisselin 1984: 150). Leyland was inculcated into the Old Blue clique by Rossetti rather than Whistler. His first purchase may have been a pot bought as a gift for the artist in 1870; Charles Augustus Howell, who also fueled Rossetti's ardor for Old Blue, observed Leyland was "never taken with the beauty of a certain pot or any thing, he only sees such and such a corner requires a pot and then he orders one" (Merrill 1998: 169). Leyland's appropriation of Chinese porcelain as "a tasteful appointment for the artful interior" (Merrill 1998: 169) has resulted in his dismissal as a serious collector. However, he can be repositioned as a

FIGURE 8.4 Bedford Lemere (1839–1911), "The Peacock Room", 49, Princes Gate, Westminster, photograph, in E.R. and J. Pennell, *The Life of James McNeill Whistler*, Vol. I, Philadelphia: J.B. Lippincott Company, 1909, facing 208. Credit: Anne Anderson

décorateur or *metteur-en-scène*, his Old Blue part of a *tout ensemble*, even though Leyland credited Marks with converting his house into a dwelling of "perfect harmony" (Williamson 1919: 4). Marks, who is said to have supplied most of Leyland's Old Blue, inevitably recognized "what a feast of colour a great collection of Blue and White porcelain could produce" (Williamson 1919: 36); the Peacock Room was originally conceived as a *porsellanzimmer*. Marks, who had a vested interest, actively encouraged *chinamania*, as Dr G. C. Williamson, his biographer, concludes "few were more intimately concerned in the development in England of the *culte* of Blue and White Nankin porcelain" (Williamson 1919: 31).

The theme of Leyland's dining room may have been inspired by his spectacular K'ang Hsi chargers that bore peacocks on the rims; these chargers were destined for display on the west wall. As Murray Marks' trade card, allegedly designed by Rossetti, Whistler and Morris, attests, peacock feathers were a standard accessory with Chinese pots [Figure 8.2]. This coupling may be due to Rossetti; "Japanese fans made from peacock feathers were hung on the walls" at Chatham Place (Marsh 1999: 266), while a peacock joined his menagerie of beasts at Chelsea in 1864.

The color scheme for the Peacock Room was inspired by the bird's plumage, melding blue and gold with emerald green. Marks was bitterly disappointed as "it was complete of itself, not a background for porcelain or for anything else, a *chef d'oeurve* doubtless, one of the great pieces of decoration in the world." Apparently, Marks and Leyland removed much of the porcelain after Whistler had completed the work (Williamson 1919: 95). Artist Thomas Armstrong, a devotee of Whistler, confessed to disliking the color combination, which "was fatal to the precious blue china . . . the cobalt blue of the pots suffered terribly from the juxtaposition with Whistler's paint, made of Prussian or Antwerp blue" (Williamson 1919: 207). However, Merrill asserts the unexpected combination of hues was deliberate; Whistler had already juxtaposed Old Blue with various shades of peacock-blue in his dining room at 2 Lindsay Row (1998: 149). He also tested this combination beforehand in his unfinished portrait of Leyland's youngest daughter Elinor, *The Blue Girl* (c.1875), in which the background for the Chinese porcelain is Prussian Blue. He envisioned the cobalt blue porcelain as an integral component of his *Harmony in Blue and Gold*, as he entitled the Peacock Room. With *Rose and Silver: La Princesse du pays de la porcelain* (1864) as its centerpiece, the gilded spindles provided by Thomas Jeckyll framing each pot like a picture, the Peacock Room was not only a *tout ensemble* but also homage to the Old Blue pots that Whistler considered "the finest specimens of Art" (Spencer 1989: 72).

The Peacock Room caused a sensation when transported to Detroit by Charles Lang Freer in 1904. But Freer was not the first to have a Blue room in Detroit. Deming Jarvis, joint Director of the Michigan Carbon Works, had filled his dining room with four hundred pieces, accumulated over forty years, by 1901 (Anon. 1901: 135). He had forged his allegiance to Chinese art at the tender age of eighteen, ransacking the world for the finest specimens, including a Ginger jar "remarkable for its intense sapphire hue" that deserved to "rank among the finest specimens of blue and white *hawthorn* ware in the world" (Anon. 1901: 139). Avoiding the "grotesque," he had "striven after the most graceful in form and the purest in colour" (Anon. 1901: 135). This enthusiastic American collector saw his Old Blue as "essentially decorative;" a carpet was designed and woven in China to "harmonise with the ware which is the splendour of the room" (Anon. 1901: 136) [Figure 8.5].

Other collectors were more diverse in their choice of Old Blue. In Dr Hammond's New York residence, sideboards were loaded with Old Delft, Chinese, Japanese and even Siamese wares; plates, dishes and plaques formed "a natural and very suitable ornamentation for a dining room" ("Curio" 1879: 13). The impression of "an old baronial hall" was conveyed; in newspaper magnate William Randolph Hearst's baronial dining room at Hearst Castle, his guests dined on Booth's Willow pattern.

FIGURE 8.5 Artist unknown, "No. I- Mr Jarvis's Collection", photograph, Anon, "Mr Deming Jarvis's Collection of Chinese Porcelain at Detroit, USA", *Connoisseur An Illustrated Magazine for Collectors*, Vol. I, Nov 1901: 137. Credit: Anne Anderson.

Conclusion

As Stein notes, one of the greatest strengths of the Aesthetic Movement was to "make accessible to artist and audience, aesthetic producer and consumer, a range of artefacts drawn from an international inventory" (1986: 39); this conjoining of artifacts, which could be from anywhere or any time, produced a rich and complex effect that could be read as cosmopolitan. Focusing on harmony, stressing the visual composition as a whole, the arresting juxtaposition of works from different eras and worlds was intended for sensuous enjoyment. Old Blue's artistic and economic value was firmly invested in its color, thus liberating it from an historical past and geographically distant culture. It was prized for its beauty, intrinsic visual and compositional values outweighing academic.

Being consumed in the home, Old Blue made "possible a kind of creative play with form and colour and texture" (Stein 1986: 39); its meaning was ambiguous as it could be both "English Art" and "Exotic Other." As a "decorator's taste," its role in the domestic interior challenged gender boundaries, the dining room maintaining its masculine dignity through the display of Chinese, Japanese and Islamic wares. Yet this meant Old Blue retained its "commodity status, failing to sever its link with consumption" (Cheang 2001: 60). Feminine consumption was expected to integrate with "home." Conversely, masculine collectibles situated in a domestic setting can be read as transgressing gender boundaries. Masculinity was recuperated by placing Old Blue in the dining room, which becomes a material metaphor of social identity. Hence, Aestheticism appears to posit masculinity as a "cultural artifact." This suggests that Leighton was constructing a particularized masculinity; he wished to "demonstrate the nature of his own aesthetic preoccupations and the power of the artist to create, synthesise and transform" (Campbell 1999: 285). But Leighton's "gentlemanly professionalism" remains equivocal, "an anxious conjunction ... of masculinity and performance" (Stephenson 1999: 239). Leighton's allegiance to Old Blue reveals the tensions inherent in Aestheticism. Although lionized as a "thing of beauty," a Chinese vase situated in the home will inevitably raise anxieties, invoking a dangerous "other" destined to corrupt our sensibilities.

Notes

1 Misinterpreting the pattern of blossoming *prunus* branches on a field of cracking ice, Rossetti named his favorite ginger jars "hawthorn pots"; collectors still retain this nomenclature.
2 Named after *Callistephus chinensis* (China Aster), which resembles chrysanthemum.
3 These may have returned to the Manor, as eleven matching *prunus* plates can be found in the china closet.

References

Alayrac-Fielding, V. (2012), "From the Curious to the 'Artinatural': The Meaning of Oriental Porcelain in 17th and 18th-Century English Interiors," *Miranda*, 7(1) (December): 1–36. http://miranda.revues.org/4390 [Accessed June 30, 2014].

Anon (1881), "Blue and White China," *The Art Amateur: A Monthly Journal Devoted to Art in the Household*, 5(2) (July): 41–42.

Anon (1901), "Mr Deming Jarvis's Collection of Chinese Porcelain at Detroit, USA," *Connoisseur: An Illustrated Magazine for Collectors*, Vol. I (November): 135–140.

Armstrong, T. (1912), "Reminiscences of Whistler," in L. M. Lamont (ed.), *Thomas Armstrong, C. B: A Memoir. 1832–1911*, London: Martin Secker: 171–214.

Brown, B. (2003), *A Sense of Things: The Object Matter of American Literature*, Chicago and London: University of Chicago Press.

Burne-Jones, G. (1904), *Memorials of Edward Burne-Jones*, Vol. I. *1833–1867*, London: Macmillan.

Campbell, L. (1999), "Decoration, Display, Disguise: Leighton House Reconsidered," in T. Barringer and E. Prettejohn (eds.), *Frederick Leighton: Antiquity Renaissance Modernity*, New Haven and London: Yale University Press: 268–269.

Cheang, S. (2001), "The Dogs of Fo: Gender, Identity and Collecting," in A. Shelton (ed.), *Collectors: Expressions of Self and Other*, London: Horniman Museum, Universidade de Coimbra: 55–72.

Childe, T. (1890), "A Pre-Raphaelite Mansion," *Harper's New Monthly Magazine*, 82 (December): 81–99.

Christie, Manson and Woods (1896), *Catalogue of the Collection of Old Rhodian, Persian and Hispano-Mauro Pottery ... of the Right Hon. Lord Leighton of Stretton, Messers Christie, Manson and Woods, Weds July 8*.

Clunas, C. (1994), "Taste and Gender: Chinese Goods in Eighteenth-Century Britain," *Dreams of the Dragon: Visions of China and Japan*, exhibition catalogue, University of Essex: 13–17.

"Curio" (1879), "Private Collections: Dr Hammond's Bric-a-Brac", *The Art Amateur*, 1(1) (June): 13–14.

Digges, W. (1877), *A China Wedding*, purported to be played at the Duke's Theatre, Holborn. Lord Chamberlain's Collection 53187, British Library.

Dufty, A. R. ([1963] 2013), Kelmscott Manor & Estate Conservation Management Plan Consultation Draft (April): www.sal.org.uk/kelmscottmanor/cmpconsultation/Draft [Accessed June 30, 2014].

Edwards, J. (2010), "The Lessons of Leighton House: Aesthetics, Politics, Erotics," in J. Edwards and I. Hart (eds.), *Rethinking the Interior, c.1867–1896: Aestheticism and the Arts and Crafts*, Farnham: Ashgate: 85–110.

Figueiredo, P. de (2001), *The Leverhulme Collection, Thornton Manor, Wirral, Merseyside, Sotheby's 26, 27, 28 June 2001*, Vol. 1.

Goncourt, E. de (2003), *La Maison d'un artiste* (1881), 2 vols, D. Pety and C. Galantaris (eds.), Dijon: L'Echelle de Jacob.

Hillier, B. (1968), *Pottery and Porcelain, 1700–1914: England, Europe and North America*, New York: Meredith.

Hobbs and Chambers (1939), *Sale of a large portion of the Furnishings and Effects removed from Kelmscott Manor, the Home of William Morris,* Weds and Thurs 19 and 20 July 1939.
Hollingsworth, A. T. (1891), *Old Blue and White Nankin China*, Odd Volumes XXVI, Privately Printed: Chiswick Press, 1891.
James, H. (1908), *The Spoils of Poynton: The Novels and Tales of Henry James*, Vol. 10, New York: Scribner's: 3–265.
Kelmscott Manor and Estate Conservation Management Plan, Consultation Draft, April (2013) www.sal.org.uk/kelmscottmanor/cmpconsultation/Draft [Accessed June 30, 2014].
Kelvin, N. (1984), *The Collected Letters of William Morris*, Vol. I, Princeton: Princeton University Press.
Kerr, R. (1865), *The Gentleman's House, or, How to Plan English Residences, from the Parsonage to the Palace*, London: John Murray.
Lamb, C. (1823), "Old China", *Essays of Elia*, London: Morley's Universal Library, 1885: 148–149.
Litchfield, F. (1900), *Pottery and Porcelain: a guide to collectors,* London and New York: Truslove, Hanson & Comba, Ltd.
Loftie, W. J. (1876), *A Plea for Art in the Home*, London: Macmillan.
Marsh, J. (1999), *Dante Gabriel Rossetti: Painter and Poet*, London: Weidenfeld and Nicolson.
Merrill, L. (1998), *The Peacock Room: A Cultural Biography*, Washington: Freer Gallery of Art and Yale University Press.
Morris, M. (1973), *Introductions to the Collected Works of William Morris, 1910–1915*, New York: Oriole.
Neiswander, J. A. (2008), *The Cosmopolitan Interior: Liberalism and the British Home 1870–1914*, New Haven and London: Yale University Press.
Pater, W. (1990), *The Renaissance Studies in Art and Poetry*, Oxford: Oxford University Press.
Pearce, N. (2014), *Gorer v. Lever: Edgar Gorer and William Hesketh Lever*, Essays: Lady Lever Art Gallery, Liverpool Museum, www.liverpoolmuseums.org.uk/ladylever/collections/chinese/goreressay [Accessed June 30, 2014].
Pennell, E. R. and J. (1909), *The Life of James McNeill Whistler*, Vol. I, Philadelphia: J. B. Lippincott.
Pierson, S. (2007), *Collectors, Collections and Museums: The Field of Chinese Ceramics in Britain, 1560–1960*, Bern: Peter Lang.
Pinkney, T. (ed.) (2005), *We Met Morris: Interviews with William Morris, 1885–1896*, Reading: Spire Books.
Reitlinger, G. (1982), *The Economics of Taste: The Rise and Fall of Picture Prices, 1760–1960*, Vol. 2, New York: Hacker Art Books.
Rossetti, W. M. (1970), *Rossetti Papers 1862–1870: A Compilation by William Michael Rossetti*, New York: AMS Press.
Saisselin, R. G. (1984), *The Bourgeois and the Bibelot*, New Brunswick: Rutgers.
Spencer, R. (1989), *Whistler: A Retrospective*, New York: Hugh Lauter Levin.
Stein, R. B. (1986), "Artifact as Ideology: The Aesthetic Movement in its American Cultural Context," in D. Bolger Burke et al. (eds.), *In Pursuit of Beauty: Americans and the Aesthetic Movement*, exhibition catalog, New York: Metropolitan Museum of Art and Rizzoli: 22–51.

Stephenson, A. (1999), "Leighton and the Shifting Repertoires of 'Masculine' Artistic Identity in the Late Victorian Period," in T. Barringer and E. Prettejohn (eds.), *Frederick Leighton: Antiquity Renaissance Modernity*, New Haven and London: Yale University Press: 221–246.

Watson, R. M. (1897), *The Art of the House*, London: George Bell and Sons.

Watt, W. (1877), *Art Furniture, from Designs by E. W. Godwin, F. S. A., and Others, with Hints and Suggestions on Domestic Furniture and Decoration*, London: B. T. Batsford.

Williamson, G. C. (1919), *Murray Marks and His Friends: A Tribute of Regard by Dr G. C. Williamson*, London: John Lane, Bodley Head.

Hodgson, Mrs. Willoughby (1911), "Mr William Hesketh Lever's Collection of Chinese Porcelain," *The Connoisseur: An Illustrated Magazine for Collectors*, Vol. XXIX (February): 73–84.

9

At the Edge of Propriety: Rolf de Maré and Nils Dardel at the Hildesborg Estate

John Potvin

The Hallwyska Museet in central Stockholm stands as a grand and spectacular testament to the rich legacy of one of Sweden's most illustrious family dynasties. Resplendent and ornate, the family home cum museum in Hamngatan houses interiors that serve as sanctuaries to relics of a formidable and voracious collector. Described by the museum itself as one of "Stockholm's most eccentric and engaging museums," the Hallwyl Palace was completed in 1898 as a winter home for the Count and Countess Walther and Wilhelmina von Hallwyl. Designed and built by Swedish architect Isak Gustaf Clason (1856–1930), the blueprint for the conservative yet up-to-date modern house was largely determined by the Countess's ever-expanding collections and the Count's need for office space from which to run the family's empire. Since its inception, the house was designed as a showcase for and memorial to the cultural importance of the family's various collections.

In addition to the display of the Countess's various assortments of *objets d'art*, the museum also boasts one of Sweden's most lauded (expressionist) portraits, that of the Count and Countess's controversial grandson, Rolf de Maré (1888–1964). The picture depicts de Maré proudly staring out at the viewer, one hand on his hip with the other in his side pocket, silhouetted by a dimensionally disproportionate representation of his mansion on the Hildesborg estate in Skåne.[1] Colorful and captivating, the painting as such is rather unremarkable artistically. Painted in 1916 by his then lover and life-long friend, Nils Dardel (1888–1943), the picture, however, stands as indexical of a dubiously complicated cultural legacy in which subjectivity, the modern interior and Orientalism provided the very foundation for scandal.

With this as an, albeit brief, cultural backdrop, this chapter turns its attention to the intersubjective queer legacy engendered by de Maré and Dardel. In his own home in Hildesborg, de Maré set out to design his own interior landscape whose community was populated by some of Sweden's most important cultural figures, queer or otherwise. The collected objects and the spaces they occupied would not only prove inspirational to Dardel, who took up residence at Hildesborg on several occasions, but also would become the material basis for the public shaming of its residents. My intention here is to explore the braiding of interior design, collecting and painting, and how, together, they engendered a queer narrative. A crucial facet of this narrative is a focus on various forms of fabrics. Deployed to furnish the interior, fabrics, textiles, carpets and skins, I argue, served to blur boundaries between East and West. At the center of this conjuncture is a queer Orientalism wherein the fantastical hybrid interior becomes a site at once of pleasure and shame, transience and comfort, heritage and sexual emancipation. All too often, the erotic and the sexual are attached to the interpretations of homosocial and/or homosexual Orientalist spaces and paintings. Here, however, I do not seek to deny the sexual, but rather to extend the discussion to include an investigation of how a queer orientation might complicate the relationship between modernism, sexuality and Orientalism.

Collecting, community and creativity

Countess Wilhelmina von Hallwyl was single-minded and steely in her determination when it came to her collecting practice, and the family's wealth afforded her the ability to let her passions run freely. Her pursuits ran along more conventional lines, focusing her attention primarily on Western European porcelains, weaponry, silverware and Northern European painting. From an early age, de Maré occupied himself with the business of collecting, learning alongside his grandmother as she acquired, cataloged and displayed her vast collections. The closeness with his grandmother and the countless hours he spent aiding her in her noble endeavor provided an ideal and fertile environment in which to learn about objects and their value and significance. With this informal training, de Maré set out to define the parameters of his own collecting interests, which he quickly established on the occasion of his first of numerous trips outside of Europe in 1910. On the occasion of his father Henrik's fiftieth birthday, de Maré traveled to India and Ceylon, which not only inspired the direction his initial collection would take, but also provided the seeds for a love affair with the dance and performance rituals of the countries he visited; a passion that would continue to grow throughout his life.

Both the collecting and his focus on dance would provide the embryo for de Maré's most important cultural contributions, the benefit of which we still enjoy today. De Maré amassed an impressive collective of rare objects from around the world, a collection around which he formed the AID (*Archives internationales de la Danse*) in Paris in 1931, the first of its kind in the world. Today, however, the largest portion of his archive comprises the majority of objects housed by the Dance Museum in Stockholm, where a foundation was established shortly following his death in 1964. The importance of this donation to the museum is a testament to the collector's attention the ephemera of world dance. De Maré's commitment to and belief in the cultural importance of dance is far too extensive to outline here, and much of the attention paid to de Maré by curators and historians has largely been restricted to his contributions to this field (see Baer 1995; Näslund 2009).

In March 1912, the same year that he met Dardel, de Maré was given the lease to Hildesborg by his grandparents with the expectation that he farm and assume the management of the land. While his grandparents occupied the estate's grand castle, the young heir set out to rebuild a pre-existing villa on the grounds and christened it Park Villa. Completed in 1913, the interior design of the villa was arranged by both Dardel and de Maré's mother Ellen, who carved friezes on either side of the fireplace. Importantly, de Maré's interpretation of Swedish homeliness was largely premised on an interior landscape heavily populated by objects acquired in foreign, non-Northern European locations. In her extensive exploration of private collecting practices, Susan M. Pearce argues that

> [c]ollections are sets of objects, and, like all other sets of objects, they are an act of the imagination, part corporate and part individual, a metaphor intended to create meanings which help to make individual identity and each individual's view of the world. Collections are gathered [. . .] lifting them away from the world of common commodities into one of special significance, one of which "sacred" seems the right word.
>
> (1995: 27)

In 1913 Sweden, de Maré's collections of foreign objects used extensively as a means to decorate his home would only serve to heighten the foreign and perverse element attributed to his domestic interiors, spaces in which exotic desires, pleasures and vices were enlivened and enacted.

Jean Baudrillard asserts, "[i]f the feeling of possession is based on a confusion of the senses (of hand and eye) and an intimacy with the privileged object, it is also based just as much on searching, ordering, playing and assembling" (1996: 88). On his long, extensive trips, de Maré accumulated an impressive and rare collection of Asian, American and African artifacts. De Maré's keen interest in dance and its central position in his collection served to expand at once the sensory and phenomenological aspect of his collection, but also provided a different dimension of the assembling, as these would help to inspire one of his greatest contributions to modern dance, the inauguration of the Ballet Suédois in 1920 in Paris. Introduced by their mutual friend Dardel, de Maré took up another love affair in spring 1918 with a struggling ballet dancer, Jean Börlin. Börlin was a dancer in the *ballet de corps* for the Royal Stockholm Opera, but de Maré believed his lover to be far more talented than his current position enabled and provided him the means to set out on his own. Two short years later, on March 24, 1920, Börlin made his solo debut on the stage of the Théâtre des Champs-Élysées in Paris. Located in one of the city's most luxurious milieu in Avenue Montaigne, de Maré purchased a seven-year lease on the theater where, for five years, the Ballets Suédois impressed, annoyed, bemused and entertained critics and fans alike. The ballets that Börlin created for the troupe were largely designed and choreographed around three core inspirational themes: idyllic, pastoral expressions of Swedish folklore; kinetic materializations of two-dimensional modern art (which formed the second major focus of de Maré's collecting praxis); and stylized interpretations of the dance cultures of, in particular, sub-Saharan Africa, the Maghreb and Thailand. In its decidedly modernist vision of dance that purposefully turned its back on traditional ballet, Börlin's repertoire took up the project the Ballets Ruses had established the previous decade of breaking cultural and artistic barriers. Largely premised on static poses rather than fluid movement, Börlin set out to blur what he and de Maré saw as artificial boundaries marking East from West, two-dimensional art from three-dimensional performance. In his 1920 performance of *Dervishes*, for example, Börlin set out create a hybrid performance that seamlessly fused Eastern mysticism with Western balletic athleticism. The simple yet luxurious backdrop, designed by M. Mouveau, illuminated in gold and mauve, silhouetted the spiraling dancers in costumes of red, blue and white, designed by the choreographer himself [Figure 9.1]. As dance scholar Ramasy Burt concludes, "*Dervishes* takes its place alongside other avant-garde and modernist works (both earlier and later) that explore ritual, autohypnotic movement" (1999: 223). Although the practice originated in Turkey, it was likely on a trip to Algeria with de Maré that Börlin came into contact with the moving rituals of the dervish. In *Dervishes*, the ballet dancer transforms this Oriental homosocial ritual into an ecstatic display of his own physical mastery, blurring the boundaries of traditional ballet and physical meditation.

Oriental impressions

Between 1911 and 1912, de Maré embarked on a year-and-a-half-long world tour that focused his attention on Ceylon and India, once again, as well as Siam, Indonesia, China, Japan and the USA. Early on in the trip, upon completion of the Ceylonese and Indian portion of his journey, the young collector proudly wrote in a card to his father that he sent "home

FIGURE 9.1 *Dervishes*. Costumes, lead dancer and choreography by Jean Börlin with décor by M. Mouveau. *Comoedia Illustré* (November 20, 1920): 56. Reproduction: John Potvin.

3 crates of curios from" the two countries, whose contents included amongst others "a number of antique cloths with marvelous hand embroideries" (in Näslund 2009: 55). Upon arrival in Thailand, the articulate, well-bred and decorous de Maré charmed his way into becoming a member of the Swedish delegation, serving as the equerry to Princess Maria of Sweden. His appointment was a purposeful means to gain an invitation to the exclusive and much anticipated coronation of King Vajiravudh (Rama VI) of Siam in December 1911. While the Court Huntsman Gustaf Lewenhaupt who formed part of the Swedish delegation described the event in his memoires as part "theatrical event," part "*Thousand and One Nights*," de Maré was less impressed by the opulence of the coronation, disappointed by the Western clothes worn by the court's officers and courtiers (Näslund 2009: 56). What he longed for instead was a supposedly more authentic, indigenous spectacle befitting an Oriental monarchy unfettered by Western influence. Notably, however, the specially decorated interior space evoked in him Orientalist delight and wonderment. His vivid description is worth quoting at length, not the least for the impression it made on him:

> A Buddha, glistening with gold and jewels, with the tall crowns; beneath him, the golden throne. The temple in the background, also of gold inlaid

with enamel. The spectacle cannot possibly be described in writing. His Majesty sat perfectly motionless for about 10 minutes, only his eyes moving. None of his retinue could be seen—only the Buddha-King, whom his subjects invoked to the sound of intoxicating music. The King then made a short speech—still motionless and as it made of stone—before the curtains were drawn again. The Buddha vision had vanished [...] In full regal splendor he was carried on his throne under a canopy to the main temple, where a service of thanksgiving was to be held.

(in Näslund 2009: 57)

Despite de Maré's purported inability to put into writing the event and its environment, he nevertheless manages to conjure some of the most savory sensory impressions. The "glistening" Buddha, itself "a vision" which ritualistically appeared and disappeared from view, the intoxication of the music and the controlled, motionless king help to suggest a performance and ritual at once regal and decidedly exotic to Western eyes.[2]

Continuing his whirlwind tour, de Maré arrived in China in March 1912. In contrast to the grand spectacle of the coronation, in his diary he described Canton, for example, as nothing short of a nightmare, where a

never-ending stream of shouting, grimacing Chinese flows through these alleys, for everyone shrieks and makes as much noise as possible to give themselves a chance of getting by. Silk-clad mandarins jostle with naked coolies, all of them trying with a grimace to avoid unduly violent collisions with the sedan chairs in which high-ranking Chinese are carried. A morning spent strolling around here leaves one utterly giddy, for the air is saturated with opium incense and the odours of fish.

(in Näslund 2009: 66)

Despite their apparent differences, this evocative description of Cantonese street life is similar to that of the coronation in the way it attempts to evoke sensory impressions of the exotic, filtered through the not uncommon Western expressions and experiences of difference (and hence its effect on pleasure) and long-held Eurocentric perceptions.

Vivid though de Maré's sensory-infused impressions were of China, Japan surprisingly left a far more dulled, if not entirely disappointed, impression on the world traveler. The country, which had so occupied the collective imagination of Europeans since it was opened to the West in the 1850s, proved to be nothing like the representations he had come to know and the impressions he had fashioned in his mind's eye (Näslund 2009: 67). Set against the backdrop of fantastical descriptions and widely coveted colorful Japanese *Ukiyo-e* prints, how could de Maré not be underwhelmed faced with the mundane realities of early twentieth-century modern life? Not unlike what he witnessed in Thailand, Japan was not left untouched by Western influence, the outcome of ever-increasing global trade and cross-cultural pollination. Nonetheless, both China and Japan proved exceptional hunting grounds for a voracious collector whose appetite was sated by objects acquired only while abroad. As Michael Camille beautifully evokes, "pleasure—not as a passive and merely optical response but as an active, productive and shaping stimulation of all the senses—is the fundamental experience at the foundations of the act of collecting" (2001: 164). Unlike with his grandmother's collections, the objects de Maré acquired during his travels provided the very foundation that would inspire both his own interior design and consequently a number of Dardel's paintings.

De Maré was a generous man, providing both Dardel and Börlin with trips, which would have been out of their reach and that would inform and alter the course of their creative output. These trips also provided their benefactor with opportunities to supplement his already extensive and ever-expanding collection. In 1914, for example, he and Dardel traveled to North Africa, which was followed by an extended holiday in Spain and Tenerife in 1916. While on a second trip in Japan in 1917, this time with Dardel, de Maré elected to return to Sweden on May 14, 1917, after only one month. For his part, Dardel stayed to familiarize himself with the visual arts of the country while also assuring the continued development a budding relationship with Nita Wallenberg, whose father, Gustaf Wallenberg, was the first Swedish envoy to Japan.

Dardel's six-month stay in Japan would, first and foremost, have a profound impact on his painting practice and would alter the course of his personal life. The artist took watercolor lessons from a local artist, learning first-hand various practices of a country whose interest in flat areas of saturated coloration coupled with a lack of attention to perspectival depth and shadowing had long imprinted itself on the visual culture of Western Europe and was well suited to Dardel's already expressionist style; the influence of Japanese art would remain discernible in his work well into the 1930s. A member of one of the most powerful and wealthy families in Sweden, Nita was secretly engaged to Dardel in the summer 1917. However, the rumors that circulated widely about Dardel's past dalliances and louche lifestyle in Paris and Hideslborg soon reached the Swedish envoy, who swiftly forced Nita to end her relationship with the painter. Dardel's various addictions and voracious sexual appetite, after all, were not easily folded into a grand Swedish dynastic narrative.

Much has been made of Dardel's broken relationship with Nita, over-determining its impact on the content of his *oeuvres*. Ingemar Lindahl, for example, is among a number of scholars who have concluded that paintings like *Crime passionnel* from 1921, to be discussed in the section that follows, is a direct, if dream-like, representation of the heart-breaking rejection of Dardel by his fiancée. While there can be no doubt that the break-up in 1919, and subsequent marriage to Thora Klinckowström in 1921, are clearly legible as themes in numerous paintings from the period, reading these pictures uniquely against this solitary and, as a result, stultifying background has obscured the layered meanings, I assert, these picture possess. Moreover, this univocal interpretative strategy has also purposefully obscured the meaningfully exotic and queer intersections in Dardel's *oeuvre* and how these were played out within the interiors of Hildesborg, in particular. While undoubtedly a colorful character who indeed led a life worthy of sensationalized biographies, the preponderance of reading his *oeuvre* through the biographical has meant, with little exception, that Dardel's work has rarely managed to escape the lurid events associated with his personal life, negating any larger cultural implications or cross-cultural dialog in which his work clearly participates. The writings of Erik Näslund, Karl Asplund and Ingemar Lindahl have established the intellectual parameters of the scholarship on Dardel, all deploying his biography as the sole means through which to understand the artist's work.

Portals: Carpets/skins/textiles

In a rare extant photograph taken of the salon at Hildesborg, transnational objects seem to willfully cavort with one another to evoke a deep and otherworldly exoticism [Figure 9.2]. Tapestries, rugs and skins become the rich surfaces on which to display Buddha heads, Buddhist ceremonial bowls and various curios from around the world, decorative debris from countless travels. In the apartment Dardel acquired for de Maré in 1920 in the bohemian enclave of Saint-Germain-des-Prés in rue Saint Simon, the Swede elected to reconstruct a version of his exotic villa salon [Figure 9.3]. In this second iteration, however, the space forms a balanced hybrid comingling of Western furniture and Eastern objects and fabrics. The Chinese dragon tapestry once housed in Park Villa is seen mounted beside a baronial dark wood fireplace upon whose mantel is set a large bronze Buddha head. Velvet armchairs befitting a bourgeois domestic interior since the nineteenth century are silhouetted by an expansive Chinese embroidered wall-hanging, which takes up nearly the entire surface of the wall. A polar bear skin rug rests overtop a Turkish or Persian rug and beside a lush silk low-to-the-floor daybed. In this space, like in Park Villa, the eye is constantly stimulated in a landscape of endless visual delights. The various interiors de Maré constructed in both his homes, each room ostensibly different from the next, attempted a balancing act in the combination of various elements of his vast collections of modern art[3] and objects amassed from around the world. These various objects were not locked away in cabinets of curiosity or under glass, but were placed in close proximity to everything which occupied and everyone who visited his Paris home. As Griselda Pollock has noted, "[p]henomenological space is not orchestrated for sight alone but by means of visual cues refers to other sensations and relations of bodies and objects in a lived world" (1988: 165).

However, this panoply of sensations and phenomenological experiences within the modern interior has been associated, at least since the nineteenth

FIGURE 9.2 Salon interior of Rolf de Maré's Park Villa, Hildesborg, Sweden, c.1913. Dansmuseet, Stockholm.

FIGURE 9.3 Interior of Rolf de Maré's salon at 2 Saint-Simon, Paris, c.1920. Dansmuseet, Stockholm.

century, with a perceived decadence and even a degenerated, weakened mind. Evoking a deep-seated *fin-de-siècle* malaise that all too often was wedded with a homophobic retrenchment of gender norms, French physician and theorist Max Nordau asserted that "[t]he present rage for collecting, the piling up of dwellings, of aimless of *bric-à-brac* ... has established an irresistible desire among degenerates to accumulate useless trifles" (1892: 27). Nordau was deeply invested in the phenomenological impressions that both objects and interiors conjured when he noted how

> [e]verything in these houses aims at exciting the nerves and dazzling the senses. The disconnected and antithetical effects in all arrangements, the constant contradiction between form and purpose, the outlandishness of most objects, is intended to be bewildering.... He who enters here must not doze, but be thrilled.
>
> (1892: 11)

Fin-de-siècle anxieties coupled with an ever-increasing modernist distrust of and disdain for ornament as advocated by domineering figures like Adolf Loos (1870–1933) who aimed to design architectural interiors devoid of objects that over-stimulated occupants' minds and bodies. Not unlike Nordau, Loos saw ornament and decoration as not only the signs of degeneration, by 1908 when he penned his infamous essay "Ornament and

Crime," but were themselves indexical of crime, that is, the very tangible markings of the decline of Western civilization itself.

Aided by his extensive collection of skins, carpets and textiles, de Maré's design ethos evokes a sort of return to an exotic or even primitivized (read degenerate) vision of the modern interior that shares an affinity with Gottfried Semper's mid-nineteenth-century notion of the "clothing of architecture." For Semper, there exists a constant interplay between the function and purpose of architecture and clothing, both acting as forms of enclosure, protection and sheath through which the body occupies space. In this interplay is engendered a different reciprocity between surface and depth. Semper notes that "[i]n all Germanic languages the word *Wand* [wall], which has the same root and basic meaning as *Gewand* [garment], directly alludes to the ancient origin and type of the *visible* spatial enclosure" (1862: 248). Through this commonly shared etymological origin, Semper moves to make a claim, as a result, for how the clothing of the body and of space function similarly to provide the material conditions of subjectivity itself. For Semper, architecture's origin was to be found in textiles, best expressed in the tents of nomadic tribes. Textiles, along with ceramics, possessed both aesthetic potential and practical function, the twined benefits for creating hearth and home. Textiles also possess a dual function, for at once they provide protection as much as they maintain a flexible surface; this duplicitous nature thus delimited the characteristics of one of four core elements of architecture: enclosure.[4] As Semper states: "[t]he wall is the architectural element that formally represents and makes visible *enclosed space as such*" (1862: 247).

As Solmaz Mohammadzadeh Kive shows in Chapter 3, carpets formed a vital and dynamic aspect of Orientalist private collections and public exhibitions. Although her inquiry focuses attention on Islamic art and decorative objects, she notes how the use of carpets and textiles helped Orientalist displays and exhibition interiors to recreate purportedly authentic spaces and overall impressions, forgoing attributing any importance to any one object. In this way, textiles provide a deep and rich conduit in the construction of experiential knowledge and the production of meaning. By citing Robert Goupil's "Oriental Room" of 1888, characterized as straight out of *The Thousand and One Nights* and F. R. Martin's collection made public in the General Art and Industry Exhibition of 1897 in Stockholm, Kive maintains that textiles and carpets furnished "rich backgrounds against which many diverse objects were unified," a common practice, she claims, which was used in the exhibition of Islamic art and decorative objects. Through the use of textile surfaces, displays such as those noted by Kive act as sites of transformation that materialize loaded, wholesale meanings, which are, in turn, grafted onto the way all objects in that space are read, understood and experienced.

Spaces of crime, spaces of passion

Hung in the very interior it represented, Dardel depicted the exoticism that infused Park Villa in *Reception* (1914). Portrayed with a palette of deep jewel tones and Dardel's characteristically elongated, ephebic corporeality, the picture's figures occupy a flattened, fantastical version of de Maré's Oriental salon. The picture not only depicts the artist himself, but also de Maré and various members of the patron's homosexual coterie who were frequently in attendance at the villa. One of the earliest descriptions of the picture has been provided by the near-contemporary critic and art historian Karl Asplund, who writes in his two-volume corpus on Dardel that the interior the artist represents is "an apotheosis of luxury, a paean in hot colours, rubean, amethyst, cornealian, the wishful dream of a nightclub owner" (1958: 109). Although the critic spares little ink on a reading of the picture, the sexual connotations are rather apparent in Asplund's dismissive formal analysis. Like the photograph described above, the space Dardel represents is defined by the way in which Oriental textiles and exoticism provide a sort of dissolution of actual or even perspective space. In the picture, the threshold into the space—the portal into exoticism—is determined by way of a draped fabric; one of many that he uses to deconstruct space only to reconstruct it as a melding of colors and textured surfaces. Whether the Chinese dragon wall-hanging, the animal skins, Asian tapestries or the occupants' clothing, textiles envelop the space of the interior and body as both become inseparable form each other in the way the pictures manages to define a clearly articulated subjectivity. Space, however fashioned, becomes the site of a queer Orientalism that begins to dissolve boundaries, even if it only alludes to "the wishful dream of a nightclub owner," and where pleasures and desires were neither defined nor confining. Elsewhere, I have argued for the significance of how the picture visualizes the liminal position these men occupied within Swedish society and how de Maré's villa at Hildesborg provided a vital space of creativity and sexual emancipation, albeit at a heavy price (Potvin 2014). Both actual and pictorial, the space is at once vivid, sumptuous and saturated in its visual stimulation, perhaps corroborating all too easily Nordau's and Loos's suspicions of decorative excess.

However, it is precisely this queer space of creativity and sexual emancipation that led social critics to attack the three men who would over the years come to occupy Park Villa. On September 8, 1920, the sensationalist periodical *Fäderneslandet* (*The Fatherland*), published an anonymous article, "En celeber omyndighetshistoria" ("A distinguished story of incapacity"), outing Dardel, de Maré and Börlin, who were said to be engaged in a *ménage-à-trois*. Although anonymous, the article is widely credited to have been penned by David Sprengel, an acquaintance of Dardel who was turned down by de Maré when he applied for the position of managing director of the Ballet Suédois. Disgruntled, the critic set out to misrepresent de Maré's grandparents who were said to be ashamed of the debauched lifestyle he was conducting in the adjacent villa on their beloved estate. Both Dardel's and Börlin's relationships with de Maré, he claimed, were not those of equals, but rather the result of these two men's desire to "pluck the golden goose of Hildesborg." Of Dardel, Sprengel was ruthless in his attacks:

> Mister "artist" himself is impoverished, which is why the "state owner" of Hildesborg became a real golden goose for him, which also made him deliver "golden eggs" en masse. Among other things the friendship was sealed through a trip around the world for which the master of Hildesborg had to pay the piper; and at Hildesborg a perverse "art gallery" was established that for the most part, however, contained works by the "master" Dardel.
>
> (Anon. 1920: n.p.)

It was here, in the domestic interiors cum art gallery of Villa Park, that the walls were covered with "perverse art." While the countless exotic objects are not cited directly in Sprengle's salacious provocations, in his reading of de Maré's interior, nonetheless, homosexuality, Orientalism and modern art overlap, variously particularized on his home's surfaces. I posit that all the collected objects, whether paintings or expressly exotic *bric-à-brac*, were all collapsed in the minds of contemporary Swedes who viewed exoticism of the so-called Orient as much as modern art with suspicion and less then veiled contempt. Sprengle's article marked the commencement of a relentless witch-hunt against the three men, which precipitated de Maré and Börlin's move to Paris (Näslund 2009; Potvin 2014).

The interior and the richly vivid textiles, rugs and skins it contained would also form the backdrop for the blood-stained palette of *Crime passionnel* (1921) [Figure 9.4]. Largely read in a conventional art-historical manner through the lens of biography, it is seen as a memorialization of Nita's rejection of Dardel. The crime of passion to which the picture's title refers is the violent murder of a lover and is often associated with France. Commonly, the violence is perpetrated at the hands of the man, who discovers his (female) lover's infidelity; however, in Dardel's canvas, it is he, the male painter, who falls victim to Nita's gunfire. Noteworthy is how the space used to stage the murderous act is de Maré's Villa Park, where Dardel was a regular long-term guest over the years leading up to de Maré's departure for Paris in 1920. For Dardel, de Maré's exotic interior becomes duplicitous in how it serves at once the space of comfort and safety that Dardel came to crave when away from Paris's nocturnal decadence, as well as the very space used to vilify Dardel and de Maré. As such, the queer Orientalism Dardel represents recalls the lifestyle refused acceptance into the Wallenberg family as much as the perversion and degenerate lifestyle Sprengle took issue with in his scathing character assassination of the residents of Villa Park. In the picture, Dardel takes his interest in collapsing perspectival space even further than he had

FIGURE 9.4 Nils Dardel, *Crime passionnel*, 1921. Moderna Museet, Stockholm.

done in *Reception*, for here foreground merges seamlessly with mid-ground, while background is only slightly suggested through a dramatic shift from the reds that dominate the composition to the deep green of the drapery and wall. Again, depth and space can only be alluded to by way of the layering of carpets, skins and textiles. Here, Semper's theory finds pictorial resonance, as textiles, carpets and skins become the primeval surfaces that enliven space and enclose subjectivity.

The bed, the site of consummated love, is rendered decidedly absent of any figures save for the alert white lap dog, which stares out at the viewer. The art historically potent sign of faithfulness and mutual fidelity, the lap dog is used here as a counterpoint to the murderous act in what functions as a putative foreground. Space is constructed as a collage of various exotic animal skins and fabrics, the very things that lead the viewer to recognize the space as de Maré's own. In Dardel's hand, the skins and fabric dissolves conventional space of the modern interior; here Orientalism and modernism cavort seamlessly to conjure a passionate world of crime and sin. As art historian Roger Benjamin asserts, Orientalist painting forms an "art of interstices, often literally made on the move" precisely because it tends toward being "eminently cross-cultural" (2003: 4). The interstices, and collisions for that matter, are asserted in the relationships between East/West, modernism/ orientalism, two-dimensional surface/three-dimensional space. Although murder and death feature heavily in Dardel's *oeuvre*, once again the choice of this particular interior as the location of the passionate undoing of a seemingly innocent love affair cannot be ignored. Here convergences and tensions construct an expressionist interior where crimes were purportedly enacted against interior design and nature itself. De Maré's interior as representation and Dardel's representations of the interior mark a hybrid site of queer excess wherein Orientalism and modern art merge seamlessly.

The patterns of the wallpaper and bedding that it silhouettes insinuate the continued influence of expressionism more broadly and French fauvism, in particular, in Dardel's work. Perhaps more exactly, the picture conjures the omnipresent arabesque patterns of Henri Matisse, with whom Dardel studied briefly in 1910. Like many other contemporary modernist Orientalists, "[i]n the pivotal years just before the First World War, [Matisse] created a scenography of the Orient that enabled [him] to redefine the image of the body, especially, but not exclusively, the female body" (Wollen 1987: 5). In addition to a similar understanding of color and its application within and beyond the picture frame, Dardel also shared in common with Matisse an unreserved appreciation of the decorative. The body, especially the female body, for Matisse was the product of an all too easy, and too common, melding of the exotic with the erotic, an aspect in which Dardel is largely uninterested. However, we would do well not to deny the erotic facet of the two pictures discussed here. After all, it was precisely Dardel's so-called degenerate modern art that hung on the walls of a space likened to a "wishful dream of nightclub owner" and in which these men were said to be engaged in a *ménage-à-trois*. While it is certainly accurate to examine Orientalist painting and interiors as products of "cultural cross-reference," rather than through a "theory of 'Otherness'" (MacKenzie 1995: 55), we would do well to consider that one interpretative strategy does not necessarily preclude the other; for, it is precisely when notions of otherness, however determined or imposed, are faced with various cultural positions and antagonisms that creative pathways and representational dissidence are enlivened. This, I posit, is certainly true of the cultural position de Maré and Dardel occupied and the representational strategies they deployed.

Suspending space

Whether materially conceived by de Maré through his collections or visually through Dardel's canvases, the cultural currency of the modern interior is achieved through cross-cutting, multi-dimensional representational strategies, and reveals as much about the subjective as it does about the intersubjective or, more precisely, the ways cultural agents set out to read interiors at a given time. In his reading of Semper, architectural historian Mark Wigley asserts that, as part of the construction of space, textiles are the "mask that dissimulates rather than represents the structure [...] As its origin in dissimulation, its essence is no longer construction but the masking of construction" (1995: 12). In de Maré's interiors and Dardel's expressionist renderings of them, textiles take on the form of walls by dissolving the very thing they are meant to conjure, breaking down spatial boundaries as much as conceptual limitations meant to confine these men and the interpretations of the interiors they occupied. As a space of representation, in Dardel's hands, de Maré's interiors evoke how Orientalist fantasy and pleasure trump any sense of architectural permanence. Carpets, embroidered fabric and animal skins act, like in the *One Thousand and One Nights*, as a mode of transportation, nomadic and adaptable to other spaces (such as a new flat in Paris). As an all-too-common and well-rehearsed exotic trope, these "magic carpets" serve as a means of dissolving material and spatial boundaries to conjure an hybrid Oriental haven in which it was possible to live out and perform sexual and gendered identities antithetical to those expected outside the enclosure of de Maré's home. These men's collective use of Orientalism is not the conduit toward eroticism, as so often has been the case, but rather provided the orientation toward a cosmopolitanism that stands in sharp contrast to the moribund parochialism of traditionalist Sweden and the limitations of being bound to one place at any one time.

Notes

1 The southern Swedish estate was purchased by the Count and Countess von Hallwyl in 1908 as the family's summer retreat.
2 On the occasion of the coronation, de Maré was himself decorated with the Coronation Order of the White Elephant.
3 When de Maré met and took up with Dardel in 1912, the collector embarked on the second stage of his passions, that of modern art. So impressive was his collection, which included work by Fernand Léger, Pablo Picasso and Marie

Laurencin, for example, that it would form unquestionably the largest and most significant portion of the Moderna Museet's collection of early twentieth-century European art. This exceptional bequest to the museum also included a number of important works by Dardel, including those works discussed in the final section of this chapter.
4 Semper argued that architecture comprised four core elements: enclosure, hearth, mound and roof.

References

Anon. (1920), "En celeber omyndighetshistoria," (September 8): n.p.
Asplund, K. (1958), *Nils Dardel*, 2 vols, Stockholm: Sveriges Allmänna Konstförenings.
Baer, N. van Norman (ed.) (1995), *Paris Modern: The Swedish Ballet 1920–25*, Seattle: University of Washington Press.
Baudrillard, J. (1996), *The System of Objects*, London: Verso.
Benjamin, R. (2003), *Orientalist Aesthetics: Art, Colonialism, and French North Africa 1880–1930*, Berkeley: University of California Press.
Burt, R. (1999), "Interpreting Jean Börlin's 'Dervishes': Masculine Subjectivity and the Queer Male Dancing Body," *Dance Chronicle*, 22(2): 223–238.
Camille, M. (2001), "Editor's Introduction," *Art History: Special Issue on Queer Collecting*, 24(2) (April): 163–168.
Lindahl, I. (1980), *Visit Hos Excentrisk Herre: En bok om Nisls Dardel*, Stockholm: Bonniers.
Loos, A. (1908), "Crime and Ornament," in M. Ward and B. Miller (eds.), *Crime and Ornament: The Arts and Popular Culture in the Shadow of Adolf Loos*, Toronto, YYZ Books, 2002: 29–36.
MacKenzie, J. M. (1995), *Orientalism: History, Theory, and the Arts*, Manchester: Manchester University Press.
Näslund, E. (1988), *Dardel*, Stockholm: Författarförlaget.
Näslund, E. (2009), *Rolf de Maré: Art Collector, Ballet Director, Museum Creator*, Stockholm: Dance Books.
Nordau, M. (1892), *Degeneration,* London: Heineman, 1895.
Pearce, S. M. (1995), *On Collecting: An Investigation into Collecting in the European Tradition*, London and New York: Routledge.
Pollock, G. (1988), *Vision and Difference*, London: Routledge.
Potvin, J. (2014), "Homosexuality/Modernism/Nationalism: Between Excess and Exile in 1920s Europe," in J. Skelly (ed.), *The Uses of Excess in Visual and Material Culture, 1700–2010*, Aldershot and Burlington: Ashgate: 183–204.
Semper, G. (1851), *The Four Elements of Architecture and Other Writings*, trans., Cambridge: Harry F. Mallgrave and Wolfgang Herrmann, 1989.
Semper, G. (1862), *Style in the Technical and Tectonic Arts, or, Practical Aesthetics*, Los Angeles: Getty Research Institute, 2004.
Wigley, M. (1995), *White Walls, Designer Dresses: The Fashioning of Modern Architecture*, Cambridge, MA, and London: The MIT Press.
Wollen, P. (1987), "Fashion/Orientalism/The Body," *New Formations*, 1 (Spring): 5–33.

PART THREE

Spaces and Markets of Consumption

Introduction

John Potvin

In her book on Oriental fables and fictions, Ros Ballaster's central claim is that "narratives move," trafficked through various networks, patterns and modes of circulation across both time and space (2007). In many ways, these stories operate similarly to other forms of commodity goods, which fill homes and interiors across the West. The production, circulation and advertisement of commodity goods possess lives and narratives that are obscured over time as much as they are expanded upon within the various interiors they occupy. Objects and commodities travel where and when individual subjects may not be able to. Exotic décor and *objets d'art* allowed people to travel through acts of consumption, to feel as though, even within their own staid, middle-class domestic dwelling, they too could partake of the mysteries and myths of the Orient, even if at times unwittingly partaking in colonial networks.

Holly Edwards shows how, over time, in the United States, for example, "the taste for exotic interiors spread from the mansions of the newly wealthy to more modest middle-class homes. This desire was fomented and fed by the burgeoning mail-order business and by large department stores like Sears, Roebuck, and Company and Wanamaker" (2000: 185). Soon, Oriental interiors became associated with places and spaces of leisure, luxury, entertainment and healthfulness, despite the often alluded to debauchery of the Orient. In the case of the spaces and markets for the consumption of Oriental wares, "[t]he cultural sphere was a partner of the economic sphere, rather than being the effect of it" (Crinson 1996: 3–4).

Through a close reading of the eighteenth-century inventories of the South Sea directors, Eric Weichel exposes the extent to which the private collections of directorial residences, more specifically the countless consumer goods gathered from throughout Asia, conjure a composite image of the deep social changes sweeping through Britain in the first half of the eighteenth century. In " 'Heraldic Fantasies in Blue and Red and Silver': Orientalism, Luxury and Social Corruption in the South Sea Directorial Houses, 1721," Weichel argues for the centrality of consumer goods in the display of not only wealth, but also public identity, connoisseurial acumen and aesthetic prowess. The transnationality of these domestic collections reveals the shifting economic realities as much as personal and professional success.

Not unlike consumer goods, natural resources and their colonial exploitation became an important means through which French Art Deco furniture designers could create luxurious items for the discerning modern home. Laura Sextro's chapter "Promoting the Colonial Empire through French Interior Design" portrays the central importance of exotic woods from colonial outposts in the creation of new techniques and design processes in the French metropolis. The exotic provenance of the woods, coupled with unique and unprecedented techniques, became the featured and much-touted selling points for manufacturers and designers alike. Through various media, consumers were enticed by the new tropical hardwoods that could help fashion a truly modern and luxurious Art Deco interior.

Seemingly on the other side of nature's spectrum, potted palms became an important imported good when establishing a truly "cozy corner" in American and British homes. As Penny Sparke describes in "Paradise in the Parlour: Potted Palms in Western Interiors, 1880–1900," tropical plants at the end of the nineteenth century became essential components of a "cozy corner" that was at once exotic, with its Kentia palms and Turkish-inspired textiles and cushions, and safe within its middle-class furnishings and architectural space. In countless photographs of women languidly lounging amidst their palm trees, the hybrid nature of these spaces moved between private leisure and colonial commerce, Western man-made parlor and tropical natural resource, exotic foreignness and domestic homeliness. Mark Crinson notes how "[t]his fascination with eclecticism has curious parallels with recent theoretical interest in hybridity; indeed, hybridity itself was a Victorian obsession. Hybrid or eclectic architecture offered by turns a fascinating or threatening object" (1996: 10).

Oriental design and entertainment have been, at least since the nineteenth century, linked in fascinating and meaningful ways, not least in the emergence of movie theaters in North America. As Camille Bédard demonstrates in "Traveling in Time and Space: The Cinematic Landscape of the Empress Theatre," the so-called atmospheric movie theater comprised an entire immersive space in which every detail, from the night sky, starry ceiling, to the clothing of the employees, provides a commercial space in which the movie-goer of the early twentieth century left their worries behind at the door to be transported to another place and time. As a case in point, the resplendent Empress Theatre in Montreal decorated by Emmanuel Briffa evoked Ancient Egypt in all its decorative glory, a well-suited interior in which to relax and view the fictional narratives cinema offers.

The significance of Oriental elements and design on the interior of leisure and entertainment remains deeply resonant even while at sea, as Anne Massey shows in "'Flights of Unpractical Fancy': Oriental Spaces at Sea from the *Titanic* to the *Empress of Britain*." On board the infamous *Titanic*, European-inspired public spaces were juxtaposed with Oriental-designed Turkish baths made available only to first-class male passengers. In her exploration of various ocean liners, Massey concludes that as Empire was downgraded to Commonwealth, so too did Oriental interiors become more common. These interiors, like all those discussed in this final Part, are spatializations of political shifts, transnational economic circuits and cultural exchanges.

Not unlike the Turkish baths on board ocean liners, a more recent form of entertainment in the form of sport and relaxation, the yoga craze, has led perhaps to the most hybrid of all contemporary manifestations of the Oriental interior, the modern yoga studio. Rounding off the third Part's emphasis on networks and systems of commodities, Lauren Bird's chapter "Posturing for Authenticity: Embodying Otherness in Contemporary Interiors of Modern Yoga," exposes how minimalist design fuses seamlessly with Indian religious and ritual objects to conjure a space of bodily rejuvenation and relaxation, while at the same time providing for a space of sociability and retreat from the detriments of the modern Western metropolis. Indeed, as Bird shows, yoga studios function as fluid contact zones, where Hindu imagery and objects enliven Western spaces of consumption of health and wellbeing.

References

Ballaster, R. (2007), *Fabulous Orients: Fictions of the East in England, 1662–1785*, Oxford and New York: Oxford University Press.

Crinson, M. (1996), *Empire Building: Orientalism, a Victorian Architecture*, London and New York: Routledge.

Edwards, H. (2000), *Noble Dreams, Wicked Pleasures: Orientalism in America, 1870–1930*, Princeton: Princeton University Press.

10

"Heraldic Fantasies in Blue and Red and Silver": Orientalism, Luxury and Social Corruption in the South Sea Directorial Houses

Eric Weichel

In 1721, at the height of the social crisis caused by one of the worst financial collapses the emerging stock-market system had yet seen in Britain, an inventory of the houses of leading figures associated with the beleaguered South Sea Company was drawn up by act of Parliament. These inventories, which give a remarkably vivid "snapshot" of individual family lives, have much potential for cultural historians interested in processes of aesthetic change, and especially for an understanding of how consumer products from Asia transformed the look, feel and experience of the interior in early eighteenth-century Britain. In this chapter, I engage in a close reading of this specific group of inventories, that is, the *Inventories of the South Sea Directors*, curated at Yale University's Lewis Walpole Library.[1] I offer an interpretation of selected examples of material goods, juxtaposed with a brief biographical analysis of their owners, to give a combined picture of the kinds of cultural hybridity that I believe are visible in the form of Orientalizing visual art, including furnishings that were displayed so prominently in the lives of the early Georgian merchant elite.

While all too few of the objects catalogued in these inventories are presently identifiable, some precious few are, and thus this catalog contributes to the memory-making processes associated with the discussion of their provenance. The value of this methodology is in how it contributes to a more sensitive, nuanced appreciation of *things* themselves, of what they were worth, of how they functioned. The period also marks a time of social and cultural change, reflected in the new admiration for "exotic" luxury items, including visual art and expensive luxury textiles and furnishings that had been produced in Asia. The printed inventories of the South Sea directorial residences are therefore important cultural documents that highlight how specific human lives were formed by, and in some sense reflected through, such a display of material objects.

The South Sea "bubble": Inventories as information

In March of 1720, the first real capitalist speculation to grip large sections of the population hit the financial markets of England, resulting from the successful bid of a largely defunct trading enterprise, the South Sea Company, to take over government debt (see Carswell 1960; Cowles 1960; Dale 2004). Initially a business venture that traded in a quota of 4,800 West African slaves to Spanish South America, the South Sea Company had fallen under the directorship of Sir John Blunt (1655–1733), a brilliant financier who had successfully transformed an armories business into a more sophisticated and complex market company, one that was able to assist in bailing out government loans (Walsh 2008, ch. 8: 1). Blunt's powers of speculation were astute, and in response to a sustained advertisement and propaganda campaign, he was able to similarly reinvigorate the South Sea Company, attracting investors from across the spectrum of the landed and mercantile gentry.

Women, whose abilities to invest in real estate were severely curtailed, were particularly prominent as investors on the emerging stock market, and their involvement is much noted in correspondence, memoirs and visual satires of the time. In William Hogarth's engraving *The South Sea Scheme* [Figure 10.1], amidst the social madness and hubbub caused by the wildly fluctuating market, well-dressed women jostle with each other to enter a doorway, above which is posted the sign "Raffeling for Husbands with Lottery Fortunes in Here." Elizabeth Moleworth, wife of the fifth son of an Irish Viscount, wrote to the Prince of Wales' mistress Henrietta Howard on June 25, 1720, at the height of the South Sea craze, saying "to tell the truth, I am almost South Sea mad ... I cannot, without great regret, reflect that, for want of a little money, I am forced to let slip an opportunity which is never like to happen again" (1824: June 25, 1720; see also Ingrassia 1998: 17–40). Some investors were canny enough, or unprincipled enough, to

FIGURE 10.1 William Hogarth, *The South Sea Scheme*, etching and engraving, 1720. The National Gallery of Art (Washington, DC), Rosenwald Collection.

sense that many people were simply hoping to capitalize on the general "get-rich-quick" ideals underlying the whole venture, and realized that a devastating collapse was imminent (Hoppot 2002; Sornette 2003: 9–13; Temin and Voth 2004; Dale, Johnson and Tang 2005; Carlos and Neal 2006: 498–530). The formidable Sarah, Duchess of Marlborough, was one of the latter, and although she and her husband had invested heavily in the scheme, she—with what her descendant Sir Winston Churchill called "her almost repellent common sense"—backed out of the investment at its peak, profiting by the almost-obscene sum of approximately £100,000, and writing " 'tis not possible by all the arts and tricks upon earth long to carry 400 000 000 of paper credit with 15 000 000 of specie. This makes me think that this project must burst in a little while and fall to nothing," although she was not averse to extending "heavily secured loans to some of her more bullish peers" (1936: 1032; see also Walsh ch. 8: 3).

Inevitably, the bubble did burst, and there were some truly spectacular bankruptcies, while many families, even of the old aristocracy, lost most or all of what they had. Carr Hervey, for example, eldest son and heir of the Earl of Bristol by his first wife, was forced to sell his estate of Aswarby, which he had inherited from his mother, and died in 1723, after falling into a cycle of heavy drinking and gambling doubtless aggravated by stress and depression (Hayton, Cruikshanks and Handley 2002: 349). George I himself was not immune, and neither was his official mistress, Melusine von der Schulenburg, the Duchess of Kendal, or his (possible) half-sister who many thought was his mistress, Sophia von Kielmansegg: both of whom were heavy backers in the scheme. James Craggs the elder, a prominent financier, committed suicide over the scandal, and with so many of the Hanoverian regime's leading figures involved in the ruin of thousands of the English elite, the public outcry against the collapse became national business [Figure 10.2]. The directors of the company were particularly singled out for criticism. In 1733, when she was angry with a clergyman who had swindled her, Lady Betty Germain jokingly wrote to Jonathan Swift that she had a mind to "revenge myself of the innocent for the sake of one bishop and minister that I say have cheated, fleeced and flead me, just as if they had been south sea directors" ([June 5, 1733] 1814: 706).

In response to the crisis, Parliament drafted a special resolution that forbade the directors and their associates from leaving the country; a second act demanded, in an unprecedented move, that their estates, assets, debts and material goods be valued by independent appraisers, and the results

FIGURE 10.2 Printed for Carington Bowles, *A monument dedicated to posterity in commemoration of [the] incredible folly transacted in the year 1720*, etching, not before 1764. Lewis Walpole Library, Yale University.

published for public perusal. Spencer Wilmington, Speaker of the House, gave the publishing commission to the "Kit-Kat" club member Jacob Tonson.

Inventories of possessions and goods from the eighteenth century have long been recognized as important primary sources for historians of visual and material culture, but often these take the form of probate inventories, or wills, which catalog the estate of a deceased person in order to legalize the transference of goods from one generation to the next. Inventories can sometimes also take the form of country-house catalogs or records of auction sales. More rarely, some sort of emergency, such as the goods appraised to be lost in a disaster, such as a fire, can spur the production of appraisals of the contents of homes. Due to their very contemporaneity, the *Inventories of the South Sea Directors* are therefore an unusual and idiosyncratic snapshot of the lives, material possessions and personal tastes of the men and women who were at the forefront of a new and powerful capitalist system of transatlantic trade, in which the re-export of cloth, the import of raw materials, and the aesthetic and cultural importance of "exotic" lands in Asia played a vital, central part.

Robert DuPlessis's study of household inventories from the period reinforces this point. Textiles, as he points out, were "major items of consumption among all segments of the populace. Irrespective of age, gender, ethnic group, locality or occupation, cloth and the clothing and furnishings fashioned from it constitute the second biggest item, after food, in household budgets" (2005: 73, 77, 81, 82). In this context, it is significant that the directors were exempted from reporting on the "necessary wearing apparel" of themselves and their families when cataloging their investments, debts and the contents of their estates. While those textiles that were recorded (especially printed Indian cloth) have thus an extreme importance as marking the directorial residences as being particularly crucial indicators of the vogue for Orientalizing interiors, other art objects, especially porcelain and furniture, can also reveal much about the specificity of individual or familial life histories and their relationship to Asian or Asian-inspired luxury goods.

John Fellowes: A typical entry in the ISSD

Sir John Fellowes, or Fellows (c.1671–1724), was one of the richest, most aristocratic of the men to be associated with the South Sea Company, as well as its primary representative for negotiations with the Bank of England. Fellowes was also the recipient of a title, having been created 1st Baron Fellows of Carlshalton. His dwelling house in the old Jewry, London, had seventeen rooms, plus those "over the stables" and the "footman's room." Paintings were in at least one of the rooms in the garret, characterized simply as "a picture," but "four painted pictures" were on the staircase. The contents of the first rooms were bedrooms, almost certainly upstairs, and are relatively minimal in comparison with the more luxurious material goods downstairs.

This is a pattern followed in subsequent lists of possessions for the rest of the directorial residences, unless specifically otherwise marked. These upstairs rooms were, however, still characterized by strong color schemes—purple, blue and green—and the use of printed Indian fabrics is very evident, with "flowered Callimanco curtains" present in at least three of the rooms, as well as "a callico quilt" and a "blue china quilt" in others. Room number nine is exemplary of the more sumptuous bedrooms on the second floor, and in fact quite typical of the nature of the entries in the *Inventories*.

> Twelve crimson Genoa Damask chairs, and serge cases, a crimson damask sattee and case, four glass sconces with double branches, a peer glass in a glass frame, a Chimney glass, and two glass nosels, three pairs of crimson mantua silk window curtains, vallance, and rods, a brass hearth, shovel, and tongs, and iron-back, and a pair of dogs, a wallnut-wood card table.
> (1721: "Fellowes")

Number ten is similar in palette choices and material for textiles, as well as the prevalent use of glass, but also included "eighteen pieces of china, six silver tea-spoons, and a strainer." Another staircase is indicated, likely suggesting further rooms were on the ground floor, and these are the most sumptuous of all, with products from an astonishing range of origins for good listed, including "ten Morocco leather chairs," "a Dutch oval table," "a Japann'd tea table," "fifteen pieces of china," and "a large Turkey carpet." The effect must have been a gloriously sensual one, with rich tones of color present in the textiles, the shimmer of glazed porcelain and the dull gleam of gold from the lacquered table.

Fellowes' country house at Carshalton contained far more works of art than did the town house, suggesting country houses were thought more appropriate sites for the display of painting than the town residences, at least by the old aristocracy, who had generations of art acquisition to deal with. The Gallery at Carshalton, of course, was the prime loci for the display of painting, and contained "seventeen chairs, a couch, a squab, and pillow, an old sattee, two Spanish tables, and carpets, and six old cushions, thirty two pictures, an old clock without a case," while "the great staircase" also contained "forty-four painted pictures great and small" as well as a giant lantern affixed to a complicated system of lines and pulley to facilitate its lighting. Lanterns of this size were significant markers of status in the eighteenth century, worthy of comment by visitors (Moore 2002: 42).[2] The room labeled "no. XV" was apparently reserved for the drinking of tea, and contained, besides the usual mohair chairs, stools and covers, "fifty six black and white prints ... a Japann'd tea table, sixteen pieces of china, a wallnut-wood card table, and a wainscot closestool," marking a fascinating correlation between practicality, ornament and function in the tea ritual, especially given the diuretic properties of caffeine (and the comparative rarity of bathrooms in even the grandest of eighteenth-century houses).

"A true picture of the famous skreen": Women, Coromandel screens, and the South Sea scandal

Among the unique works of visual art at Carshalton were "seven black and white prints of the cartoons," the only narrative subject of visual art to be mentioned by name in the Fellowes inventory and undoubtedly referring to engravings after Raphael's Sistine Chapel cartoons, which had been acquired by the English crown in the early seventeenth century. The Raphael cartoons were on permanent display in Hampton Court, and were located in a special purpose-built gallery adjoining the major rooms of state; their presence at Carshalton is a gesture of aristocratic solidarity in taste. Orientalizing goods included "a large blue and white China jar," probably a rolwagon or large porcelain jar produced in Asia for the export market, and "an eight-leav'd India paper screen." Folding screens, which originated as a format in East Asia and were often made of lacquer, were highly desired trade goods in the houses of the British elite, who demanded such goods from the "Coromandel" eastern coast of India. Attracted by its fine natural harbor, extensive cloth-producing industries and rich natural resources, British traders and merchants were quick to found a settlement at the port of Vizagapatam, on the north shore of the Coromandel coast, and it was from Vizagapatam that many of the large, transoceanic shipping frigates left India for Europe, their holds straining with cargos of printed cloth, lacquered furniture and the much-cherished Chinese and Japanese porcelain, which was sold here via middlemen (Hamling 2010: 131; Jaffer and Corrigan 2001: 172).

Folding screens, likely from the Coromandel coast, are also recorded in the house of Sir John Blunt, who as senior director, probably bore the greatest responsibility in triggering the South Sea scandal. Blunt's house "in Birchin lane" was well appointed, comfortable and well stocked with visual art and other specialized cultural objects, including Orientalizing items of furniture and material culture. The Blunt residence was liberally stocked with china of all kinds, but the greatest numbers are recorded in the dining room, which also held a "Japan'd cabinet," referring to the process of decorating furniture with lacquer in imitation of the best kinds of products from Edo-period Japan, and "4 china-jars, 2 bowls, 32 small pieces of china, 36 cups and sawcers, and tea-pots. 2 dozen of china handle knives and forks. In the closet in the dining room some china and glass-ware." Blunt's colleague Richard Hawes, at his recently purchased estate at Kittering in Northamptonshire, was similarly sumptuous in his display of Orientalizing textiles and furniture, including "a looking glass in a Japan Frame" in "the chamber over the great parlour and dining room." The great parlour itself had two "Japan'd" tea tables and an extensive collection of china, including "8 cups, 9 saucers, 2 slop basons, 2 large saucers, a tea-pot, 2 large beakers,

2 bottles, a jar, a sugar dish and cover." Like the Blunt residence in Birchin Lane, Kitterling boasted India screens, including a "4 leaf painted screen" and a "six-leaf red kersey screen" in a garret near the garden.

The close association between Coromandel screens (and Oriental interiors in general) and the South Sea bubble in the minds of the early eighteenth-century British society is highlighted in one satire by the well-known engraver Bernard Picart [Figure 10.3]. In "A true picture of the famous skreen . . .," the government's involvement in the financial scandal is wittily exposed by showing the Duchess of Kendal, the King's official mistress, hiding behind a Cormandel folding screen: her skirts are visible behind its decorated folds, pointing to her role as a semi-official broker between the monarchy and the royal court and the South Sea directors. Women's involvement as independent investors, their tastes in exotic Asian luxury products, and the role of the stock market in catering to these new habits in

FIGURE 10.3 Bernard Picart, *A true picture of the famous skreen describ'd in the Londn. journal no. 85 (Satire on the Duchess of Kendall)*, etching, 1721. Lewis Walpole Library, Yale University.

consumption, are all regular themes in South Sea satires, but few other visual representations of the period draw such an explicit link between social corruption, the court, the tastes of elite women, and the Oriental interior.

Porcelain and lacquer

While the small country house of Blunt and Hawes' colleague Sir William Chapman (c.1670–1737) at Hampstead, in Middlesex, was likely a far more modest structure than Fellowes' ostentatious residence at Carshalton, the catalog of goods present there is indicative of the comfortable, colorful and sensual atmosphere that such small country retreats possessed, and of their undoubted appeal for family members desperate to leave the harried routines of city life behind. Down in the gardens at Hampstead, the summer house contained "four chairs, marble table, a parcel of china ware," which accords well with what we know about more famous summerhouses. For example, Henrietta Howard, mistress of the future George II, had a lovely little cottage, heavily painted on the inside with glaring colors, built on the grounds of her residence at Marble Hill in Richmond. Designed to house part of her impressive collection of porcelain, the building would have been easily recallable in the minds of many of the major cultural figures of the day, including her friend and correspondent Lord Chesterfield (Borman 2007: 226).[3] The collection in this "cheyney room" reached such vast numbers that it "defeated the inventory clerks" valuing her estate after her death in 1767: they decided to value only the best pieces (Wilson 2009: 207). Like Henrietta Howard's summerhouse, Chapman's little garden structure filled with china would be a potent marker of taste, wealth and privilege, marking the family as one in touch with international trends in garden architecture and design.

The recorded possessions of fellow director Sir Theodore Janssen (c. 1658–1748), "Knight Baronet," who lived in a house in the newly constructed Hanover Square, is exemplary of the aristocratic lavishness of Orientalizing decoration that characterized the houses of most of the directors who had any claim to a title in the peerage. "Five large pieces of china" along with a "green china [chintz] bed" were in the second upstairs bedroom, and it is tempting to attribute them to *famille verte* porcelain from China that imitated the green-hued variety of *imari*-ware issuing from Japan, while the third had two further green chintz beds and a picture. More works of art were in the neighboring fourth bedroom, which housed "nine small pictures, fourteen pieces of china, A chints bed lined with silk ... An india japan chest, a turkey work'd carpet," and "three china bottles," reflecting how the directorial residences showcased a *bricolage* of Oriental objects with highly distinct, and also highly hybrid, origins: Indian printed chintz cloth, Chinese export porcelain, a carpet imitating Turkish textiles, and an Indian-made chest worked with lacquer in the Japanese fashion. Four pieces of china and a yellow cloth bed and counterpane were in the ninth bedroom, while the tenth contained "two small India cabinets," the eleventh featured a "gilt leather six leaf screen" as well as a "fire screen," while the twelfth had an astonishing forty-one pieces of china, no bed and yet another India cabinet, as well as a chimney-piece mirror with "glass arms" of the family. Bedroom thirteen had a "japan'd screen, two japan'd tables and leather covers" and two "family pictures," while the eighteenth room, probably the dining room, showcased "thirty china dishes and thirty-six plates."

Sir Harcourt Master's (1670–1746) houses "on Tower-Hill and Greenwich" had a collection of material goods that are particularly informative about the rise of a new Rococo style in England, and well demonstrate the close association between elite women's tastes and consuming habits, and the sharp rise in exoticism within the interior. Women's interests in Asian consumer goods during this period was a direct by-product of their lack of formal access to classical education and their concomitant love of cultural products that existed outside the traditionally patriarchal framework of Greco-Roman aesthetics. In her dressing room, Lady Elizabeth Master displayed "A Peer-glass, a Chimney glass, a pair of wall stands, 11 India prints ... a parcel of China plates, cups, sawcers, and some delft plates," which perfectly illustrates how some women with access to imported goods inaugurated a new, less formal and more cosmopolitan aesthetic in their semi-private spaces. Elite women's interest in Asia was given a prestigious pedigree through the political efforts of Queen Mary and other noblewomen at the late seventeenth-century court to stress social commonality through shared tastes in exotic Asian products (Weichel 2014). Queen Mary's innovatively "excessive" display of Asian ceramic art continued to be influential in early Georgian interior design, sparking a climate in which the rococo flourished, with its whims, extravagancies and tongue-in-cheek use of motif-pastiche and bricolage culled from patterns on china, wallpaper and textiles, and possibly also "Indian" prints like those on display in Lady Master's dressing room.

Hugh Raymond

Of all the entries, those relevant to Captain Hugh Raymond (d. 1737) are the most specifically indicative of how personal participation within the South Sea scheme had the potential to change social norms and how exotic goods within the early eighteenth-century British interior reflected individual life histories. In his capacity as a prominent London ship-builder and captain, Raymond personally visited Asia several times: he "commanded the *Duchess* 1702–1705 on a voyage to and from Calcutta, and again 1705–1708 on a voyage to Fort George," which he also visited from 1709 to 1712 in command of the *Bouverie* (Bowrey 1993: xlvii). The inventory of his family's residence records a characteristic jumble of worn furniture in "the Nursery-Chamber" at Marine Square, including chests of drawers and battered tables, but "in the room next to the nursery" was "a black table, three Japan'd wig-boxes, three family pictures . . . sixteen china dishes, nine odd sawcers and a small jar" and "one Japan bowl."

Wigs, as I have written elsewhere, are fascinating signs of masculine fashion, and of course their use in this period is mostly limited to (elite) men from Western Europe, so the "japan'd wig boxes" owned by Raymond are intriguing mixtures of cultural adornment (Weichel 2008). "In the two pair of stairs room" was "a Japan'd chest and stand, a small cabinet and stand, three family pictures, one small ditto, a black hearth and furniture, two large bowls and dishes china, three small large and one dish and jar, and one broke, nineteen sawcers, thirteen cups" and "three china images," the first record in all of the published inventories of the directorial residences to refer specifically to porcelain figurines and statuary. Objects of this kind would become such a major fixture of English Rococo decoration over the course of the next four decades. "In the back room up two pair of stairs" was "a set of Irish stitch'd hangings" as well as "two china bowls and dishes, two small ditto, a sugar dish and sawcers, a large punch bowl and ladle, &c. japan'd." In the dining room, "a Leathern skreen, two black card tables, 7 family pictures, a tea-table and furniture, two turkey carpets . . . one jar, three brockes, seven brachers china, and *one pair of lions, and two more on horseback*" (italics mine).

The Raymond inventory is thus the first in the entire corpus of *ISSD* contents to connect specifically to the emergence of a Francophile Rococo mode of decoration via the sight, novel at the time, of Chinese figurines. The "lions" are almost certainly *fu* guardian lions or the *shishi* lion dogs that were produced in great numbers throughout China and Japan during the seventeenth century. The Ashmolean museum at Oxford holds one particularly evocative example of lion or lion-dog ceramics: formerly in the Reitlinger collection, it is late Edo Kakeimon-ware polychrome overglaze porcelain from about 1680, and with its distinctive snarl, lovely riot of enameled decoration and glaring eyes, it is an object completely at odds with the dominant mode of classicizing aesthetics prevalent in Britain as in Western Europe as a whole; a comparable object, dated slightly later, is in the Victoria and Albert Museum [Figures 10.4 and 10.5]. The Raymond house was riddled with porcelain figurines, including those in the "back parlour," which contained "two china bowls and covers, two small jars, four small images, two becars, a fire skreen . . . ten India pictures, a Tea-Table and furniture, a Tea-table, four pair of pistols, a feather whisk with a silver handle." In the "fore parlour," "a black card table, a small tea table, four cups and saucers . . . five china dishes, twenty-eight plates, five small bowls, two mugs, one bottle, two tea-pots, four cups, one jar, four small basons . . . some broken china." "On the stair case, eighty-two large and small pictures . . . one japan cistern . . . three dozen drinking glasses," while even the back kitchen contained further small pictures and more china, and spaces as prosaic as the "compting house" had an array of china,

FIGURE 10.4 Model of a lion-dog, porcelain, painted in overglaze enamels; Japan, Arita kilns (Kakiemon type), Edo period, 21.0 cm × 19.1 cm, 1660–1690. © Victoria and Albert Museum, London.

FIGURE 10.5 Japanese export porcelain figure of a lion-dog, decoration in overglaze enamels, Arita kilns (Kakiemon type), Edo period, 1670–1700, 12 cm × 14.2 cm. © Victoria and Albert Museum, London.

including "two tea pots, one slop bason ... fifteen china dishes, seventeen plates, three small bowls, three tea-pots, nine cups, five saucers, two japan'd cups, one family picture, a stove and furniture, and about seventy books" (1721: "Raymond").

Raymond's country residence in Essex at Saling Hall was much less liberally bestowed with china than was his town residence. A close reading of the *ISSD* shows that Saling Hall's interior was decorated with some very personal symbols of Oriental colonialism. For Raymond and his family, and perhaps for many of the newly ennobled directors, expensive examples of imported East Asian porcelain were vital markers of *urban* status—of connection to the markets, ports and ships that were the backbone of their wealth. They did less entertaining in country than would be expected of a family with a more established, land-centered aristocratic life, and thus a more extensive network of social, familial and political connections. By purchasing Saling Hall, Raymond was advertising his newfound social status: the old Jacobean manor had been previously owned by the Carter family, who sold it to Hugh Raymond in 1717, a mere three years before the South Sea scandal.

Hugh Johnson, who lived at Saling Hall for many years, notes that while Raymond was in Asia, he "commissioned an early example of Chinese armorial porcelain known as the Saling Service," and also describes these wonderfully hybrid pieces, combining European coats-of-arms with Chinese and Japanese aesthetics created to allure to foreign buyers, as "heraldic fantasies in red and blue and silver" (Johnson 2006: 335). These "heraldic fantasies" are undoubtedly among the pieces recorded in the inventory as "in the hall," where "nineteen small china basons, ten plates, four small dishes, thirty-three cups, and twenty-eight saucers, four tea pots, and a milk pot, some glasses and deflt ware" were on show. Two pieces have survived and are retained in the Johnson collection; they have never, to my knowledge, been previously been the focus of any scholarly attention.

An early armorial service of this kind would have been a heady accoutrement of (recently achieved) nobility when displayed so prominently in the Raymond family's newly purchased Jacobean manor. Armorial services are the rarest and most expensive of all Chinese export porcelain, and involved a lengthy, transnational (indeed, pan-global) process of cultural exchange, in which the coat of arms of the patron was shipped, via the East India Company, to the city of Jingdezhen, ceramics production capital of the Qing empire (Le Corbeiller and Frelinghuysen 2003: 24; Bailey and Litzenburg 2003: 96; see also Howard 1994: 34, 56, 81–84). Many noble families in England directly commissioned one-of-a-kind porcelain services from China that were specially decorated with their coats of arms. British ceramic production, in response, began to replicate the "foreign colors" produced for the export market by China, most notably in the delicate pinks and golds of the so-called *famille rose* porcelain inspired by orders from Europe. Complete services, including dinner plates, teapots, serving trays and sets of matched vases in fives, called garnitures, were then shipped back to England with the coat of arms embedded in more traditional forms of Chinese floral decoration (Mudge 1986: 140; see also Richards 1999).

Just as Raymond's proudly displayed armorial porcelains were exhibited in the annexed aristocratic architectural space of Saling Hall, these relics of a lost history are decorated with an annexed set of symbols, "heraldic fantasies" that mimicked the outward forms of lineage, social security and noble rank. Unlike noblemen such as Carr Hervey whose sources of income were almost exclusively tied to land and its agricultural revenues, Raymond, as an important naval figure, would have been able to bolster his income through the private sale of luxury goods like imported Chinese figurines, some pieces of which he evidently kept to decorate his new houses in London and in Essex. These small porcelain works are thus direct results of colonial interaction. Through annexing an old feudal manor formerly belonging to an ancient family, and by decorating that manor in a fashionably Orientalizing style that stressed his personal connection to the exotic lands of Asia, Hugh Raymond signaled his suitability for aristocratic status, his ability to compete with more traditionally established families with long lineages, and his position at the forefront of a newly emerging capitalist economy.

One object, now found in the Musée Guimet, that well represents the kinds of "figures on horseback" imported by Raymond and other South Sea captains is a Qing export porcelain figurine of a European cavalier, made sometime in the first quarter of the eighteenth century. The rich hues of violet, rose and cerulean that displayed in its enamel over-glaze decoration are a fitting counterpoint to the kinds of pink-hued enamels, brought to the forefront in the comparatively brief transitional reign of Yongzheng (1722–1735), that were just coming to fashion in this time. This work is an exceptionally vivid manifestation of the cross-cultural currents at play in the development of a new pan-Eurasian, even globalized aesthetic. It is, also, a weird object, strange in its individuality and idiosyncratic distinctiveness, unusual and precious. This porcelain figurine is almost like a *Europerie*, showing a stylized, abstracted, even fantastical European man on horseback, his distinctive clothes shot through with fluorescent hues of color, wearing the characteristic tri-cornered hat characteristic of early eighteenth-century elite masculine fashion.

The Guimet object is thus a culturally hybrid object and is also very Francophile in that it is aware of, and even caters to, the new taste in exquisite shades of rose that characterized the French court during both the Orleans regency and the Yongzheng rule. The French painters of the Régence, Nicolas de Largillière, Antoine Watteau and their followers Pater and Jean de Troy were distinctive within art-making practices at the time for their use of shades of pastel pinks and purples, entirely at odds with the brilliant blues, reds, yellows and greens of the classical French academy, represented by artists like Le Brun and Poussin. Instead, as has been much noted, French art switched to a different form of emotional expression, stressing the diminutive, the distinct, the esoteric and the seemingly frivolous above the immediate, triumphant, grandiose norms of the seventeenth-century Baroque. The early Rococo also sought renewed inspiration in the visual repertoires of the East, and much of that has to be allowed to the look and feel of objects exactly like this one, or those that littered the Raymond home, and others like it, as signs of economic and professional prestige.

Ceramic art objects like these belong neither to the creator culture or to the culture that consumes the end product, because they are thought to represent either opposing cultural poles; representations of the strangeness (or uniqueness, distinctiveness, or precious weirdness) of Asia, to Captain Raymond and his family, they are simultaneously representative of the "precious weirdness" of Europeans to East Asian artists, who found inspiration and economic benefits from the creation of idealized Otherings of extra-cultural identity. Raymond's *fu* lions and export porcelain figurines, therefore, deserve a theoretical reconceptualization, as does his individual participation in the shifting tastes of early eighteenth-century British consumers. His own economic activities in Asia, and his own personal travels, were able to effect a small degree of cultural change in and after his lifetime, as the wealthy merchant class, building on the established tastes of elite British women, developed a shared interest in the "precious weirdness" of stylistically hybrid works of art.

Oriental interiors and social change

I have given these case studies in such detail because I believe they offer a real chance to critically interrogate what we know about the early eighteenth century in Britain, and what we know more specifically about culture and art of this period. The globalized trading and consumption practices of early capitalism went hand-in-hand with economic aggression, dangerously speculative and exploitative financial risks, the construction of vast networks of transnational shipping, and a concomitant flood of luxury consumer goods, including furniture, textiles, and foodstuffs, into a market that had been previously reliant on hand-made craft. As a consequence, craft suffered and a new globalized aesthetic emerged, but this aesthetic is one that was heavily dependent on the aristocratic tastes of a hereditary elite who buttressed their social position by direct involvement in trade as well as through marriages. Families like that of John Fellowes, whose residence at Carlshalton included engravings after the Raphael cartoons at Hampton Court and a lavish tea-room, were building on the visual and social traditions and tastes of the aristocratic elite. Individuals like Sir John Blunt, who came out of the mercantilist world of the London financiers, were willing to take huge risks for the chance of the huge social rewards that came with the newly emerging speculative system, and, as the 1720 South Sea crisis reveals, these rewards had a heavy price in terms of the ruin and descent into poverty suffered by many members of the directorial families. Art, especially art made in a foreign place or made in imitation of a foreign style, was and is the concrete, physical reminder of how culture and lifestyle, even on the immediate, most personal of levels, can and does change in response, not only to the demands of a fluctuating economy, but to the new stimuli of increased economic access to a far-away country.

Hugh Raymond's *fu* lions and guardian statuettes of export porcelain, likely acquired over the course of his career as a naval captain for the East India Company, are markers of these processes of social change. No mere trinkets, these objects were striking physical reminders of colonialism, and of economic and military processes of interaction and oppression, for the Raymonds' peer group of elites. They also functioned as potent signs of early eighteenth-century Britain's respect for China's technological prowess and ancient decorative repertoire, thus paying homage to the tremendous aesthetic and artistic achievements of East Asia. The Saling Hall armorial service, some few precious pieces of which do survive, are therefore important records of the transnationality of the British country house in the early eighteenth century. Itself a marker of continuity, stability and privilege, the country house came to display treasures from other lands, making it culturally oscillatory, representing and recapitulating works from far across the Eurasian supercontinent in an appropriative, acquisitive gesture of admiration. The sheer desire expressed by British consumers for such unique pieces of East Asian statuary, and the profits to be made by an East Indiaman captain in personally trading them, itself points to the quality of these goods, their inherent seductive, aesthetic values.

The *Inventories of the South Sea Directors* can thus provide us with an enhanced view of visual art in the Georgian world, especially in their focus on the materiality and preciousness of goods obtained, or influenced by, the cultural spheres that were outside traditional systems of British thought, aesthetics, and expression. They also provide a wonderfully sumptuous reading of the world of material goods that surrounded specific individuals and their families in early Georgian Oriental interiors.

Notes

1 The manuscript is grouped according to individuals, without sequential pagination outside of the individual lists, so unless otherwise footnoted, all references are from *Inventories of the South Sea Directors*, Quarto 63 721 P258, hereby called *ISSD*, followed by the name of the merchant whose possessions are being cataloged. The name-based nature of the cataloging system is the most direct method of finding these citations in the volume.

2 In July of 1735, the Rev. Jeremiah Milles commented on the lantern at Houghton that "in ye middle of [the Hall] it hangs by a gilt chain, a very noble lantern; which is so famous for its size" (Moore 2002: 42).

3 In 1739, Howard wrote to well-known architect Henry Herbert, 9th Earl of Pembroke, that her "Cheyney room will make you stare, if not swear . . . I must tell you 'tis the admiration of the vulgar, but my vanity would be entirely gratified if it shou'd meet with your approbation" (Borman 2007: 226).

References

Inventories of the South Sea Directors (1721), Lewis Walpole Library MSS Quarto 63 721 P258, London: Jacob Tonson.
Letters to and From Henrietta, Countess of Suffolk, and her Second Husband George Berkeley, 1712–1767, vol. 1 (1720), London: John Murray, 1824.
Bailey, A. and T. Litzenburg (2003), *Chinese Export Porcelain in the Reeves Center Collection at Washington and Lee University*, Lingfield: Third Millenium Publishing.
Borman, T. (2007), *Henrietta Howard: King's Mistress, Queen's Servant*, London: Jonathan Cape.
Bowrey, T. (1679), *A Geographical Account of Countries Round the Bay of Bengal, 1669 to 1679*, New Delhi: Asian Educational Services, 1905, 1993.
Carlos, A. and L. Neal (2006), "The Micro-Foundations of the Early London Capital Market: Bank of England Shareholders during and after the South Sea Bubble, 1720–1725," *The Economic History Review*, 59(3) (August): 498–530.
Carswell, J. (1960), *The South Sea Bubble*, London: Cresset Press.
Churchill, W. (1936), *Marlborough: His Life and Times*, vol. 2, Chicago: University of Chicago Press.
Cowles, V. (1960), *The Great Swindle: The Study of the South Sea Bubble*, London: Collins.
Dale, R. (2004), *The First Crash: Lessons from the South Sea Bubble*, Princeton, NJ: Princeton University Press.
Dale, R., J. Johnson and L. Tang (2005), "Financial Markets Can Go Mad: Evidence of Irrational Behaviour during the South Sea Bubble," *The Economic History Review*, 58(2) (May): 233–271.
DuPlessis, R. (2005), "Cloth and the Emergence of the Atlantic Economy," in P. A. Coclanis (ed.), *The Atlantic Economy during the Seventeenth and Eighteenth Centuries: Organization, Operation, Practice and Personnel*, Columbia, SC: University of South Carolina Press: 72–95.
Hamling, T. (2010), *Decorating the Godly Household: Religious Art in Post-Reformation Britain*, New Haven, CT, and London: Yale University Press.
Hayton, D., E. Cruikshanks and S. Handley (2002), *The House of Commons, 1690–1715*, vol. 1, Cambridge: Cambridge University Press and the History of Parliament Trust.
Hoppot, J. (2002), "The Myths of the South Sea Bubble," *Transactions of the Royal Historical Society*, vol. 12: 141–165.
Howard, D. S. (1994), *The Choice of the Private Trader: The Private Market in Chinese Export Porcelain Illustrated from the Hodroff Collection*, London: Zwemmer for the Minneapolis Institute of Arts.
Ingrassia, C. (1998), *Authorship, Commerce and Gender in Early Eighteenth-Century England: A Culture of Paper Credit*, Cambridge: Cambridge University Press.

Jaffer, A. and K. Corrigan (2001), *Furniture from British India and Ceylon: A Catalogue of the Collections in the Victoria and Albert Museum and the Peabody Essex Museum*, Salem, MA: Peabody Essex Museum.

Le Corbeiller, C. and A. C. Frelinghuysen (2003), "Chinese Export Porcelain," *The Metropolitan Museum of Art Bulletin*, 60(3): 1–60.

Johnson, H. (2006), *A Life Uncorked*, Berkeley: University of California Press.

Moore, A. (2002), "Aedes Walpolianae: The Collection as Edifice," in L. Dukelskaya and A. Moore (eds.), *A Capital Collection: Houghton Hall and the Hermitage*, New Haven, CT: Yale University Press: 1–54.

Mudge, J. M. (1986), *Chinese Export Porcelain in North America*, New York: Riverside.

Richards, S. (1999), *Eighteenth-Century Ceramics: Products for a Civilized Society*, Manchester: Manchester University Press.

Sornette, D. (2003), *Why Stock Markets Crash: Critical Events in Complex Financial Systems*, Princeton: Princeton University Press.

Swift, J. and W. Scott (eds.) (1814), *Epistolatory Correspondence of Swift*, vol. 2, Edinburgh: Constable.

Temin, P. and H. J. Voth (2004), "Riding the South Sea Bubble," *The American Economic Review*, 94(5) (December): 1654–1668.

Walsh, J. (2008), *Keynes and the Market: How the World's Greatest Economist Overturned Conventional Widsom and Made a Fortune on the Stock Market*, Hoboken, NJ: John Wiley.

Weichel, E. (2008), " 'Fixed by so much better a fire': Wigs and Masculinity in Early Eighteenth-Century British Miniatures," *Shift: Queen's Graduate Journal of Visual and Material Culture*, 1: 1–25.

Weichel, E. (2014), " 'Every other place it could be placed with advantage': Ladies-in-Waiting at the British Court and the 'Excessive' Display of Ceramics as Art Objects, 1689–1740," in J. Skelly (ed.), *The Uses of Excess in Visual and Material Culture, 1600–2010*. Aldershot and Burlington: Ashgate: 41–62.

Wilson, T. (2009), " 'Playthings still?' Horace Walpole as a collector of ceramics," in M. Snodin and C. Roman (eds.), *Horace Walpole's Strawberry Hill*, New Haven, CT, and London: Yale University Press for the Yale Center for British Art and the Victoria and Albert Museum: 200–219.

11

Promoting the Colonial Empire through French Interior Design

Laura Sextro

> *Here is traditional art and modern art. Here is rustic oak, bourgeois walnut, plush palisander, formal mahogany. And here the same is satinwood, elm burl, thuya, amboina burr and* bois des îles *made fashionable and which cause one to dream of mysterious countries: Cuba, Mexico, Saint-Domingue, the Ivory Coast, Rio.*
>
> (Lévitan 1931)

In an advertising approach new to furniture manufacturers, the Lévitan sales catalog from 1931 begins by boldly depicting the colonial origins of wood that the company used in furniture design. The images that introduce the catalog feature eighteen frames illustrating the use of wood in Lévitan's furniture-manufacturing process: from the woods felled in the forest, to mill, port, stockyard, workroom, to the finished product on the showroom floor [Figure 11.1]. The first frame of the catalog portrays the logging process in Koundé, a forest in French Equatorial Africa, and specifically shows two railroad cars stacked with felled trees weaving through the tall tropical forest of what the catalog captioned as "rare species" (Lévitan 1931). While not all of the furniture utilized colonial wood, Lévitan's marketing strategy relied on tracing a colonial provenance for the wood that would make its furniture more valuable and appealing to both French woodworkers and the public at large. This advertising scheme demonstrates

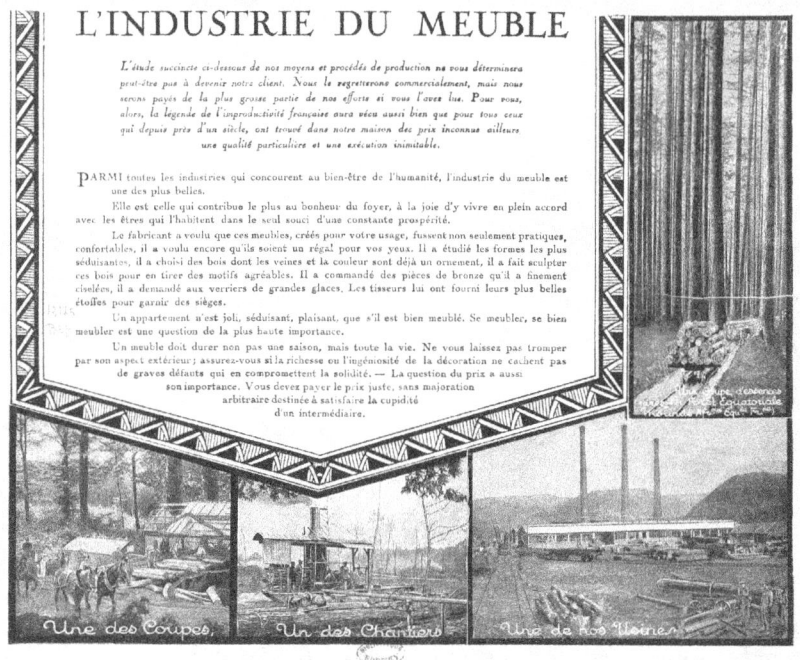

FIGURE 11.1 First page of Lévitan's 1931 furniture catalog depicting the harvesting and transport of French colonial hardwood. The upper frame reads "A harvest of rare species from Koudé, in Equatorial Africa, A.E.F" (Lévitan 1931). © Bibliothèque Forney / Roger-Viollet.

that, by 1931, wood from *outre-mer* had earned a reputation of quality and prestige, especially when it came to its use in furniture.

In a larger context, the use and promotion of colonial tropical hardwoods in furniture production in inter-war Paris gave new meaning to modern interior design. Exotic woods from French colonies had been used in furniture since the seventeenth century, but by the 1920s the rise of French Art Deco design gave new impetus to the use of colonial wood. Indeed, a salient feature of Art Deco—often overlooked—is the centrality of the use of tropical hardwood. Displays at Parisian international expositions, in Paris-based design literature and furniture catalogs, helped popularize the modern-style furniture and with it the material benefits from the French-colonial relationship. Exotic tropical hardwoods were used and promoted in new ways, linking the importance of the provenance of the materials with their celebrated aesthetic attributes.

This chapter builds on Edward Said's *Orientalism* (1978) to broaden how we understand the aesthetic outcome from the convergence of colonial politics, metropolitan commerce and colonial raw materials. Said explains that Europe created and maintained its power over the colonial "other" through sets of discourses created in academic circles, public imagination and corporate institutions. Orientalism also provides a useful framework for assessing the processes by which the colonies were appropriated in modern interior design in inter-war France. Colonial political and social structures facilitated the importation of colonial materials and encouraged its incorporation into French metropolitan culture. The diverse sets of interests of forest experts, furniture manufacturers, decorative art and woodworking authors lauded the decorative properties inherent in the tropical woods and increasingly used colonial provenance as a way to sell high-end modern furniture and interior design. Not only did French interior design appropriate materials from its colonies, the very modernity of the luxury models relied on the colonial materials. French public displays of interior designs at the Parisian expositions of 1925 and 1931 demonstrated both the growing economic reliance and modern aesthetic dependence of French designers on the colonial. In both material ways and rhetorical strategies, the French colonies influenced the look and significance of the French modern interior. This chapter explores how various media that promoted colonial wood revealed how the raw materials of modern design embodied the deeper economic, aesthetic and political significance of colonialism in inter-war France.

Didactic display: Colonial woods at the 1925 Decorative Arts Exposition and within the woodworker profession

The explicit marketing of colonial wood in France and its use in modern design were years in the making. Historically, French furniture makers used domestic woods and they used exotic hardwoods in higher-end furniture design when colonial woods became available as French territorial interests expanded overseas. Tropical hardwoods from French colonies, designated in French as *bois des îles* or *bois des Indes* had been used in French furniture for centuries, but furniture makers provided little information about the origins of the materials (Dobie 2007: 18, 19; Pastore 2007: 37–47). By the latter half of the nineteenth century, when France began to invest more money in and create more extensive government policies for its colonies, the availability of exotic wood grew. With increased intervention in the colonies, colonial wood became ever cheaper in France (Auslander 1996: 350).

By the late 1920s and early 1930s, publications and displays of this material made explicit the French colonial provenance. Drawing attention to the wood's point of origin made clear that the timber had become available because of the existence of French-colonial trade networks. A number of forest experts and engineers, under the auspices of the French government, sought to educate both woodworkers and the public at large to "assimilate" wood from the colonies into metropolitan needs. The furniture industry was one such potential market for colonial materials.

Displays of interior design at both the 1925 Exposition Internationale des Arts Décoratifs et Industriels Modernes and the 1931 Exposition Coloniale Internationale were important opportunities for both the French government and businesses to advertise the growing metropole-colony relationship. These inter-war expositions proved to be an important means of displaying the convergence of colonialism—and with it colonial woods— with changes to furniture design. Organized by state offices and commercial enterprises, the 1925 Decorative Arts Exposition (from which the term Art Deco was coined almost four decades later) consisted of various pavilions that displayed French designs and modern industry by groups of individual designers, magazine publishers, department stores and transportation companies. While the majority of the presentations were French, at least a dozen foreign countries presented their modern designs in the foreign section. Architects and decorative artists aspired to create attractive, modern displays to commodify the decorative arts designed for the modern home, offices, ocean liner cabins and department store window displays.

Several presentations at the 1925 Decorative Arts Exposition made explicit the contributions of colonial wood to French modern interior design. Under the auspices of the Service Technique des Bois Coloniaux and on behalf of the Minister of the Colonies, forest expert André Bertin displayed samples of colonial wood in an annex to the French African pavilion. The samples from forests in the Ivory Coast, Gabon and Cameroon served to show how the tropical hardwoods could be used to fashion interiors, from balustrades and stairs to interior paneling (Ministère du Commerce et de l'Industrie 1925: 318). In addition, the technical aspects of how to use the wood and the artistic effects that could be achieved were displayed in the Grand Palais, a large permanent building that for the purposes of the exposition housed woodworking machinery for specific industrial and educational uses. The trade organization Trancheurs-Dérouleurs presented a large display of colonial wood and its use in *ébénisterie* that showcased a series of panels of exotic veneer ("Nos Bois Coloniaux dans l'Ébénisterie" 1925: 967). Lastly, there were live veneer demonstrations using a large machine to slice colonial wood for the various furniture-making industrial sectors present at the exposition ("A l'Exposition des Arts Décoratifs" 1925: 999).

In the years following the 1925 Decorative Arts Exposition, efforts to promote the use of colonial wood expanded, including explanations of woodworking. *Travail du Bois*, a monthly woodworking journal begun in 1923, was circulated widely in Paris, the French provinces and abroad. Directed toward an audience of woodworkers and factory owners, many of the articles discussed the properties of wood and taught modern woodworking practices. Several articles in this trade journal captured the inter-war interest in the growing availability of woods from the colonies particularly because new woodworking techniques would allow woodworkers to take advantage of the desirable modern decorative qualities afforded by the unusual grain patterns and vibrant colors.

In essence, the woodworking articles in *Travail du Bois* instructed woodworkers to take command over the wild or unknown properties of colonial wood for metropolitan purposes, essentially Orientalizing the raw material. Between 1926 and 1928, André Bertin co-authored with engineer Julien Petitpas fourteen articles in a series titled "L'Usinage des Bois Coloniaux." The articles explained how to manufacture objects using colonial wood, focusing in part on the inherent physical characteristics of French colonial African wood and on the modern advances in technology needed to work with it. For example, Bertin and Petitpas explained that woodworkers in the late 1920s should no longer be intimidated to cut dense tropical hardwood. Previously, woodworkers shied away from using tropical hardwoods because methods they used to cut domestic woods either splintered the tropical varieties or broke their machines. But with improvements in planers and saws and a better understanding of colonial wood properties, woodworkers could successfully cut through the irregular silicon deposits found in colonial woods that had previously made them difficult to cut (Bertin and Petitpas 1926: 241). According to Bertin and Petitpas, because the new advanced scientific studies informed engineering solutions, the quantity and quality of processed colonial wood would improve and make it ideal for metropolitan needs.

Another *Travail du Bois* series of articles "L'Utilisation des Bois Exotiques," later titled "L'Utilisation des Bois Coloniaux," placed greater emphasis on explaining aesthetic virtues of tropical wood to a metropolitan woodworking readership. In fact, the change in title alone between its 1928 inception and 1931 series continuation indicates a growing emphasis to promote woods that came from the colonies. This article series sought to educate professionals in the aesthetic value of colonial wood in response to changes in design as well as the growing availability for its use in metropolitan industries. Authors at *Travail du Bois* recognized there was an advantage to intentionally using the French geopolitical economy as a way to market tropical wood.

The significance of colonial wood in modern design

Concurrent with growing efforts to educate and encourage metropolitan woodworkers to use colonial wood, literature from design commentators also illustrates an increasing awareness of colonial wood in French modern interior design. Discourses about design did not convey a need to master colonial raw materials, however, but instead celebrated that the use of colonial wood in design responded to modern needs, both in French colonial trade and in style. Commentary on modern design at the 1925 Decorative Arts Exposition and in design literature demonstrates that the design attributes of colonial wood and access to those materials enabled by the strength of French colonial trade helped make modern design possible.

The geopolitical context for the 1925 Exposition was a key factor in the way the colonies were represented in modern design. The French displays were a demonstration to visitors not only the extent to which the country had recovered from the devastation of the First World War but also the continued position of the French at the forefront of taste, innovation and design in the decorative arts (Benton 2003: 141). While a significant rationale for this exposition was to introduce and affirm a new contemporary aesthetic, part of it was made possible by colonial materials. Observers at the exposition described the overall style of French furniture design as "simple and costly, unadorned yet assertive ... produced by proportion and a richness of material rather than by elaborate carving or applied ornament" (Paris 1925: 265). Although the general catalog's attribution of materials used for furniture design was uneven, some commentators noted that much of the exotic wood used in luxury furniture design was obtained from French colonial possessions (Richards 1926: 44).

The exposition featured spectacular displays of the explicit use of colonial materials in the booths sponsored under French and French colonial auspices. In 1925, the importance of the colonies and colonial trade as a validation of French imperialism and as a key element of French national identity influenced the exposition's layout and the politics of display. Staged on the periphery of the exposition site, the presence of the colonial pavilions figuratively buttressed a French imperial identity. Though represented literally, France needed the colonies for the raw materials necessary in the domestic production of luxury goods such as furniture. In this way, the French preoccupation with design for modern living and the normalization of the French colonial connection—what Rydell refers to as *coloniale moderne*—were clearly accentuated (Rydell 1993: 61–62, 67–68).

Indeed, both the United States and British trade commissions that attended the exposition commented on how the colonial connections supported the use of colonial woods as an important feature of French luxury furniture production:

> In the modern movement rare woods notable for their beauty of grain and color form a very important decorative element in connection with furniture and wall treatment. Most of these woods are obtained from the French colonial possessions in Guiana, Africa, Indo-China and Madagascar.
> (Richards 1926: 44)

While the United States trade commission, appointed by the Secretary of Commerce to attend the 1925 Exposition, noted that some other woods used in French furniture design were acquired from "other parts of the globe," the commission report itemized only the "most important kinds that figure in the French furniture" and whose provenance was specific to the French colonies (Richards 1926: 44).

As the director of the artistic and technical section of the 1925 Decorative Arts Exposition, Henri-Marcel Magne wrote extensively about the event. In his applied arts manual *Décor du Mobilier: Meubles et Sièges* (1928), published under the auspices of the Conservatoire Nationale des Arts et Métiers, Magne continued to favor artistic trends presented at the 1925 Exposition and encouraged a stronger collaboration between industrial arts and the artistic and creative abilities of craftsmen. As an instructor at the school for whom he published his manual, Magne's book traces the evolution of contemporary design and encouraged the already burgeoning use of colonial wood in modern furniture to meet the needs of the French modern interior.

Décor du Mobilier posits that material choices for furniture responded to the contemporary needs to create functional furniture. Magne describes what he considered successful furniture traditions from the past to the current day addressing both style and social context. He argued that by his present day the opportune availability of colonial wood contributed to the changes in style to modern furniture design. By the turn of the twentieth century, "the timber from the French colonies offered to cabinetmakers a marvelous variety of wood of which the elegance is unparalleled because of the beauty of the grain and the richness of color" (Magne 1928: 20). Magne was particularly enthusiastic about African colonial woods for their many color variations that opened up a new gamut of decorative options (18). Of the two-dozen wood types, the color palette was rich and varied and included: whitish-yellow Gabonese zebrawood with dark-grain stripes or bands of color; Indochinese pink and wine-red palisander and bright orange *santal rouge*; and more colonial woods which were golden yellow, brown ochre and red brown. Magne also made specific reference to colonial woods that could compete with wood from non-colonial sources, such as mahoganies from Madagascar that could aesthetically compete with the most beautiful mahoganies from Brazil.

In addition to the decorative properties, Magne thought colonial woods should be used because of their influence on the French colonial economy. "The exploitation of our colonial forests presents the double advantage of providing low-cost valuable wood while not unfavorably influencing our balance of trade" (Magne 1928: 22). He explained that of the 147,000 tonnes of colonial wood that France received in 1924, a mere 47,000 tonnes was destined for furniture design, but the total export of wood from the colonies was at least twice these amounts. Considering the export data,

Magne felt that the French should be able to utilize even greater quantities of colonial wood to make and decorate furniture (22). In his view, not only were the artistic and design considerations important, but the non-artistic realms of politics and colonial economies also influenced the selection of materials for French design.

As proposed by *Décor du Mobilier*, furniture design responded to social needs, where contemporary style and furniture's form reflected current social values. Whereas in the eighteenth century, furniture designers were concerned with making chairs that could accommodate women wearing corsets, by the twentieth century, clothing was not a driver for furniture design. Instead, the perceived needs of a modern, fast-paced French society and changes to housing shaped the simplified form interior design would take. Advances in modern technology allowed for the use of new materials. Magne explains that newly available colonial materials, from wood to artificial tortoiseshell, could be used to decorate modern furniture which "avoids carvings that are difficult to clean" (Magne 1928: 212). Colonial woods could contribute to making it possible to create a simplified design that was elegant, streamlined and easy to clean [Figure 11.2]. Overall, Magne's study demonstrates that colonial wood brought decorative advantages to creating functional modern design that takes advantage of French colonial trade opportunities.

FIGURE 11.2 Depiction of an ideal bedroom set displayed at the 1925 Decorative Arts Exposition, as discussed by Magne in *Décor du Mobilier* (Magne 1925). © Victoria and Albert Museum, London.

The colonial connection on display

While the use of colonial wood in modern design became prevalent in the early 1920s, particularly in the 1925 Decorative Arts Exposition, by the 1931 Colonial Exposition colonial wood was center stage. In 1925, there was only partial recognition or awareness of colonial materials, whereas by 1931 colonial origins of raw materials were made explicit or at least broadly assumed. Furniture sales catalogs and concerted marketing efforts made in conjunction with the 1931 Colonial Exposition called attention to the provenance of exotic wood through visual display and printed form. By specifying that the "exotic" was in part "French colonial," materials used in the modern interior assumed a new meaning that explicitly referenced colonialism.

In May 1931, the Ministries of the Colonies and of Foreign Affairs opened the gates to the International Colonial Exposition in Paris. The vast advertising campaigns, press coverage and the exposition itself were all intended to promote a pro-colonial message which, in turn, demonstrated the advantages of being a colonial power (Golan 1995: 114–116). On the one hand, the exposition was a venue through which colonial promoters (including the French government) advertised the humanitarian and economic interests they claimed to have promoted abroad. On the other hand, it could be seen as a means to justify French colonial endeavors and to demonstrate that colonization provided economic benefits to the metropole (Ageron 1984; Morton 2000).

Jean Meniaud, the director of the Service Technique des Bois Coloniaux (under the auspices of the French colonial government), proclaimed: "in the evolution of modern decoration an interesting, strong market opportunity for our colonial woods [presented itself] at the 1931 Exposition" (Meniaud 1931: 58). The use of colonial wood, Meniaud asserted:

> responds to the tastes of the clientele and will grow quickly. It is also the same in beautiful interior joinery, in store layouts and decoration. Because of their warm colors and their grain patterns these woods make effects that cannot be obtained by French woods. There is a tendency to replace painting, fabric or wall paper with veneers of colonial wood and this new form of decoration, [which] one can observe in storefronts, bars, cafés or restaurants, halls of hotels or diverse offices, calls on joinery, doorframe, parquets and assorted woods making harmonious ensembles.
> (Meniaud 1931: 57)

Meniaud sought to promote colonial woods for variety of uses and he championed their aesthetic qualities for their use in interior design and furnishings.

Struck by the aesthetic qualities of colonial wood, the official French government report on the 1931 Colonial Exposition explained the intrinsic connection between modern design and colonial wood. Author of the report Marcel Olivier asserted that the 1925 Decorative Arts Exposition in Paris had previously demonstrated the union between decorative artists and manufacturers with the commitment to utilize quality materials in the production of a new decorative style. Modern design required beautiful materials at the same time that it became necessary to find uses for materials from overseas possessions. According to Olivier, colonial materials had become an important component to French modern design. Using exotic woods in the metropole both served the colonial project and satisfied the responsibility of modern design:

> Particularly concerning wood, the lesson put forth by the [1931] Colonial Exposition must not be lost. We now know all that we have to gain by facilitating exchange with our colonies with the metropole, by methodically establishing the exploitation of forests, completed by a rational organization of shipping transport, by river and sea [...]. For luxury *ébénisterie*, one can use twenty different tree species, such as various mahoganies, bright red padouk, walnut from Gabon, bilinga, bubinga and veined zebrawood (*zingana*). Add to these West African woods palisander from Madagascar, amaranth, teak and partridge wood (*wacapou*) from French Guiana and palisander (*trac*) from Indochina, etc.
>
> (Olivier 1933: 425–426)

Olivier's expository remarks about the use of colonial wood reminded the reader of its centrality to modern design.

Colonial wood exhibits were scattered throughout the 1931 Colonial Exposition. At the main entrance to the exposition, a small collection of buildings in a section titled "Bois Coloniaux" was dedicated to presenting all aspects of the colonial wood industry. These buildings and displays created symbolic visual distinctions by demonstrating how the raw materials directly contributed to French metropolitan industries. Their interior design presentations provided examples of the uses of colonial wood in modern design. The Sous-Groupe du Bois, a collaborative organization of various metropolitan and colonial timber organizations, presented model interiors of an office and a library outfitted with modern-style furniture made using colonial woods. In order to garner interest, the Sous-Groupe du Bois also hosted a contest during the exposition to promote the wider use of wood in furniture and decoration ("Les Bois à l'Exposition Coloniale" 1930: 298). Commentators from within the industry were optimistic about the various decorative designs that the woods would inspire (Petitpas 1931).

Furniture ensembles in the Palais des Industries de Luxe demonstrated that colonial materials used in modern interior design had (and could have) a prominent place in modern French and wealthy colonial homes. The various displays contained high-end items made of colonial materials to sell to a metropolitan audience and a colonial clientele. The overall theme of this Luxury Industry Pavilion, including the formal reception room, featured ensembles for an imagined colonist's dwelling. The Art Deco designers who contributed luxury furniture models to this pavilion used colonial design schemes and materials. Well-known interior designers and design firms participated, such as Jacques-Emile Ruhlmann, Jules Leleu, René Prou for Bon Marché, Maurice Dufrêne for Galeries Lafayette, the department stores Au Louvre and Le Printemps, the interior design group Décoration Intérieur Moderne (D.I.M.) and the furniture manufacturer Lévitan (Liste Officielle des Exposants 1931: 86–90). These presentations made clear that modern luxury design relied on a newly enhanced French-colonial trade network for access to precious materials and that an "exotic" aesthetic could be used to market the designs.

Furniture ensembles from the manufacturer Lévitan presented in the exposition demonstrated an aesthetic that melded the modern and the colonial. The firm's "Bedroom" installation used amboyna burl for the bed, dresser and chair to achieve what it considered to be the epitome of modern design. As the furniture catalog stated about the design: "Nothing which is useless, nothing which is not necessary. The creator of this splendid bedroom saw that everything was at the same time simple and noble ... The shimmer of fabric on the reflection of the amboyna, harmony of beige and pink: it is pure art!" (Lévitan 1935). The decorative qualities of the tropical wood coupled with the zebra-striped bed cover utilized exotic wood to achieve an opulent and dramatic effect. Additionally, the Lévitan "Dining Room" ensemble, made of Rio palisander, achieved a look made "with simple resources attained the peak of luxury and elegance" (Lévitan 1935). Lévitan marketers found their presentations at the Colonial Exposition so successful that photographs of the 1931 ensembles became part of the advertising scheme and were reprinted in their furniture catalogs of 1933 and 1935(Lévitan 1933, 1935) [Figure 11.3].

The Lévitan furniture models relied on the decorative attributes of exotic wood in their designs, whether the wood came from the French colonies or from other tropical environments. Although not all Lévitan's timber originated in the colonies (e.g., Rio palisander was from Brazil), its exotic characteristics clearly evoked the colonial. Thus, whether the woods were colonial or not, the furniture designs at the 1931 Colonial Exposition and in the catalog demonstrated the importance of a presumed use of colonial materials in the firm's modern design concepts. The 1930s Lévitan model ensembles regularly employed mahogany, palisander and amboyna as well as occasional uses of zebrawood and *bois des îles* (*vavona*) in more upscale versions. Lévitan's marketers found their presentations at the Colonial Exposition to be so successful that these furniture ensembles became part of their advertisement schemes for modern furniture during the mid-1930s. The "Modern Furniture and Decoration" sales catalog of 1933 romanticized the use of exotic woods, claiming they had a mysterious allure that was

FIGURE 11.3 Page from Lévitan's furniture catalog promoting their award of the Diplôme d'Honneur for the furniture designs and displays of the *Salle à manger* and *Chambre à Coucher* at the 1931 Colonial Exposition (Lévitan 1933). © Bibliothèque Forney / Roger-Viollet.

translated through furniture design (Lévitan 1933). While the company's catalogs and exposition presentation conflated colonial provenance with a more generalized exotic and non-Western appellation, the manufacturer continued to sell lines of furniture based on the firm's technical and artistic command in handling exotic wood.

Perhaps the most spectacular interiors were staged in the two Oval Salons on the entry level of the Permanent Colonial Museum. Albert Laprade, the main architect for the Colonial Museum, chose Art Deco interior designers who belonged to the Société des Artistes Décorateurs. As both Romy Golan and Patricia Morton have noted, the designers chosen for the Colonial Exposition were already well versed in decorating for a clientele who expected some kind of colonial motif (Morton 1998: 369; Golan 1995: 106). Laprade picked well-known interior designers Jacques-Émile Ruhlmann and Eugène Printz to transform and decorate the oval-shaped rooms into offices for the colonial officials Paul Reynaud and Maréchal Lyautey, respectively. Both Ruhlmann and Printz designed the office furniture in the Art Deco style with simple, hygienic, bold lines, using both solid wood and veneers of varnished colonial woods for desks, side tables, lamp-posts, doors and wood paneling. Ruhlmann and Printz imagined official French-colonial state offices to be adorned in modern furniture. Since both designers actually used these offices during the exposition, these staged interiors became a functional reality.

Although there is some inconsistency as to the provenance and types of wood used in the furniture and interior design in the Oval Salons, visitors were led to believe that the materials used originated in the colonies. Ruhlmann's designs for Reynaud's office used ebony from Madagascar (some accounts opined this was Macassar ebony) in the room's parquet, window surrounds, doors and a desk whose top was covered in shark-skin (Morton 1998: 117; Camard 1984: 225; Bayer 1990: 42). The "Bloch" desk and several oversized "Elephant" chairs in the room had actually been designed for clients and for the salons of the Société des Artistes Décorateurs in the late 1920s, but they were now adapted for the 1931 Colonial Exposition (Camard 1984: 110, 222). Printz's room on the opposite side of the museum entrance presented an office for Lyautey, also known as the Salon Maréchal. Printz made the doors with a geometric inlay of Gabonese palm wood, and used rosewood and ebony from Gabon (or several types of mahogany) for the circular patterned parquet (Morton 1998: 372). "Lyautey's desk," a table, and lamp-posts were also made of palm wood (*patawa*) (Morton 1998: 372).

Conclusion

The French modern interior in the inter-war period was a space in which gains from the empire were advertised. Nowhere was this more apparent than in the displays of interior designs at the Parisian expositions of 1925 and 1931. In addition to the displays, which relied on the availability and use of colonial materials, the expositions generated much discussion, and many publications extolled the aesthetic, technical and economic attributes of colonial wood. Woodworkers were taught how to figuratively "tame" raw materials from the colonies, to "civilize" them through uses in the metropole and to support an imperial economy for the supply of colonial wood. By the 1931 Colonial Exposition, a variety of institutions and individuals recognized the successful exploitation of colonial timber and its significant influence on French metropolitan culture and the post-war economy. Colonial wood also factored into the French public imagination through advertisements and model interiors. The real or assumed provenance of the wood in furniture design became an important element in acknowledging how the French *outre-mer* contributed to the fashionable "exotic" aesthetic.

The colonial ethos that was articulated, used and assumed in modern design is, on the one hand, an Orientalist one. A seemingly international and democratic interior design style was in fact inherently rooted in capitalist, national and colonial practices. The cultural appropriation of materials from the French empire normalized the asymmetrical colonial economic and political relationship. Thus, the multivalent meaning in the aesthetic of the inter-war French modern interior provided a new *raison d'être* for French colonialism.

On the other hand, the hybrid forms that French modern furniture design took provide another dimension to understanding the contribution of colonial wood. Though French designers developed the style of the furniture, colonial materials inspired the form. The integral nature of colonial wood to high-end modern design referenced by the Lévitan catalogs suggest that French identity and modern furniture could not have achieved the success they did without the availability of colonial wood. While the modern designs that used colonial wood showcased a certain progress of civilization by appropriating colonial materials, the luxury models that incorporated colonial wood also created a new entity that was not purely French nor purely colonial, but a new streamlined form that was equally colonial and metropolitan.

References

"À l'Exposition des Arts Décoratifs," *Travail du Bois*, September 1925: 999.
Ageron, C. (1984), "L'Exposition Coloniale de 1931: Mythe républicain ou mythe impérial?" in P. Nora (ed.), *Les Lieux de Mémoire. 1, La République*, Paris: Gallimard.
Auslander, L. (1996), *Taste and Power: Furnishing Modern France*, Berkeley: University of California Press.
Bayer, P. (1990), *Art Deco Interiors: Decoration and Design Classics of the 1920s and 1930s*, London: Thames and Hudson.
Benton, C. (2003), "The International Exhibition," in C. Benton, T. Benton and G. Wood (eds.), *Art Deco 1910–1939*, London: Victoria and Albert Museum.
Bertin, A. and J. Petitpas (1926), "L'Usinage des Bois Coloniaux," *Travail du Bois*, May: 241.
"Les Bois à l'Exposition Coloniale Internationale de Paris," *Travail du Bois*, November 1930.
Camard, F. (1984), *Ruhlmann, Master of Art Deco*, New York: Abrams.
Dobie, M. (2007), "Orientalism, Colonialism, and Furniture in Eighteenth-Century France," in D. Goodman and K. Norberg (eds.), *Furnishing the Eighteenth Century: What Furniture Can Tell Us About the European and American Past*, New York: Routledge.
Golan, R. (1995), *Modernity and Nostalgia: Art and Politics in France between the Wars*, New Haven: Yale University Press.
Lévitan (1931), Furniture sales catalog, Paris: Établissements Lévitan.
Lévitan (1933), *Ameublement Moderne*, Furniture sales catalog, Paris: Établissements Lévitan.
Lévitan (1935), *Art Moderne*, Furniture sales catalog, Paris: Établissements Lévitan.
Liste Officielle des Exposants, Exposition Coloniale Internationale (1931), Paris: Mayeux.
Magne, H.-M. (1928), *Décor du Mobilier: Meubles et Sièges*, Paris: H. Laurens.

Meniaud, J. (1931), *Nos Bois Coloniaux*, Paris: Agence Générale des Colonies.
Ministère du Commerce, et de l'industrie, des postes et des télégraphes (1925), *Catalogue Général Officiel: Exposition Internationale des Arts Décoratifs et Industriels Modernes, Paris, Avril–Octobre*. Paris: Impr. de Vaugirard.
Morton, P. A. (1998), "National and Colonial: The Musée des Colonies at the Colonial Exposition, Paris, 1931," *The Art Bulletin*, 80: 357–377.
Morton, P. A. (2000), *Hybrid Modernities: Architecture and Representation at the 1931 Colonial Exposition, Paris*, Cambridge, MA: MIT Press.
"Nos Bois Coloniaux dans l'Ébénisterie," *Travail du Bois*, August 1925: 967.
Olivier, M. (1933), *Exposition Coloniale Internationale de Paris 1931: Rapport Général*, Vol. 5, part 1 (Les Sections Coloniales), Paris: Impr. Nationale.
Paris, W. (1925), "The International Exposition of Modern Industrial and Decorative Art in Paris, part 1, Interior Architecture," *Architectural Record*, 58, no. 3 (September): 265–277.
Pastore, C. (2007), "Mahogany as a Status Symbol: Race and Luxury in Saint Domingue at the End of the Eighteenth Century," in D. Goodman and K. Norberg (eds.), *Furnishing the Eighteenth Century: What Furniture Can Tell Us About the European and American Past*, New York: Routledge: 37–47.
Petitpas, J. (1931), "Le Bois à l'Exposition Coloniale," *Travail du Bois* (August).
Richards, C. (1926), *Report of Commission Appointed by the Secretary of Commerce to Visit and Report upon the International Exposition of Modern Decorative and Industrial Art in Paris, 1925*, Washington, DC: Department of Commerce.
Rydell, R. (1993), *World of Fairs: The Century-of-Progress Expositions*, Chicago: University of Chicago Press.
Said, E. (1978), *Orientalism*, 1st edn., New York: Pantheon Books.
Travail du Bois, Paris: Société de publications mécaniques, (referencing articles from years 1923–1936).
"L'Utilisation des Bois Coloniaux," *Travail du Bois* (October 1931 to September 1933).

12

Paradise in the Parlor: Cozy Corners and Potted Palms in Western Interiors, 1880–1900

Penny Sparke

> *We may find ourselves surrounded with imagery of tropical luxuriance, while the forms and fragrance of real plants will complete the delusion.*
>
> (H. J. Cooper, "The Art of Furnishing on Rational and Aesthetic Principles" 1879: 5)

In the postcolonial early twenty-first century, much work still needs to be undertaken to fully unravel the cross-cultural influences that occurred during the era of European imperialism and colonization and the early years of international trade and travel. In particular, its effects upon material and spatial culture and everyday life need more attention as it was within those arenas that new cultural norms and practices were established. The complex transnational effects of eighteenth- and nineteenth-century European imperialism and colonization in this area are only just being addressed and the tools with which to undertake that work still to be fully defined (Wild 2000). Inevitably, much was lost, or re-constructed, in translation.

While a significant amount of work has been done on the effects of European culture and style being imposed on to colonized nations, and on recapturing the indigenous, local cultures that were eclipsed as a result, less has been done to unpack the meanings of the reverse movement of culture, that is, on the cultural influences of the colonized nations on the colonizers (King 1984). In the area of material culture and the decorative arts, this has, to date, been mostly focused on the influences of trade relations with China and Japan and, to a lesser extent, India (Sato and Watanabe 1991). It has become clear from this work that, in the colonising countries, so remote were the origins of those cultures and styles that the boundaries between them became porous and that, for many, they merged into a single phenomenon that simply stood for exoticism and "otherness" in the broadest sense of the terms.

The work undertaken by the cultural theorist Edward Said in the late 1970s has helped us focus on the fact that what he called "Orientalism" (which for him was linked primarily to the culture of the Arab, Islamic world), was a Western construct which, in his eyes, acted as a form of active and deliberate marginalization. By depicting the Oriental other as irrational, lazy, sensuous and feminine, he claimed, it was understood as being all the things the West was not, that is, rational, industrious and masculine (Said 2003). Homi Bhabha took that debate one step further, however, venturing beyond the binary situation outlined by Said to posit the existence of a "Third Space" that was hybrid in nature and which understood cultural categories as being in a permanent state of transformation (Rutherford 1990: 207–221).

While that debate continues within the world of cultural theory it has also impacted on the ways in which historians of material culture and the decorative arts understand their objects of study. While Said's work helps them to understand that the view of the "other" tells us more about the viewer than the viewed, and that they have to be diligent when deconstructing the myths that have been created within the context of transnational cultural exchange, Bhabha's ideas helps them grasp the fact that most material cultural manifestations are inevitably hybrid in nature, the results, that is, of continually ongoing transformations and combinations of the complex cultural influences that have helped form them. This study recognizes the importance of both these insights. In the context of the subject under discussion—the inclusion, that is, of tropical palms which originated in a wide range of geographical areas, the Caribbean and Central and South America among them, in an otherwise exclusively Oriental setting—Bhabha's notions of "transformation" and "hybridity" are highly relevant.

This account of exoticism and otherness (which, in the context of this chapter, are both Oriental and tropical in their origins) in the late nineteenth-century Western domestic interior offers an example of the ways in which new and complex meanings can be constructed in that space through the appropriation and display of multiple objects and styles presented as a whole. Given the huge propensity for hybridity in that context, both within individual objects and in their combinations in a spatial setting, care is required in unpacking their complex and often seemingly internally inconsistent cultural meanings. Given also, that the only access to them in combination is through photographs the heavily posed, seemingly consistent and misleadingly static nature of the imagery in question needs to be taken into account.

The cozy corner

A photograph of the New York-based interior decorator Elsie de Wolfe (1867–1950), taken in 1896, just before she refurbished her 122 East 17th Street home, situated on the corner of East 17th Street and Irving Place, in the French eighteenth-century style, shows her reclining on a sea of silk-covered, patterned and embroidered cushions and surrounded by lush potted palms and an aspidistra [Figure 12.1]. Closer inspection reveals a carpet of Middle-Eastern origin covering a low plinth beneath her feet, and, to her right, two inlaid, Turkish-style side tables with what appear to be Middle-Eastern-style metal bowls (used as plant holders) positioned on them.

FIGURE 12.1 The Interior Decorator, Elsie de Wolfe, lounging on a cozy corner, in her house at 122 East 17th Street, New York, 1896. Reproduced with permission from the Museum of the City of New York.

In spite of Miss de Wolfe's overtly Western, high Victorian "Aesthetic" dress, and the William Morris-style wallpaper located behind her, the Oriental flavor of this complex scene is indisputable. Reminiscent of a Turkish harem—or at least of one that had been widely seen in European paintings and photographs that we now call Orientalist—it sits within the early nineteenth-century French painting tradition of the odalisque—a slave or concubine in a harem who was depicted as a sexually available woman—most notably embraced by the artists Eugene Delacroix and Jean Auguste Dominique Ingres. In the photograph of de Wolfe in her Irving Place home, however, the overtly erotic, early nineteenth-century naked odalisque, was replaced by a fully clothed, highly fashionable figure located in an albeit equally exotic (although less overtly suggestive) "cozy corner."

Also widely referred to as a "Turkish Corner," the "cozy corner" was a reconstruction of a highly informal lounging area, originally found in harems (or at least represented as such by male Orientalist artists who were, ironically, forbidden to enter them), that found its way into, firstly, artistic and, later, style-conscious middle-class domestic interiors of the mid-1890s in both Europe and the USA. The extant photographs that depict examples of that particular late nineteenth-century domestic decorating genre present their female subjects as dreamy, reflective, relaxed (perhaps even work-shy), frequently overtly sexual and embedded within a carefully constructed theatrical set denoting physical comfort and luxury. The set usually comprised a low carpet- or fabric-covered plinth, draped patterned fabrics and cushions, and a range of furniture pieces and decorative items, including inlaid tables, metalwork (occasionally a hookah or a lamp), and frequently exotic plants, usually palms.

While this depiction would have been denounced as a false construction by Said, created by the West (the colonizing Occident) in order to undermine the Orient (the colonized East), in the context of the history of the interior, it can be understood, quite simply, as a Western decorating fashion—linked to late nineteenth-century Aestheticism as it entered the popular arena. Arguably, it ultimately said less about the Orient per se than about Western social aspirations in an urban setting. Seen from that perspective "Turkish Corners," and the so-called "Oriental Interior" as a whole, can be seen to have represented the idea, or ideal, of a liberal household, one in which artistic practices were embraced, beauty was prioritized and femininity was ever present. The first "Turkish corners" existed in homes that were inhabited by an artistic avant-garde that was situated at the margins of society. By the 1890s, they had entered the houses of a wider range of middle-class homemakers who had sufficient fashion sense and social know-how to understand that to appear to be marginal, and to be seen to embrace artistic values in the domestic sphere, positioned them firmly as members of upwardly mobile, sophisticated, metropolitan middle-class society. The home-makers in question acquired their knowledge about the kind of interiors that would communicate this message from contemporary magazines and advice books, as well as from access to model interiors presented at exhibitions and in photographers' studios.

Oriental interiors were rarely stylistically pure. Indeed, they did not need to be. Rather, they occupied a spectrum, one end of which was inhabited by *Gesamtkunstwerk* interiors, within which every element was indisputably either directly derived from or inspired by the East, or a Western idea of the East, and the other end by decorating schemes that merely contained, say, an item of Turkish metalwork or a Turkish or Persian carpet—sufficient signs of the presence of the Orient in an otherwise eclectic setting. Of all the Oriental symbols used in domestic settings, the carpet was, perhaps, the most widespread and it quickly became a key element within the basic vocabulary of the language of Victorian domesticity. Indeed, it could also be found outside the private arena, bringing domesticity to a wide range of semi-public and public settings including hotel lobbies and even lunatic asylums.

The "cozy corner" was part of a wider fascination with all things described at the time as "Oriental" that had penetrated fashionable, middle-class interior décor by the end of the nineteenth century. Broadly speaking, it signified an interest in the past and with the sensuous, the bodily, the feminine and the decorative. It contrasted strongly with the more rational "proto-modern" design style that emerged at the end of the nineteenth century, which was epitomized by the work of the William Morris and the members of the Arts and Crafts Movement. This widely disseminated decorative idiom, which featured vernacular country chairs and textiles featuring patterns abstracted from natural forms, has tended to dominate historical accounts of the period, as well as design historical discourse, eclipsing the fashion for all things Oriental (Naylor 2001). The two styles frequently co-existed in a single setting, however: Oriental metalwork could be found in the drawing room of William Morris's Kelmscott House, built in London's Hammersmith, for example, while the dining room of the same home featured a Persian carpet and a chest full of more Oriental metal-ware.

Although the West had been entranced by the art and culture of the Middle East for centuries, and numerous European examples of interest in countries from that part of the world influencing the interior schemes of the nobility and the wealthy in the eighteenth century existed, that interest resurfaced in the nineteenth century, reaching the peak of its popularity in the mid-1890s when aspirational middle-class home-makers began to emulate an interior style that had already been manifesting itself in more rarefied artistic circles. Leading artists, architects and designers of the day led the way: In Britain, for example, Owen Jones demonstrated a strong interest in the Islamic decorative arts in his 1956 book *The Grammar of Ornament*, which proved hugely influential; and in 1890, the artist Frederick Leighton included an Arab Hall in his London home. It combined stylistic features inspired by Syria, Egypt, Persia, Damascus and Algeria, among other exotic locations.

"Turkish taste," formed an element of French décor throughout the nineteenth century (Grier 2010: 38), while, on the other side of the Atlantic, the taste for all things Oriental was manifested by, among other examples, the Moorish Revival mansion designed for the circus impresario P. T. Barnum in New York in 1848 by the architect Leopold Eidlitz. Other notable instances of the fashion for the style on the East Coast of the USA included the "Persian"-style home—"Olana"—designed in 1872 by Calvert Vaux for Hudson River painter Frederick Edwin Church. In 1893, the Columbian Exposition in Chicago featured a Turkish village and bazaar, as well as a "Streets of Cairo" exhibit, both of which proved hugely popular. Indeed, the bazaar offered all the items required by home-makers to create their own "Turkish Corners." By the mid-1990s, the popular Oriental style had become a pan-Western phenomenon represented by loose melanges of settings, furniture items and artifacts which, although they had their origins (fictionally, if not factually) in North Africa, Turkey, and the Middle East, could be bought locally.

Above all, the cozy corner served to undermine the high formality of the mid-nineteenth-century parlor, the furniture items of which had required a quite different and much more controlled set of postures and a greater degree of formal social interaction on the part of its inhabitants. It introduced a new level of personal privacy, relaxation and interiority into the home and, above all, a new, sexualized and independent image of the domesticated woman. In the image discussed above, for example, de Wolfe (a professional actress at the time) was assuming a very specific pose for the photographer. Suggesting independence and reflection, she achieved this by holding her head and looking into the middle distance. The idea of interior decoration becoming an important medium through which women could express their individual creative identities was in line with the tenets of Aestheticism (Gere and Hoskins 2008: 8). De Wolfe was at one with her personal identity and her domestic privacy. However, it was a posed privacy, visible to the many visitors who came to admire the fashionableness of the interior décor on display. De Wolfe and her partner, the theatrical agent, Elizabeth Marbury (1856–1933), opened their house in Irving Place on Sunday afternoons to a gathering of celebrity cultural figures, including Dame Nellie Melba. Their aim, in so doing, was undoubtedly to have some of that celebrity status rub off from them and, when de Wolfe turned from being an actress to an interior decorator, to attract clients.

The potted palm as exotic "Other" in the late nineteenth-century middle-class home

The set for the posed privacy expressed in the de Wolfe photograph was achieved through a combined use of textiles, furnishings and a range of decorative items, including potted palms and an aspidistra. The last were not an obligatory component of cozy corners. However, records exist of other examples in which they were included and they certainly served as a visual complement to the other elements used to construct that particular theatrical setting.

While palms are associated with many of the geographical areas that can be described as Oriental—Southern Asia, North Africa and Southern Turkey among others—they have their origins in a wider range of tropical locations. They are seen as highly exotic natural objects, therefore, linked with the ideas of warmth, sensuousness and relaxation. In the nineteenth century, they had the capacity to inject a level of exoticism into the West that could supplement Oriental settings but which could also be added to a wide range of other domestic settings and styles. While, that is, when accompanied by the other necessary components of that interior decorative scheme, or language, they could contribute to a specifically nineteenth-century Oriental exoticism, they also provided exotic otherness in more conventional nineteenth-century middle-class interiors. In Britain, that otherness not only evoked the sumptuousness and warmth of a tropical environment but also, given many of their countries of origin, the authority of the British Empire.

The link between palms and Orientalism was not new however. Numerous eighteenth- and nineteenth-century paintings and photographs of Oriental scenes, including fantasized images of harem interiors, created by European travelers and others, depicted palms. This was both because they often existed in the locations of choice (when those locations were in tropical zones) but also, undoubtedly, because of the tree's inherent visual elegance and abundant capacity to contribute to the picturesque nature of a work by providing height, a visual softness, which contrasted with architectural solidity and regularity, and, frequently, a convenient framing device. As such they came to play a significant role within Oriental iconography and were therefore, not surprisingly, frequently included in nineteenth-century interiors that expressed an Oriental theme, such as the one in de Wolfe's New York home. They were by no means restricted to such interiors, however, as has been suggested, but took on an important role in countless late nineteenth-century middle-class domestic interiors across a wider stylistic spectrum, introducing an element of exoticism into them.

The roles played by the Oriental style and potted palms in the middle-class home were both related and distinct: They both injected a sense of otherness and exoticism into interiors that derived from the distance of their geographical origins and their cultural difference. Where they parted company lay in the difference of the specifics of their geographical origins in many cases and in the fact that another face of palms' otherness lay in the fact that they were a symptom of the industrialising world needing to keep one foot in the natural world. By bringing nature inside, in the form not only of plant and flowers, but also of birds, fish and reptiles, the Victorians sought to avoid a split between nature and culture and, thereby, avoid alienation from the pre-industrial world that they had all but abandoned,

Oriental-style furnishings and potted palms in the home both had their roots in Western colonization—the former through the Europeans exerting their power over the Islamic World and the latter through the European colonization of places in a range of geographical locations, including Asia, the Pacific Islands, Africa and the Americas. The introduction of both helped fulfill a deep desire—one that had already been met by the aristocracy through the embrace of chinoiserie and *japonisme*, as well as citrus fruit trees—to inject exoticism into the home.

As they did in paintings and photographs, so within interior settings palms frequently provided a frame, a set of stage side curtains as it were, for all the other interior elements—rugs, cushions, hangings, metalwork, tables and a range of other decorative objects among them—in either an Oriental-style ensemble or in a more conventional nineteenth-century home in the neo-Classical, neo-Tudor, neo-Gothic, *japoniste*, or Arts and Crafts styles, or, quite frequently, a mixture of some or all of them. Palms also offered sculptural elegance and architectural structure. They could perform the role of screens and their presence frequently served to offset the effects of clutter and stylistic mixing, enabling eclectic settings to appear unified. They also added height where it was needed and the color green to complement the widespread use of deep reds that pervaded the Victorian parlor. Although they could not emulate their exotic role, indigenous ferns frequently provided a cheaper alternative that could offer some of the same aesthetic benefits.

The journey of palms into the middle-class home, via the conservatory, was initially less a response to the requirements of taste, however, and more to ones of scientific inquiry. However, as the century progressed, they became increasingly aestheticized and integrated into the fashionable interior, both in wealthy country houses and in more modest middle-class dwellings. Palms brought with them the exoticism of the tropics, as well as memories of empire and of an un-tamed world in which nature had held sway over culture. In Britain, the first large-scale glass and iron palm houses were built in the grounds of the Duke of Devonshire's home, Chatsworth House (1837–1840) in Derbyshire, designed by Joseph Paxton who went on to create the Crystal Palace that housed the Great Exhibition held in Hyde Park in 1851. Between 1844 and 1848, the enormous palm house at Kew came into being. So popular were the palm houses and the 1851 exhibition that they fueled a fashion for the creation of palm houses in public parks. This was followed by a rash of domestic conservatories (made possible by the recent development of sheet glass) attached to the homes of the wealthy and of the urban *nouveau riche* [Figure 12.2].

In Liverpool, for example, one of the country's most important ports at which numerous merchant ships arrived filled with imported plants, the Isla Gladstone conservatory was built in 1896 in Stanley Park, which itself had opened twenty-six years earlier. The conservatory was stocked with a large

FIGURE 12.2 Nineteenth-century conservatory in the Gothic style at Orton Hall, Peterborough. Photograph: Penny Sparke.

collection of exotic plants, including palms. At exactly the same time, not far from the Park in Aigburth Vale, the furnisher and decorator S. J. Waring (1837–1907), who was to became a partner in the well-known British furnishers and decorators Waring and Gillow (following a merger in 1897), bought a house which he called Palmyra (the name of both a type of palm and of a place in ancient Syria [Corner 1955: 285]). Waring added to the rear of the early nineteenth-century villa an octagonal-roofed conservatory which led to a sequence of elaborate, intersecting glass houses [Figure 12.3]. He filled the conservatory with exotic plants, mostly palms but also a few ferns, as well as with some garden furniture and a standard lamp, thus transforming it into an outside parlor. A paper Chinese lantern hung from one of the metal beams. The glasshouses were linked to the rear of the house through the addition of some Moorish-style arches and tiles (reminiscent of those depicted by Owen Jones in his *Grammar of Ornament* (1856), which had been inspired by the Alhambra in Granada). Just as de Wolfe had added a mirror to the rear of her cozy corner to create an enhanced sense of space, so S. J. Waring also injected one into the middle archway at the rear of his house. In the same year in which he built his conservatory, the *Journal of Horticulture and Practical Gardening* reported that S. J. Waring's gardener, Mr Pattinson, won a prize for a palm grown at Palmyra, showing the extent of the furnisher's commitment to nurturing that exotic plant.

Interestingly, Waring did not limit his interest in palms to the conservatory, but also introduced some small examples into his dining room [Figure 12.4]. In spite of the overtly Oriental flavor suggested by the name of the Waring

FIGURE 12.3 Palm House at Palmyra, Aigburth Vale, Liverpool, 1896. Reproduced by permission of English Heritage.

FIGURE 12.4 Dining room in Palmyra, Aigburth Vale, Liverpool, 1896. Reproduced by permission of English Heritage.

home, that style was notable by its absence in the interior décor. Instead, the dining room was highly conventional in its familiar eclecticism and historicism: It featured Chippendale-style dining chairs, some French eighteenth-century-style electric sconces, a Japanese-style bamboo firescreen and a neo-Tudor molded plaster ceiling. The only sign of Orientalism—as was the case in so many middle-class homes of the period—was the presence of either a Turkish or a Persian carpet on the floor. To that small taste of exoticism was added the presence of three small palms, one of them placed at the center of the dining table.

Advice literature and the exotic home of taste

While the owners of country houses had decorators undertake their interior schemes, including the positioning of their potted palms, middle-class urban dwellers were left to make their own decorating decisions. In helping the latter engage in the fashion for both Orientalizing the domestic interior, and rendering it exotic through the introduction of potted palms, the role of two bodies of advice books—those focusing on furnishing and others oriented towards the activity known as "window gardening"—cannot be underestimated. It is impossible to know how much they actually influenced practice, but they undoubtedly played a key role in communicating the ideals to which home-makers aspired.

In the first category, Mrs Haweis, for example, a widely read advisor on furniture and furnishings to British home-makers, devoted a chapter of her book *Beautiful Houses* to a description of Alma-Tadema's house in Regent's Park in which she noted the existence of a conservatory, complete with a hammock, palms and Chinese lanterns and, in the interior itself, the use of hanging textiles instead of doors, which gave the house, in her words an "Oriental character." Both features seemed to get her seal of approval (Haweis 1882: 25).

Where advisors on plants in the home were concerned on both sides of the Atlantic there was a strong consensus about the beauty and superiority of palms over other plants. There was also a significant interest in indigenous ferns placed in Wardian cases as they were deemed to be the best alternative to palms for those for whom the latter were a financial impossibility. This strategy was discussed at length by Shirley Hibberd in his influential book *Rustic Adornments for Homes of Taste*, first published in 1856 but reprinted in 1857, 1870 and 1895. The final edition contained a chapter entitled "The Fern-Case" which described the plants in question as being of great beauty and as playing a key role in the "circle of household adornments" (Hibberd 1987 [1856]: 136). Attention was also paid to fern stands, which could, according to Hibberd, be acquired in a number of desired styles, presumably Oriental among them. Palms were included in a chapter dedicated to window gardens and enclosed exterior window cases, but they were not considered at length in the text. They were visible, however, in an illustration depicting a conservatory leading from a dwelling-house (Hibberd 1987 [1856]: 240).

Hibberd's engagement with the Oriental style came to the fore in a discussion about indoor bird cages. In the 1856 edition, he highlighted one fantasy creation in particular that was designed for "Homes of Taste" by Mr William Kidd. With its repeated decorative arches, abstract patterning and onion-shaped domed top, it had a strong mosque-like appearance. Its presence in the book demonstrated Hibberd's awareness of the role played both by nature, in its many forms, and by styles derived from distant lands, as exotic, tasteful others in the 1890s home, however modest. He also included an illustration of a parrot house "in the Moorish style" which he claimed was "well adapted for use as an open bird and vine-house during summer" (Hibberd 1987 [1856]: 256). He went on to explain that "[a] collection of parrots and paroquets would have a splendid effect in such a building and give it a true oriental appearance." Evidence of Hibberd's acute awareness of the contemporary vogue for all things Oriental was reinforced by a discussion of a fiction that in his view "beat the 'Arabian Nights' out of all hope of competition" (Hibberd 1987 [1856]: 250).

Because of their elegance and architectural structure palms were seen as being particularly useful in the area of table decoration. In his 1874 book *Domestic Floriculture: Window-Gardening and Floral Decorations, being practical directions for the propagation, culture and arrangement of plants and flowers as domestic ornaments*, F. W. Burbridge illustrated a table decorated with palms. The display featured multiple palms with a large one at the center surrounded by others of descending height. The plants' pots were concealed beneath the table's surface, supported by a metal structure secured beneath it (Burbridge 1874: 142–143). In *Floral Decorations for the Dwelling House* of the following year, Annie Hassard repeated the same idea of placing palms on tables with their pots positioned beneath, explaining that she did exactly this for two tables she designed for Royal Horticultural Society shows at South Kensington and Birmingham. The specific plants she used on those occasions were a "graceful pair of Pteris tremula and . . . a pair of Chamaedoreas," the former a type of fern and the latter a small palm from the Americas (Hassard 1875: 14).

Across the Atlantic, "window" and "parlor" gardening also became popular household pursuits, modeled upon European examples. Henry T. Williams's book, *Window Gardening*, of 1862 and 1972, and Edward Sprague Rand's *The Window Gardener* of 1863, 1870, 1871 and 1882, both embraced the exotic implications of bringing nature—in the form of plants and tropical birds—to accompany furnishings inspired by the styles from distant lands, into the home. Ferns were given special attention once again, but Williams also devoted a section of his book to palms explaining that the discovery of dwarf versions made it a much more flexible plant for the interior (Williams 1872: 262). As a result, he recommended using palms as table decorations. Williams predicted prophetically that "they will soon be the favorites of our parlors" (1872: 262). He also pointed out that, although many palms grew to be very big, their growth was slow and they could be used in rooms for considerable periods of time (Williams 1872: 264). Rand adopted a more practical approach and explained of palms that, "[t]heir stiff foliage is well adapted to endure the impure air of apartments and is not injured by gas . . . Where plants are needed for effect, and little attention can be given, palms . . . . are eminently useful" (Rand 2009 [1863]: 123).

The last decades of the nineteenth century and early years of twentieth century saw palms used as part of fashionable decoration move beyond the home and into a wide range of semi-public and public spaces, including ones in hotels, ocean liners, department stores, seaside winter gardens and "people's palaces." The idea of the "palm court" emerged at that time, a space in which guests, shoppers and audiences could take tea in a fashionable environment while being entertained by music, often played by a "palm quartet." Palm courts emerged in huge numbers across both sides of the Atlantic—examples included those in the Langham and Ritz hotels in London and the Plaza hotel in New York; Harrods in London and Au Printemps and the Galeries Lafayettes in Paris; the ocean liners *Aquitania*,

Olympic and *Titanic*; the English winter garden at Blackpool; and the "People's Palaces" in London and Glasgow. To a significant extent, their appeal undoubtedly lay in the exotic ambiance provided by the plants themselves. By 1914, the palm court had mostly disappeared from view, however.

Conclusion

In describing his theory of culture in the context of cultural translation, Homi Bhabha has described the importance of understanding incompleteness. "Translation," he has explained, "is also a way of imitating, but in a mischievous, displacing sense—imitating an original in such a way that the priority of the original is not reinforced but by the very fact that it can be simulated, copied, transferred, transformed, made into a simulacrum and so on: the 'original' is never finished or complete in itself" (in Rutherford 1990: 210). The use of both the Oriental style and the potted palm in interiors continued to be copied and transformed through the course of the nineteenth century, sometimes in isolation and sometimes in conjunction with each other (as in the de Wolfe photograph). While based on a set of fairly stable themes—those of exoticism, escapism and aspiration—both their material and spatial languages as well as their contexts and meanings continued to evolve over half a century.

Taken together with Said's insights into the fact that "otherness" in a colonizing culture is usually more fiction than fact, Bhabha's ideas help make sense of the nature and meaning of the exoticism present in de Wolfe's Irving Place home, as well in the other examples of both Oriental and palm-filled interiors discussed in this chapter. While there was not necessarily any inherent logic, consistency or authenticity in their contents the effects of the whole had a validity that was meaningful to contemporaries. At a time of rapid industrialization, urbanization and growing international political unrest in Europe and the USA, the escapist appeal of distant lands and of the increasingly remote world of nature, represented by the inclusion of a Turkish carpet and an exotic potted palm in the home, served to help assuage the anxieties of two continents.

References

Burbridge, F. W. (1874), *Domestic Floriculture: Window-Gardening and Floral Decorations, being practical directions for the propagation, culture and arrangement of plants and flowers as domestic ornaments,* Edinburgh and London: William Blackwood and Sons.

Cooper, H. J. (1879), *The Art of Furnishing on Rational and Aesthetic Principles,* London: C. Kegan Paul.

Corner, E. J. H. (1955), *The Natural History of Palms*, Berkeley and Los Angeles: University of California Press.
Gere, C. and L. Hoskins (2000), *The House Beautiful: Oscar Wilde and the Aesthetic Interior*, London: Lund Humphries in association with the Geffrye Museum.
Grier, K. (2010), *Culture and Comfort: Parlor-Making and Middle-Class Identity, 1850–1930*, Washington: Smithsonian Books.
Hassard, A. (1875), *Floral Decorations for the Dwelling House*, London: Macmillan.
Haweis, Mrs E. (1882), *Beautiful Houses*, New York: Scribner and Welford.
Hibberd, S. (1856), *Rustic Adornments for Homes of Taste*, London: Century and the National Trust, 1987.
King, A. D. (1984), *The Bungalow: The Production of a Global Culture*, London: Routledge.
Naylor, G. (2001), *The Arts and Crafts Movement*, London: Studio Vista.
Rand, E. S. (1863), *Flowers for the Parlor and Garden*, New York: General Books, 2009.
Rutherford, J. (ed.) (1990), *Community, Culture, Difference*, London: Lawrence and Wishart.
Said, E. W. (2003), *Orientalism*, Harmondsworth: Penguin Books.
Sato, T. and T. Watanabe (1991), *Japan and Britain: An Aesthetic Dialogue, 1850–1930*, London: Lund Humphries.
Wild, A. (2000), *The East India Company: Trade and Conquest from 1600*, London: The Lyons Press.
Williams, H. T. (1872), *Window Gardening: Devoted Specially to the Culture of Flowers and Ornamental Plants for Indoor Use and Parlor Decoration*, New York: Henry T. Williams.

13

Traveling in Time and Space: The Cinematic Landscape of the Empress Theatre

Camille Bédard

A promenade in Notre-Dame-de-Grâce (NDG) Park, Montreal reveals an unexpected building across Sherbrooke Street West: the Egyptian-inspired Empress Theatre. Mirage or reality? The movie theater is resolutely distinct from the surrounding built environment: its elaborate façade, adorned with hieroglyphs, lotus flowers and busts of Ramses, is an invitation to enter another world.

This chapter examines the case study of the Empress Theatre of Montreal, built in 1927 [Figure 13.1]. Designed by the architect Alcide Chaussé (1868–1944), the Empress was decorated by the artist Emmanuel Briffa (1875–1955), who placed Egyptian motifs throughout the building to simulate Ancient Egypt. Developed by the Austrian-born architect John Eberson (1875–1954) in the 1920s, the typology of the atmospheric movie theater is a make-believe architecture of exotic destinations. Authenticity is not the ultimate goal of the exotic décor, but rather illusion, through which the Empress revisits the Orientalist divide between East and West. The Empress will also be analyzed as a space of cinematic tourism, in which traveling and discovery are facilitated by the fictive nature of cinema. This combination of reality and fiction, which collapses several sites within a single building, is a form of what Michel Foucault has termed "heterotopia." As a space of cultural translation, the exoticized movie theater blurs traditional geographical boundaries to create a space of hybridity which confers a

FIGURE 13.1 Empress Theatre, Montreal, 1928. Royal Architectural Institute of Canada.

decisive role onto the users of the building. The experience of the atmospheric movie theater thereby empowers movie-goers to transcend the materiality of the building and shape their own *architecture of the imagination*.

The atmospheric movie theater

The presentation of Thomas Edison's Kinetoscope in a converted shoe store on Lower Broadway in New York City in April 1894 marked the birth of the seventh art of cinema (Morrison 2006: 22). Built predominantly in the USA between 1913 and 1932, with a peak in the 1920s, movie palaces were characterized by their lavish decoration and enormous size. The average seating capacity was between 1,800 and 2,500, and up to 6,200 in the case of the Cathedral of the Motion Picture: the Roxy Theater of New York City (Herzog 1981: 15). Inspired by the classical architecture of European palaces and opera houses, movie palaces sought to elevate moviegoing to a form of respectable entertainment, in opposition to nickelodeons which were associated with the working class because of their low admission price, small seating capacity and sedate interiors. The credos of film mogul Marcus Loew, "We sell tickets to theatres, not movies," and of movie theater architect S. Charles Lee, "The show starts on the sidewalk" (Valentine 1994: 9), testify to the new role of building and space played in the cinematic experience. Indeed, the movie palace era marked the beginning of theatre design as buildings became attractions in their own right (Morrison 2006: 25).

As grandiose as it was, the classical architecture of movie palaces called for a second wind in the 1920s to support the insatiable desire of expansion of film moguls. Architect John Eberson found inspiration for the atmospheric movie theater while wintering in Florida:

> I was impressed with the colorful scenes which greeted me at Miami, Palm Beach and Tampa, where I saw, happy, gaily-dressed people living constantly under azure skies, and amongst tropical spendor. Visions of Italian gardens, Spanish patios, Persian shrines and French formal garden lawns flashed through my mind, and at once I directed my energies to carrying out these ideas.
> (Kinerk and Wilhelm 1998: 215)

The new typology of the atmospheric, or "stars-and-clouds," theater transported film-goers to dreamlike fantasies, far away from their daily routines. The architectural reference was no longer Ancient Greece or Rome as in classical movie palaces, but rather exotic cultures such as Egypt, China, India or Moorish Andalusia. World fairs, travelogs and archeological discoveries cultivated this taste for exoticism and inspired the make-believe architecture of movie palaces. Illusion, a crucial element in the design of these spaces, reached its zenith with atmospheric movie theaters: the immersive auditorium simulated inside the building a deceptive outdoor space.

Two criteria define the typology of the atmospheric movie theater. On the one hand, side walls had to reproduce elements that evoke exterior architecture such as balconies, roofs and windows, as well as vegetation and sometimes animals. Eberson himself was known for using stuffed peacocks in his projects (Kinerk and Wilhelm 1998: 221). On the other hand, the ceiling needed to be treated like a sky vault, painted in blue with small stars, either painted directly on it, integrated into it through light bulbs or projected onto it (Martineau 1988: 53).[1] The illusion of the nocturnal sky of the atmospheric movie theater was completed by the effects of the Brenograph, "a super magic lantern that not only projected song slides for the organ interludes, but an endless variety of scenic effects by means of multiple lenses and moving slides and intricate fades and dissolves" (Hall 1961: 201). Among the various effects listed in the 1928 catalog of the Brenkert Light Projection Company are aurora Borealis, flying angels, fast-moving dark storm clouds, ocean waves, volcano in eruption and falling roses (Hall 1961: 202). The nickname of "soft-tops" stems from the mock-up nighttime ceiling, compared to more conventional movie theaters referred to as "hard-tops" because of their plain ceiling (Cameco n.d.: 2).[2]

Inaugurated in 1922, Eberson's Majestic in Houston is the first atmospheric movie theater, an imitation of an Andalusian courtyard (Hall 1961: 95). This theme of Moorish Andalusia was especially popular, as noted by the theater critic W. F. Gladish: "among the so-called atmospherics houses, there are probably more of the Spanish design of architectural influence than all the others put together. Chinese, Egyptian, Babylonian and other effects are conspicuous by their absence" (Kolomeir 1987: 42). Atmospheric theaters can be further divided in their representation and imitation of foreign cultures in the built form. The first subtype of atmospheric theater refers to a single culture, such as the Mayan-inspired Fisher in Detroit, designed by Graven and Mayger in 1928. The second subtype combines references to various cultures within the same building in an architectural melting-pot, such as the Oriental by the Rapp brothers, which opened in 1926 and featured a combination of Cambodian, Indian and Thai ornamentation.

The distinction between the depiction of a single or multiple cultures sheds light on the biased perception and representation of the East by the West, defined by postcolonial theorist Edward W. Said as "Orientalism." Such a theoretical framework reveals the artificial divide between the fabricated entities of the familiar (Europe, the West, "us") versus the strange (the Orient, the East, "them.") (Said 1978: 43). The Western fascination for the East emerged from the discovery and translation of Oriental texts as well as the Napoleonic invasion of Egypt in 1798 (Said 1978: 42). For the West, the Orient evoked mystery, fantasy and magic, as well as sensuality and eternity. Such romanticized perceptions and representations of the East is based on cultural stereotypes, which distort reality. Said argues that "the Orient is less a place than a *topos*, a set of references, a congeries of characteristics, that seems to have its origins in a quotation, or a fragment of a text, or a citation from someone's work on the Orient, or some bit of previous imagining, or an amalgam of all these" (1978: 177). In short, the Orientalist discourse of power crystallized the myth of the Orient in the Western imagination.

Among the thousands of North American movie theaters, only thirteen atmospheric movie theaters were built in Canada between 1927 and 1931 (Russell 1991: 172). Some were "true" theaters while others reproduced the exotic ambiance, without conforming entirely to Eberson's criteria. The Spanish-inspired Runnymede Theater, which opened in 1927 on Bloor Street West in Toronto, is the first Canadian movie theatre to use the atmospheric genre. The Canadian versions feature the same over-representation of Spanish-inspired movie theaters as in the United States; the Empress is the only Egyptian-themed atmospheric movie theater of Canada. Through the perception, reception and experience of this make-believe architecture, film-goers construct their own architecture of the imagination, a hybrid space which acknowledges the affective and intangible essence of architecture.

The Empress Theatre

Inaugurated in 1918 right at the border of the city of Westmount that prohibited the building and operation of movie theaters on its territory at the time, the Empress was the second movie theater to open in Notre-Dame-de-Grâce after the Westmount or Claremont (Pelletier 2012: 103). The fast-growing anglophone middle-class neighborhood—from a population of 5,000 inhabitants in 1914 to 30,000 by 1930—was a perfect location for small-scale movie theaters (Corporation de développement économique communautaire Côte-des-Neiges/Notre-Dame-de-Grâce 2013).[3]

The 1,550-seat Egyptian-inspired movie theater is a collaborative project between Alcide Chaussé, an expert on fire prevention, and the Maltese-born theater decorator Emmanuel Briffa. During the movie palace era, this type of partnership was frequent: architects were in charge of the structural aspect of the building, the safety and comfort of its patrons, and optimization of circulation patterns, while decorators sought to astound movie-goers with flamboyant decoration. After its inauguration on May 19, 1928, the Empress operated as a second-run movie theater for three decades until its brief conversion as the cabaret Royal Follies in the early 1960s. After the subdivision of the auditorium into two smaller rooms, the movie theater took on a new identity as Cinema V, a repertory film center with second-run, art and cult films. It was acquired by Famous Players in 1987 and operated as a first-run two-screen movie theater until August 11, 1992, when a minor fire occurred in the theater.

Situated at the intersection of Sherbrooke Street West and Old Orchard Avenue, the location of the Empress in a residential neighborhood allowed for a generous façade of seventy-six feet in width, which is uncommon for downtown movie theaters because of expensive real estate values. Moreover, its location across the street from NDG Park confers a broad panorama on the wide façade. Camouflaged behind the trees of the park, the Egyptian movie theater progressively appears in the descent to Sherbrooke Street West. This processional approach connects two vital spaces for the social life of the neighborhood: the cultural landmark of the movie theater and the public space of the park. This approach from the north reveals the Empress's façade from a high-angle shot, a majestic vista whose stunning impact emphasizes the distinctiveness of the Egyptian-inspired movie theater in the predominantly "white" and anglophone middle-class neighborhood.

The cinematic Egyptian complex includes two sections. The main section is the movie theater itself, while a slightly recessed mixed-use section composed of apartment units, offices and stores rounds up the corner of Old Orchard Street (Empress Cultural Centre 2013). The tripartite cast stone façade of the theatre is composed of a highly decorated central section with two flanking side bays. The central section is clearly demarcated by two pilasters and a giant Ramses head surmounted on each of them. The busts of the pharaoh thus interrupt the hieroglyphic inscriptions of the cornice, a rupture emphasized by the sun-disc motifs which crown them. The low reliefs of an Egyptian couple in profile frame the large windows of the mezzanine level, while palm leaves decorate the capital of the pilasters. Four groups of lotus flowers are repeated between the two pilasters, a horizontal motif which balances the verticality of the façade. In the early days of the Empress, a vertical electric marquee attached to the central engaged column further divided the façade in two. The symmetrical side bays feature similar Egyptian motifs: palm-leaves capitals, hieroglyphic inscriptions, sun-disc motifs and lotus flowers. In brief, the Empress's façade is a spectacular and unified ensemble: its monumental framing pilasters are reminiscent of the pylons and obelisks of the Temple of Edfu in Upper Egypt, 251–237 BCE (Cohen-Rose 1996: 97).

The lobby on the ground floor is the least ornamented section of the building because of the inclined terrain and irregular corner site (Kolomeir 1987: 39). The asymmetrical plan of the movie theater being ill-suited for a vast entrance lobby, Chaussé simplified the lobby to its only essential constituent: the ticket office. Stores outside the lobby further limited the space available, a restriction which Briffa turned into an opportunity to highlight the décor of the mezzanine. After the simple and functional space of the lobby, the make-believe architecture unfolds on the mezzanine with the rest room[4] whose walls are painted with vegetal motifs and hieroglyphs, simulating hanging drapes [Figure 13.2]. The rest room features a fireplace, painted with Egyptian figures in profile and sun-disc motifs "to symbolize the ancient rite of tending the sacred fires" (Royal Architectural Institute of

FIGURE 13.2 Rest room on mezzanine floor, showing fireplace, Empress Theatre, Montreal, 1928. Royal Architectural Institute of Canada.

Canada 1928: 396). In Chaussé's plan, however, an electric fountain is drawn in lieu of the fireplace. Suited to the Egyptian theme and tropical climate, the fountain was likely considered discordant with Quebec's harsh winters, and so further helps to remove movie-goers from the mundane.

Despite the elaborate façade, the auditorium of the Empress remains the focus of the building. The Empress, however, is not an atmospheric theater in the sense of Eberson's definition, since the ceiling is divided into five vaults with domes, painted in blue with pale stars of the early evening (Lanken 1993: 127). The ceiling of a "true" atmospheric theater would be uninterrupted to simulate the nocturnal sky, hence the nickname of "soft-top." Nonetheless, the immersive atmosphere of the Empress's auditorium is effective. Framed pilasters topped with a pharaoh's bust, similar to the giant Ramses heads of the façade, interrupt the *trompe-l'œil* panels of the side walls. The fictive landscape of the side walls features columns of ancient temples, pyramids, sphinxes and giant figures in stone [Figure 13.3]. Highly detailed pilasters, incised with hieroglyphic inscriptions in the same horizontal bands ending in papyrus leaves, frame the proscenium arch. On either side of the stage stands a life-size statue of an Egyptian girl carrying a vase which is tipping forward into a fountain. The asbestos curtain of the proscenium contributed to this make-believe Egyptian ambiance when it

FIGURE 13.3 West wall, from balcony, Empress Theatre, Montreal, 1928. Royal Architectural Institute of Canada.

FIGURE 13.4 Proscenium arch and asbestos curtain, Empress Theatre, Montreal, 1928. Royal Architectural Institute of Canada.

was drawn between performances. The asbestos curtain features a *trompe-l'œil* painting, with a pylon[5] in the receding distance, surrounded by decorated pilasters and palm trees in the background which reinforced the perspectival effect [Figure 13.4]. The *trompe-l'œil* landscape extends the illusion of reality from the space of the auditorium to the fictive space beyond in an ethereal crescendo: the screen, the movie and the imagination.

Heterotopia: The intersection of near and far

As an immersive and thematic environment, the atmospheric movie theater belongs to the typology of themed spaces, which cultural anthropologist Scott A. Lukas defines as "the use of an overarching theme, such as western, to create a holistic and integrated spatial organization of a consumer venue" (2007: 1). Theming, however, is not an authentic representation of reality but a projection of desire based on simulation, immersion and narrativity. Theming is a limited inclusion of a given theme, a stereotype and approximation of time, an event, place, person or culture (Lukas 2007: 272). Among themed spaces, Egyptian-inspired movie theaters have a particular status related to the affiliation between Egypt and cinema. Antonia Lant notes that Egyptology had a legacy for cinema since "[even] before the arrival of cinema, writers on Egypt associated that culture with magic, preservation and silent, visual power—all qualities that anticipate the character of cinema" (1992: 104). Egypt itself is singular in the colonial project because of its geographical location as Europe's entry point to the East. Egypt is not just *any* Other, but a gateway to other Other(s) (Lant 1992: 98). This distinctiveness resulted in a fascination for Egypt, or Egyptomania, which consists in the borrowing "of the most spectacular elements, from the grammar of ornament that is the original essence of ancient Egypt art" (Humbert et al. 1994: 21). The Egyptian Revival is linked to specific historical events such as Napoleon's Egyptian campaign (1798–1801), the deciphering of hieroglyphics by Jean-François Champollion in 1822, the opening of the Suez Canal in 1869 and, in the case of atmospheric movie theaters, the discovery of the tomb of Tutankhamun by Howard Carter in November 1922 (Humbert et al. 1994: 22, 508). In brief, Egypt was a significant geographical reference for atmospheric movie theaters as the border between East and West and translated into a gateway from the real to the imaginary.

Several decades before atmospheric movie theaters made their appearance, themed exotic movie theaters were introduced in world fairs and amusement parks. According to the architect and theater historian Craig Morrison, "the buildings and surroundings of the World's Columbian Exposition—a sort of stage set, an illusion, an outdoor theatre—had a profound and lasting effect on the design of places where Americans gathered for enlightenment and fun" (Morrison 2006: 173). In 1893, the World's Columbian Exposition of Chicago crowned the unparalleled European colonial expansion between 1815 and 1914, fueled the Oriental Renaissance and epitomized the fascination for the exotic. With its staggering attendance of twenty-one million visitors, the Chicago World's Fair contributed to the dissemination of stereotypical representations of the East through themed spaces. As simulacra, these partial representations of exoticized cultures are each "subject to conditions of time and place. All of these images are partial and contrived; none is 'true' or 'accurate'" (Edwards et al. 2000: 14). Indeed, the aesthectic of quotation, or pastiche, deconstructs chronological order and geographical borders to enable the emergence of spaces of cultural translation.

A direct descendant of the exoticized pavilions of world fairs and amusement parks, the Empress testifies to the fascination for Egypt and its adaptation in the built form. Briffa selected motifs such as sphinxes, pharaohs and pyramids that would have been readily identifiable as foreign and exotic by the audience. According to Said, Orientalism is based on a structure of myths which have led to its standardization and cultural stereotyping in the Western mind (1978: 6). As such, "[the] idea of representation is a theatrical one: the Orient is the stage on which the whole East is confined. On this stage will appear figures whose role is to represent the larger whole from which they emanate" (Said 1978: 63). The make-believe ambiance of the Empress Theatre thus relies on the circularity of specific motifs which synecdochically stand for Egypt, among which the sphinx is the most representative and widespread motif of Egyptomania because it is instantly recognizable (Humbert et al. 1994: 22). In the Empress, the sphinx appears on the background of the painted landscape of the auditorium's side wall and over the cornice of the auditorium. Several Egyptian motifs such as busts of pharaohs, sun-disc motifs, palm leaves, lotus flowers and hieroglyphs are repeated inside and outside the movie theater. Hieroglyphics materialize this architecture of make-believe: the drawings only can be understood, their cryptic signification being left to experts. Atmospheric movie theaters are thus deceptively authentic: such Orientalist spaces project an idea of the exoticized Other, without entirely giving access to it. Their foreignness flirts with the everyday while being resolutely distinct from it, a tension which reinforces their ability to move film-goers.

The Empress and other Egyptian-inspired buidlings do not merely replicate Egypt, they consolidate the exotic with the local in a hybrid process, which engenders a sort of heterotopia. Introduced by Michel Foucault in 1967, heterotopias are places "capable of juxtaposing in a single real space several spaces, several sites that are in themselves incompatible" (Windover 2009: 217). In opposition to utopias, which are sites with no real place, heterotopias may be located in reality, although they are outside all places: its real sites are simultaneously represented, contested and inverted. Noteworthy is that Foucault classifies the movie theater as a heterotopia. Nonetheless, as noted by architectural historian Michael Windover, Foucault's description of the movie theater as a "very odd rectangular room, at the end of which, on a two-dimensional screen, one sees the projection of a three-dimensional space" (1984: 47) is far from the excessive decoration and ornamentation of the atmospheric movie theater (Windover 2009: 222). The atmospheric movie theater, however, is a form of heterotopia because of the malleability of time and space intrinsic to the building type.

Although the Empress refers to a single culture, the movie theater remains a heterotopia because it consolidates places that are foreign to one another. The building itself is a simulation of Egypt, but located in Montreal; it screens movies made in Hollywood but filmed in numerous locations. Such spatial hybridity is enabled by a temporal fracture which allows film-goers to escape momentarily from the humdrum of daily life. This temporary break from traditional time is also the fourth principle of the heterotopia, as either an indefinite accumulation of time or celebration of its transitoriness. The movie theater fuses durability and ephemerality. The building itself is permanent, but the movies it "houses" leave only fleeting impressions, a reminder of Baudelaire's definition of modernity as a combination of the eternal and the fugitive (Baudelaire 1995: 13). As a heterotopia, the Empress facilitates the coexistence of multiple realities that could not have met otherwise: East/West, permanence/transience, materiality/virtuality. The temporary escape it offers thereby leads to another type of discovery, not a physical but an imaginary exploration of unknown destinations.

Imagination: Fictive and affective tourism

The destination of this cinematic trip is not exactly the site simulated by the building, but another space with endless possibilites: the imagination. In atmospheric movie theaters, spectators become visitors (Bruno 2002: 62). As noted by architectural historian Amir H. Ameri, in "this exotic and Oriental imaginary, the moviegoers were transformed into visiting tourists in a foreign displaced and displacing land, where film stood in the same relationship to the real, as Orient did to Occident" (2011: 88). The atmospheric movie theater of the Empress is a displaced Egypt in the predominantly "white" neighborhood of NDG. It is also a displacing space, in which for a small fee, movie-goers are offered "opportunities to see and experience (again, largely virtually) spaces that not too long beforehand had generally been unavailable to any but colonizers" (Windover 2009: 221). Cinema and tourism are both mass phenomena and leisure activities for pleasure and spectacle consumption (Bruno 2002: 82). The peculiarity of the Empress is that it offers both activities: cinema as the primary focus of the building and tourism as its second.

This cinematic tourism is two-fold: the spatial experience of the movie theater is a form of traveling in itself since it enables the discovery of Egypt through the fictive but realistic landscapes painted on the side walls and asbestos curtain of the auditorium. In the Empress, two life-size statues of Egyptian women on each side of the proscenium arch reinforce the illusion of reality [Figure 13.5]. A similar human presence enhanced the fictive Egyptian décor of the *Champollion*, one of the three Messageries Maritimes steamships launched between 1924 and 1926 (Humbert et all 1994: 524). In the niches of the first-class stairway, two painted-wood statues of Egyptian women provided a foretaste of the destination [Figure 13.6]. The statues' elaborate jewelled neckpieces are a token of luxury: in the *Champollion*, the journey to Egypt was not only symbolic, but real, Egypt being the final goal of the trip. Although only a partial discovery of Egypt, cinematic tourism was embraced by movie-goers since the actual trip could only be afforded by the privileged few. In both cases, however, Egyptian theming surpasses the two-dimensional surface treatment. The panoramas of the painted landscapes are complemented by the corporeality of the statues. The spatial experience is both optical and haptical, unfolding through the sense of sight, with color, light and perspectival effects, and with the sense of touch, through the depth, scale and delimitation of objects. The three-dimensional statues invade the space of the cinematic and cruising travelers, transforming the fantasy into a lived reality.

In Grauman's Egyptian Theater, an explicit reference for Montreal's Empress with its massive pseudo-Egyptian iconography, the evocation of Egypt was not solely limited to the built form: employees would wear costumes to enliven the fictive décor (Kolomeir 1987: 39) [Figure 13.7]. As noted by Ben M. Hall, "[the] Egyptian's architectural wonders were not confined to the auditorium; pacing up and down on the parapet at the end of the great forecourt was a bearded Bedouin in a striped robe carrying a spear" (1961: 211). Although

FIGURE 13.5 Fountain and part of stage, Empress Theatre, Montreal, 1928. Royal Architectural Institute of Canada.

there is no evidence of such practice at the Empress, the make-believe ambiance remains indissociable from the ethos of atmospheric movie theaters. The combination of cinema, immersive architecture and performance in the Empress results in a multi-sensorial experience: the *Gesamtkuntswerk*. This form of artistic synthesis, which harmonizes several art forms simultaneously, is associated with the operas of Richard Wagner (Knapp 1999: 7). The bodily experience of the Empress converts the predominantly visual experience of cinema into an all-encompassing event, in which movie-goers are not only passive consumers, but active participants in this culture of spectacle.

Traveling is not limited, however, to the spatial experience of the building: the narratives of movies displace and "move" film-goers. As a result, cinematic

THE CINEMATIC LANDSCAPE OF THE EMPRESS THEATRE 231

FIGURE 13.6 First-class stairway of the Champollion steamship (1924), decorated with a painting of Jean Lefeuvre. © Collection Jean-Marcel Humbert.

FIGURE 13.7 Usherettes of Grauman's Egyptian Theater, Hollywood, California, c.1922–1923. © Collection Jean-Marcel Humbert.

tourism is both an outward and inward journey. For Antonia Lant, "the use of Egyptianate elements in cinema design may thus be feeding precisely on this transitional aura, on this power to signify a passage to a new scene, a promise of changing experience" (Lant 1992: 98). The spatial sequence of the Empress activates this transition from reality to fiction. The monumental façade, which recalls the gateway of an Egyptian temple, augurs the timeless experience that awaits movie-goers inside the building. The rest room, with its vegetal and hieroglyphic motifs, provides a human scale to this immersive cinematic experience. Fiction, however, truly unfolds in the auditorium: the *trompe-l'oeil* landscapes of the side walls and asbestos curtain dissolve the enclosed space of the movie theater. After all, cinema is based on projection: the actual projection of movies on a screen, as well as the immaterial projection of hopes, desires, and dreams that propel movie-goers to places attainable only with the imagination.

The recognition of the importance of imagination in architecture challenges the assumption of the materiality of buildings. Shelley Hornstein argues that architecture not only exists as a physical entity, but also in the recollection of the physical site (2011: 3). For Hornstein, this intangible architecture lies within the memory and heart of the users. The affective experience of architecture is in accordance with the building type of the movie theater, as a space in which the whole gamut of emotions is sparked by the movies projected on the screen. The case of the Empress Theatre further attests to the crucial role of imagination in the conception and experience of architecture. Indeed, Briffa's assistant Joffre Gendron, who worked with the Maltese-born decorator from 1935, asserted that his master "[. . .] rarely did preliminary drawings for his paintings and stencils, rather sketching and creating on the spot" (Kolomeir 1987: 29). Gendron further reported that Briffa owned a book of designs, which he consulted when he sought inspiration for a new movie theater commission (Lanken 2013). The Egyptian décor of the Empress was imagined and shaped by Briffa, with his own knowledge, perception and interpretation of Egypt. For theater historian Ben M. Hall, "the movie palace architect was an escape artist. It was his mission to build new dream worlds for the disillusioned; and as he piled detail on detail, each prism, each gilded cherub, every jewel-eyed dragon became part of a whole . . . a feast for the eye, a catapult for the imagination" (1961: 94). Briffa and his assistants thus provided a basic framework that would trigger the imagination of movie-goers who, subsequently, would build their own imaginary architecture.

Conclusion

The building of the Empress Theatre captures and stimulates the imagination of movie-goers. The Empress is not any genuine depiction of Egypt. Rather, it is its creative representation through the amalgamation of several symbols and ornamental details which enhance the magical experience of cinema. For journalist and film critic Dane Lanken, the eclecticism of atmospheric movie theaters is intrinsically linked to the art of cinema: "I think that was one of the nice things about movie theaters, you could mix things, it didn't matter to have Roman columns and Native American designs altogether, it didn't matter at all. [. . .] It's all part of the same thing, being moved by the movie theater or being moved by the movie itself" (Lanken 2013). In this improbable reconciliation of East and West, the Empress is a hybrid space that challenges the fixity of geographical barriers. The movie theater is not Egypt, Montreal or Hollywood. Its physical location in Notre-Dame-de-Grâce is the only stable site of its polymorphous geography, since its real location is grounded in the imagination of each and every movie-goer. The immersive ambiance of the Empress thus empowers movie-goers to transcend the materiality of the building and shape their own architecture of the imagination.

Notes

1 The origin of the blue ceiling with painted silver stars is attributed to the Prussian architect Karl Friedrich Schinkel and his stage design for Mozart's opera *The Magic Flute* in Berlin in 1816 (Humbert et al. 1994: 405).
2 Atmospheric movie theaters would be followed a few decades later by genuine "soft-tops," the drive-in theaters, which had only the actual sky vault for a ceiling.
3 After the Empress followed the Spanish-inspired Monkland Theater in 1930, the streamlined Art Deco Snowdon in 1937 and the Kent in 1941 (Pelletier 2012: 254).
4 In this context, the rest room of the Empress corresponds to the British definition of the word, which is "a room (usually in a public building) set aside for rest and quiet," and not the American definition of "lavatory" (*Oxford English Dictionary*).
5 The pylon is "a monumental gateway to an ancient Egyptian temple formed by two truncated pyramidal towers" (*Oxford English Dictionary*).

References

Ameri, A. (2011), "Imaginary Placements: The Other Space of Cinema," *Journal of Aesthetics and Art Criticism*, 69(1): Special Issue, *The Aesthetics of Architecture: Philosophical Investigations into the Art of Building*: 81–91.
Baudelaire, C. (1995), *The Painter of Modern Life and Other Essays*, trans. J. Mayne, 2nd edn, London: Phaidon Press.
Bruno, G. (2002), *Atlas of Emotion: Journeys in Art, Architecture and Film*, London and New York: Verso.
Cameco Capitol Arts Center (n.d.), "Capitol Theater: 1930 to Present," Capitol Theater.
Cohen-Rose, S. (1996), *Northern Deco: Art Deco Architecture in Montreal*, Montreal: Corona Publishers.
Corporation de développement économique communautaire Côte-des-Neiges/Notre-Dame-de-Grâce, "Portrait of the Borough" 2009 [Accessed October 8,

2013]. http://www.cdeccdnndg.org/index.php/en/the-cdec/portrait-of-the-borough.html.

Edwards, H., et al. (2000), *Noble Dreams, Wicked Pleasures: Orientalism in America, 1870–1930*, Princeton, NJ: Princeton University Press in association with the Sterling and Francine Clark Art Institute.

Empress Cultural Centre, "History of the Empress" [Accessed October 14, 2013]. http://empresscentre.com/webE/?page_id=57.

Foucault, M. (1984), "Of Other Spaces, Heterotopias," *Architecture, Mouvement, Continuité*, 5: 46–49.

Hall, B. (1961), *The Best Remaining Seats: The Story of the Golden Age of the Movie Palace*, New York: C. N. Potter.

Herzog, C. (1981), "The Movie Palace and the Theatrical Sources of Its Architectural Style," *Cinema Journal*, 20(2): 15–37.

Hornstein, S. (2011), *Losing Site: Architecture, Memory, and Place*, Burlington, Vermont: Ashgate.

Humbert, J.-M., et al. (1994), *Egyptomania: Egypt in Western Art, 1730–1930*. Ottawa; Paris: National Gallery of Canada; Réunion des Musées Nationaux.

Kinerk, M. and D. Wilhelm (1998), "Dream Palaces: The Motion Picture Playhouse in the Sunshine State," *The Journal of Decorative and Propaganda Arts*, 23, Florida Theme Issue: 208–237.

Knapp, G. (1999), *Neuschwanstein*, Stuttgart and London: Edition Axel Menges.

Kolomeir, H. (1987), "The Neighborhood Movie House in Montreal 1925–1929: The Harmonious Whole," Master's Thesis, Concordia University.

Lanken, D. (1993), *Montreal Movie Palaces: Great Theatres of the Golden Era, 1884–1938*, Waterloo, Ontario: Archives of Canadian Art.

Lanken, D. (2013), Interview by author. Personal interview, Montreal.

Lant, A. (1992), "The Curse of the Pharaoh, or How Cinema Contracted Egyptomania," *October*, 59: 86–112.

Lukas, S. (2007), *The Themed Space: Locating Culture, Nation, and Self*, Lanham, MD: Lexington Books.

Martineau, J. (1988), "Les salles de cinéma construites avant 1940 sur le territoire de la Communauté urbaine de Montréal; Volume 1, Cahier 1: Analyse, synthèse et évaluation patrimoniale," Montreal.

Morrison, C. (2006), *Theaters*, Washington, DC: Norton/Library of Congress Visual Sourcebooks in Architecture, Design and Engineering.

Pelletier, L. (2012), "The Fellows Who Dress the Pictures: Montreal Film Exhibitors in the Days of Vertical Integration (1912–1952)," PhD dissertation, Concordia University.

Royal Architectural Institute of Canada (1928), "The New Empress Theatre, Montreal," *The Journal of the Royal Architectural Institute of Canada*: 392–396.

Russell, H. (1991), "The Capitol Theater, Cornwall, Ontario," Gatineau, Qc: Federal Heritage Buildings Review Office: 171–187.

Said, E. (1978), *Orientalism*, New York: Random House.

Valentine, M. (1994), *The Show Starts on the Sidewalk: An Architectural History of the Movie Theater, Starring S. Charles Lee*, New Haven: Yale University Press.

Windover, M. (2009), "Exchanging Looks: 'Art Dekho' Movie Theaters in Bombay," *Architectural History*, 52: 201–232.

14

"Flights of Unpractical Fancy": Oriental Spaces at Sea from the *Titanic* to the *Empress of Britain*

Anne Massey

One important, but overlooked, part of a history of Oriental interiors to date is a consideration of the spaces within the ocean liner. The interior design of these ships makes a unique contribution to this volume on the Oriental, as the liners often traveled to the Orient itself plus the styling of these ship-based interiors occupies a unique position within the discourse of design. This chapter focuses on British ocean liners; British global interests and power were served and sustained by these passenger ships that circumnavigated the globe. Imperial power was exerted and reinforced through these vessels, which physically carried passengers, mail and goods from Britain around the world and back again.[1] The ships provided vital links with North America, sailing westwards to service the huge immigrant trade and for the trans-Atlantic voyages of wealthier business and leisure travelers before the age of air travel.[2] The ships also traveled east, to Africa and Asia on these global trade routes. Despite the fact that many of these ships traveled to and from the Orient, and that shipping companies and ships were named after the Orient, the Oriental style was rarely used for the design of the exterior or interior. The style was only evident within the liminal spaces of the ships, predominately the Turkish Bath and the Verandah Café. What were the reasons for this apparent marginalization?

Historiography and the ocean liner interior

Existing scholarship on the "Oriental," particularly within the discipline of art history, tends to simplify and stereotype representations of the East in painting (Nochlin 1989). Research in the field of cultural history has explored the meanings and proliferation of the Oriental in terms of architecture and design, particularly in the work of John M. MacKenzie (1995). As MacKenzie has argued: "By the twentieth century, Orientalism had certainly become the language of pleasure and relaxation" (1995: 89). However, his convincing case studies did not extend beyond land-based examples, and did not encompass the interiors of ocean liners.

The historiography of the ocean liner itself as an object of study is dominated by histories which accentuate nostalgia and the lost luxury of transatlantic travel, many in "coffee table"-type books, which are heavily illustrated (Ulrich 1998). The main concentration of published books centers on the *Titanic*, the tragedy of the sinking contrasts hauntingly with high-class passenger travel. In terms of general design history, Greg Votolato's book *Ship* adds significantly to the field by providing a critical context for the study of ocean-going travel (Votolato 2011), whilst Philip Dawson and Bruce Peter's *Ship Style* privileges modernism in the book's account of ship exteriors and interiors (Dawson and Peter 2010). Apart from these two publications, and the author's *Designing Liners: Interior Design Afloat* (Wealleans: 2006), little recent work on the interior covers the ship, or indeed, transport more generally.

This could be due to a concentration on the domestic as opposed to the commercial in the study of the interior as an emerging field of enquiry. Such studies demonstrate a rootedness in time and space, they are landlocked, a snapshot, frozen in a particular moment (Brooker 2013). There are some exceptions, which successfully trace the changing appearance and meaning of a particular interior as representation through time (Penner and Rice 2013). The ship interior represents a challenge, in that it is a space which moves both through time and through different geographical contexts. Docking at a variety of ports, the visual culture of one nation is brought into a forced conversation with another. This transnational dialog provides the context for this chapter.

Concentrating more closely on the Oriental spaces at sea particularly, I would argue that they add an extra dimension to a consideration of the Oriental and of the Oriental interior. Not only is there evidence of some minority spaces being decorated in the Oriental style, but many of the ships also physically moved to and from the places of the Orient carrying passengers to service the British Empire eastwards, to Egypt, India, Singapore, Australia and Hong Kong and back home again. They constituted physical reminders of British power, wielded unapologetically on the world's oceans and in the world's ports [Figure 14.1]. They were the lifeblood of the British Empire, connecting trade routes and servicing the administration of this global economy. And not just the economics

FIGURE 14.1 Charles Edward Dixon RI, *Orient Line to Australia*, poster, lithograph printed in ten colors on paper laid on board and varnished, c.1912. © P&O Heritage Collection, www.poheritage.com.

of the Empire but its political structures in terms of conveying diplomats and civil servants; the defence of the Empire in the form of military personnel and its cultural infrastructure in the shape of teachers and the clergy.

Whilst the ships traveled to locations within the Orient, and beyond, their exteriors were symbolic of Imperial might and technological prowess, they were representations of modernity. There were no concessions made to the decorative devices of the Orient. Their masts and funnels towered high above their multi-decked structures. Sleek and sophisticated, they were built for speed and reliability, physically dominating the world's oceans and the shores of the British Empire. Constructed from iron and steel, their only decoration would be decision about the company colors used to paint the exteriors—red funnels with black tops for the Cunard Line, for example, and in this case the Orient Line with golden funnels represented here by the *Otranto* navigating the Suez Canal in 1912. But this is not simply a story of one-way domination. With the Oriental interiors on board the ships, there is evidence of a hybridity at work, of inter-play and transnational communication.

To understand the complex role and function of the Oriental interior at sea, it is important to first understand the more general context of ship interior design. Throughout the nineteenth and twentieth centuries, it was the naval architect who was responsible for the design of the ship's structure and layout, and it was only during construction that the design of the interiors was given any consideration by the client, that is, the shipping line (see Wealleans 2006). Therefore, ocean liners present a unique part of the history of the interior as their exteriors are essentially machines designed for movement on water. The exterior envelopes the interior spaces in a different way to land-based architecture. These floating objects of transit needed to guarantee safety of passage first and foremost. The comfort of the passenger was a secondary, but related, consideration. As Sir Colin Anderson, Chairman of the Orient Line during the 1930s, argued in his 1966 Royal Society of the Arts lecture:

> It is impossible to separate the design of ship interiors from the overpowering functional need for everything within a ship to be shipshape. There is no place in a ship for haphazard effects or for flights of unpractical fancy. In this, there is a fundamental difference between the design of a passenger ship and that of a house or even an hotel.
>
> (Anderson 1966: 478)

Anderson summarized here an attitude towards ship interior design on behalf of the shipping-line owners, which privileged the perceived practicalities of maritime travel over the styling of the ships' passenger spaces. The "flights of unpractical fancy" can be closely aligned with the Oriental interior. These were spaces for the imagination to run wild, for relaxation and bodily comfort and luxury, and far removed from the "shipshape" vision of Anderson. It is also revealing that Anderson associates "flights of fancy" with the domestic or hotel interior.

P&O ships: Serving the Empire

The floating space of the ocean liner was divided into several decks, which were then partitioned into separate areas of working for the crew and for transitory eating, sleeping, socializing and amusement for the passengers. As such, they bear a resemblance to hotel structures. The differentiated spaces on the separate decks dictated certain roles and performativity within them, even from the earliest days of commercial passenger travel within the Empire. For example, the first ship to be built for the main British company to service the Empire on the route eastwards, the Peninsular and Oriental Steam Navigation Company (P&O) was the *Hindostan*, completed in 1842. A wooden paddle steamer, the ship was 66.32 meters in length with a 10.91-meter beam and depth of 9.17 meters. It had 60 cabins that accommodated 102 passengers and 50 passengers' servants. These were unusually situated in the center of the ship, with gangways either side buffeting the passengers from the extreme heat and noise of the sea. The dining room was placed at the rear, or stern, of the *Hindostan*. Normally, the cabins would have led off the dining room, as was the case with Brunel's *SS Great Britain* (see Wealleans 2006: 13–18).

The *Hindostan* was named after the term used for British India in the nineteenth century, and the ship traveled from Southampton to Calcutta and back again from 1842 until 1864, when it was sunk by the great Calcutta Cyclone. The ship's route included Gibraltar, St Vincent, Ascension, Capetown, Mauritius and Point de Galle, which took ninety-one days in total on the first voyage. The ship entered the service to Madras, Galle, Aden and Suez that linked with the Overland Route through Egypt, before the opening of the Suez Canal in 1869 when passengers were forced to travel eighty-four miles across the desert in horse-drawn wagons. P&O offered one sailing from Calcutta to Britain per month in the 1840s, with two other ships, the *Bentinck* and the *Precursor*, which P&O brought into service for the route.

Information about the layout of the *Hindostan* can be gleaned from the ship's plans, but no other contemporary visual representation exists. A valuable, written source is the memoir by "A Madras Officer" from 1846 entitled, *The Ocean and the Desert*. This reveals the cramped and uncomfortable spaces on board these early passenger ships. The author complained of:

> The accommodations for passengers are poor, cramped, and badly ventilated, built with the intentions, evidently, of cramming as many living souls into as small a space as possible. The number of people between decks, to say nothing of the fires in the engine room, render the heat insufferable, in spite of the wind-sails down each hatchway. There are ports, fore and aft, but they are not allowed to be opened at sea. The cabins are so small, that there is scarcely room for *one*

individual, far less for two; and it is so dark down below, that you can scarcely see.

(A Madras Officer 1843: 8)

The decoration of the passenger spaces is detailed in his account of the dining room. The author refers to:

gaudy *papier mache* colourings, descriptions of various subjects; the staunchions and rudder-head, as well as the mast . . . . are all painted with flowers in the most beautifully arranged groups I ever saw, tastefully embellished with fountains and . . . other ornaments. The appearance of the whole was superb, when lighted of an evening, which it was with argaund lamps suspended from the ceiling; large mirrors at each end, and book-cases, nearly fitted up . . .

(A Madras Officer 1843: 11–12)

The furniture was constructed from mahogany and the fixtures from brass. This type of interior decoration was typical of ship interiors and more broadly, public interiors, of the time, and did not include Oriental references. This only came with reference to the name of the ship and its passengers. A report from the *Illlustrated London News* about *The Bentick* mentions the "health, comfort or luxury of oriental voyagers" (1843); so the term was in common usage by that time, to refer in general to travel eastwards from Great Britain. There was the basic style of the cabins, which contrasted with the early Victorian, Renaissance revival public interiors, resplendent with painted decoration, reflective mahogany, etched mirrors and polished brass. These interiors were designed by the ship builders, who would engage local furniture and furnishing suppliers to fit out the interiors in mainstream, popular styles; these were essentially commercial interiors. During the nineteenth century, the Oriental style was reserved for predominately land-based places of entertainment and display. Temporary exhibition spaces and seaside piers drew heavily on the style, but these were spaces of leisure and entertainment. What was needed for the interior design of ocean liners was reassurance and comfort. Travel by sea was dangerous and challenging, passengers needed to be reassured that they would eventually arrive at their chosen destination in relative safety and security, the perception was, as Anderson argued, that this was not a space for frivolity or "flights of unpractical fancy." The Oriental interior was used for the purposes of display and fantasy by adventurous collectors or artists, some linked to the sea. For example, wealthy shipping line owner Frederick Richards Leyland commissioned James McNeil Whistler to create the Oriental interior *par excellence* with the Peacock Room in 1877 (Huxtable 2013) and Lord Leighton commissioned the Arab Hall, also in 1877. The ceramicist William de Morgan contributed to the design of the Arab Hall, which included fifteenth- and sixteenth-century tiles, mainly from Damascus. De Morgan was commissioned to supply and design Oriental tiles for eight ocean liners by P&O from 1882 until 1900, but these did not contribute to an overall Oriental interior scheme.

De Morgan drew his inspiration from fifteenth- and sixteenth-century Isnik ware, using the distinctive dark blue, turquoise and white for his abstract, Oriental designs. But the tiles were not used in the cabins or main public rooms on the ships, which were decorated in historic Western European styles. The Oriental tiles were used to line the passageways, as they provided a robust facing, which would withstand the repeated wear of passengers and crew making their way between the separate areas on board. The tiles also offered a welcome coolness to the interior corridors, given the extremities of heat on board the ships. The one room for which the De Morgan tiles were used was the Smoking Room, due to nicotine staining, ceramic tiles provided the perfect wipe-clean finish. De Morgan also supplied specially commissioned tile panels for the smoking rooms, often depicting historic galleons in Arts and Crafts style, but also abstract, Oriental panels. As MacKenzie has argued, the Oriental style was often associated with particular consumer goods, particularly tea and tobacco, therefore the use of this style in the Smoking Room exemplified this trend (1995: 89).

De Morgan was commissioned by P&O directly, and subsequently by the architect T. E. Collcutt, from 1896 onwards. However, it was the Orient Line, formed in 1877 to service the journey between the UK and Australia, which was the first shipping line to use an architect specifically for the design of its ship interiors. The Arts and Crafts architect J. J. Stevenson was employed to style the Orient Line ships' public spaces, beginning with the *Orient* in 1877. Stevenson went on to design four more ship interiors for the Orient Line, using the Arts and Crafts and Aesthetic Movement styles, employing artists such as Walter Crane and Knox and Webb to create very English interior spaces, despite the name of the ships and the line. There was little acknowledgement of the Oriental which gave the Line, and the ship, its name. The Orient Line always used a professional designer to style its interiors, which gave them high design values and a homogenous quality. This continued until the 1930s, when ships such as the modernist *Orion* in 1935 entered the Australian service, with Marion Dorn rugs and modern interiors by Brian O'Rorke, all commissioned by Colin Anderson. But there was little of the Oriental in evidence on the Orient Line and its voyages via the Orient, including Port Said and Aden. The Line wanted to project a serviceable, safe image based on reliability and function, the Oriental simply did not fit with the image. There were no "flights of unpractical fancy."

The White Star Line: Floating luxury hotels

However, when the more commercially focussed White Star line is considered, the Oriental style was used, if sparingly, in the design of its interiors for the trans-Atlantic route from Southampton to New York. These were much more substantial ships, the *Olympic* of 1911 was the biggest to be launched in the world at that time, with a length of 882 feet (268.8 meters), compared to the *Orion* of 665 feet (202.7 meters). The design of the White Star ocean liner interiors was undertaken by the ship-fitting company, Aldam Heaton & Co., and presented a hybridity of style, expressing a commercial vernacular, there were "unpractical flights of fancy." White Star's *Olympic* entered service in 1911, and the *Titanic* the following year, with first-class Turkish baths and steam rooms decorated in Oriental style, comingling with a panoply of Western European styles for the more public spaces on both ships. Entire rooms in French Louis XIV, XV, XVI and Empire style were located next to each other, providing the first-class passengers with the experience of moving through time while moving on the sea. First-class cabins were decorated in Old Dutch and Modern Dutch, whilst other public rooms plundered the Georgian, Queen Anne and Adam styles. But Oriental-style interiors were used for the more private, obscure spaces on board the ship.

The Turkish baths were tucked away, comparatively low down in the ship, on F deck between the swimming pool and third-class dining room. Better to flood the third-class accommodation than the first class higher up the ship, as there were always potential leakage issues. The water in the swimming pool would be heavy (one cubic meter weighs a metric tonne) and so it would need to be situated as near the ship's center line as possible and also low down in its center of gravity. Even when the ship was sailing on calm seas, the water could be liable to move around unpredictably, which could make the ship unstable if the pool was placed at the top. The Turkish Baths would need to be situated adjacent to the swimming pool, hence they were always fitted lower down, snuggled amongst the third-class quarters.

White Star had pioneered the inclusion of the Turkish Baths on board its ships, the first being on the *Adriatic* in 1907 for first-class passengers, which was not in a specifically Oriental style. However, the *Olympic* and *Titanic*'s Turkish Baths three years later were exclusively Oriental. The ships were built to compete with the Cunard liners, *Mauretania* and *Lusitania* so there was substantial investment in building the most luxurious ships in history. Famously, and tragically, the ships also met and even exceeded the safety legislation of the time.

The Turkish baths were subdivided into various areas for the performance of cleansing and, relaxation ending in a cold plunge pool. Unlike the first Turkish bath in London, the Jermyn Street Hammam of 1862, the space was open to both men and women, but at different times to ensure propriety (Potvin 2005). Women could use the facilities from 10 in the morning until 1 in the afternoon, and men from 2 in the afternoon until 7 in the evening, at a fairly hefty extra charge of 4 shillings. The large cooling room was decorated in seventeenth-century Turkish style with two matching shampoo rooms, an intermediate room and a hot room. The walls were tiled from the dado upwards in Oriental, blue and green patterned ceramic. The dado, doors and paneling were in teak. Bronze, Arabian-style lamps hung from the ceilings, which were gilded and highlighted in red, and a drinking fountain provided another Oriental reference. The day beds were decorated in Oriental style with bolster cushions, and Oriental-style octagonal occasional tables completed the scheme. This was a space for "unpractical flights of fancy," for escape, bodily pleasure, display and relaxation. The portholes of the cooling room were covered with carved, Oriental screens, as the contemporary publicity boasted: "through which the light fitfully reveals something of the grandeur of the mysterious East" (White Star 1911: 43). The East remained mysterious for these ocean liners, present as a fantasy in the steam room, but absent as far as the actual journey went westwards from Southampton to New York and back again.

Elsie McKay and the *Viceroy of India*

The ships that traveled the line eastwards from Britain to Africa, India and Australia continued to have even fewer Oriental references. The ships did not boast the luxury of Turkish baths as they were smaller in scale and less lavish in their decoration, compared to their trans-Atlantic counterparts. P&O was also driven by the corporate needs of the Empire, rather than the commercial imperatives of the White Star line and others. The Oriental interior was used sparingly, on the P&O ships it was employed for the liminal space of the Verandah Café. First seen on the German liner, the *Kaiser Wilhelm II* in 1903 and emulated on board the *Mauretania* in 1907 this was a semi-indoor space. Situated in between the grandiose interior spaces of the public rooms and the more basic external deck space, the Verandah Cafés frequently had Oriental-style lighting plus wickerwork furniture. The space was used to serve first-class passengers coffee in a sheltered enclave, protected from the elements outside, with the option of opening doors onto the deck when the weather permitted. The Verandah Café lacked the cosseted atmosphere of the grand public rooms. On board the *Olympic* and *Titanic*, the cafés had the standard wickerwork furniture and were painted the conventional white with the addition of trellis decoration. By contrast, one example of a Verandah Café that did draw upon the Oriental style was on board P&O's *Viceroy of India*, launched in 1929 [Figure 14.2]. Here, we see Oriental-style arches decorating the windows and walls, with applied plaster decoration with a Moorish theme and a heavily carved ceiling. The ceiling mouldings use the characterstic Arabic-inspired *Rub el Hizb* symbol of two overlapping squares.

The innovative design of this space was the work of Elsie Mackay, the daughter of the Chairman of the line, Lord Inchcape, and the first woman to design interiors for ocean liners. Her work represents a transnational

FIGURE 14.2 Elsie MacKay, The Verandah Café, *Viceroy of India*, 1929. © P&O Heritage Collection, www.poheritage.com.

approach to the Oriental interior, and contrasts with the segregated approach of the *Titanic* Turkish baths. This was more of a conversation between East and West. This approach can partly be explained by McKay's own background.

McKay's references for the Oriental were partly drawn from popular culture. She had enjoyed a career as an actress in early films and on the stage, so would have known of the language of the Oriental which heavily influenced cinema and theater design during the early years of the twentieth century (MacKenzie 1995: 89–93). She was intimately acquainted with film production with as Oriental theme, as her first starring role was in the British silent film *Snow in the Desert* (1919). Indeed, the interiors she designed for the *Viceroy of India* resemble stage or film sets, and in particular the renowned Smoking Room which led into the interior of A Deck from the Verandah Cafe by means of decorative, ironwork gates [Figure 14.3]. The Smoking Room was heavily based on the seventeenth-century State Room of the old Palace, Bromley-by-Bow which had been built and decorated for James I, and reconstructed at the Victoria and Albert Museum, where Mackay almost certainly saw it and studied it carefully. Colin Anderson derided this particular interior in his canonical 1966 essay, even reproducing a photograph of it as one of his seven illustrations. He celebrated the functionalism and modernity of his own Orient Line, contrasted with McKay's design: "In the early 1920s a palatial grandiosity still pervaded even the architect-designed rooms I am

FIGURE 14.3 Elsie MacKay, First Class Smoking Room, *Viceroy of India*, 1929. © P&O Heritage Collection, www.poheritage.com.

speaking of. They tended to have classical pillars, rich metal balustrading and a high central area. We were probably the only shipowners who did not provide those favorite shipboard aids to gracious living, armour and baronial stone fireplaces" (Anderson 1966: 482).

However, even amongst the oak paneling, the carved coat of arms over the fireplace and crossed swords there were Oriental rugs and alluring glimpses of the Orient in the form of the Verandah Café which could be snatched through the iron gates beyond. The Jacobean style of the Smoking Room was also echoed in the Verandah Café space with the leaded windows and oak occasional tables with barley twist legs. This attests to the slippages that existed between the Oriental interior and other styles, the transitive nature of the Oriental, which exemplifies transnational, two-way communication. The Oriental merges with the Jacobean in the construction of two inter-related spaces, symbolic of the designer's biography. Elsie Mackay was the daughter of a British Viscount, to be created an Earl in 1929, the year of the launch of the *Viceroy of India*. However, she was born in Simla, India, and spent her early childhood there as her father was President of the Bengal Chamber of Commerce, and represented the Legislative Council of the Viceroy of India and was a member of the Council of the Secretary of State for India. Therefore, she would have grown up amongst the sights and sounds of India before traveling by sea back to the family home in Scotland, a symbol of the transnational. However, the Oriental still had no place at the heart of the ship, it was on the fringes, the periphery of the layout. On board the *Viceroy of India*, the first-class reading and writing room beyond the Smoking Room were in more conventional, Adamesque style.

The *Empress of Britain*: The oriental interior

The first example of an Oriental interior in the central part of an ocean liner is that of the Cathay Lounge on the *Empress of Britain* [Figure 14.4]. This Canadian-owned ship sailed between Southampton and Quebec, and great efforts were made by the Canadian Pacific Steamship Company to attract passengers through high design values. This was the first ship to be designed for use as both an ocean liner and a cruise ship. The ship had to be made attractive as a liner, as the trip between Southampton and Quebec was less

FIGURE 14.4 Edmund Dulac, Cathay Lounge, *Empress of Britain*, Canadian Pacific Line, 1931. Image reproduced with permission courtesy of Canadian Pacific.

popular than the route between Southampton and New York. During the winter, it was impossible to sail through the iced over waters of the St Lawrence River, and so the liner became a cruise ship and offered round the world voyages via the Mediterranean to North Africa and the Holy Land, through the Suez Canal and into the Red Sea, then onto India, Ceylon, Southeast Asia and the Dutch East Indies, before reaching China, Hong Kong and Japan and crossing the Pacific to Hawaii and California before navigating the Panama Canal back to New York. These cruises to the Orient took place during the winters of 1931 until 1939 and the outbreak of the Second World War.

At 760 feet, 6 inches (231.80 meters) in length, the ship did not exactly match the *Olympic* and *Titanic* in actual size; however, it was still large and could carry 1,195 passengers (465 first class, 260 tourist class, and 470 third class) for the voyage between Southampton and Quebec, and 700 single-class passengers for cruising. The *Empress of Britain* had eight decks, and the design of the public rooms was coordinated by their in-house designers, P. A. Staynes and A. H. Jones, who were also responsible for the design of the writing and card rooms, suites, entrance foyer, swimming pool and modern, not Oriental, Turkish baths. The Oriental interior on board was the first-class Smoking Room. Staynes and Jones coordinated a series of high-profile British artists and designers to work on the first-class public spaces. Society portrait painter John Lavery designed the Empress Room, which doubled as a cinema and ballroom in neoclassical style, with glamorous touches including a mirror ball and pink ostrich feathers. The intimate Knickerbocker Bar was designed by cartoonist W. Heath Robinson with a semi-circular bar and stools for drinking cocktails. The first-class Smoking Room or Cathay Lounge was the Chinese-inspired space for "flights of unpractical fancy." Designed by the illustrator Edmund Dulac, this was the first smoking room on an ocean liner the author has managed to trace that did not to draw on Western European historic styles. Dulac had a background of working with Oriental subject matter, as he illustrated children's books, including the *Arabian Nights* in 1907. The color scheme of the room was red and black, with silver paneling in gray ash on the walls. The ceiling was decorated with shimmering silver interspersed with a vermillion geometric pattern. This fretwork pattern was mirrored in the flooring, with its finish inlaid with Macassar ebony in the oak. The lighting in the room echoed the Oriental theme, with translucent glass surrounding the bar area with the same fretwork form as the ceiling and floor. The mirrored chimney breast reflected the diverse light sources, and was decorated with peach, gold, green and black mirrors. The furniture was red and black lacquer, upholstered in pink and white fabric, the form of the furniture echoed the fretwork theme.

The room was commented on positively by the majority of design critics, who appreciated the overall integrity of the decorative scheme. Frida Wolfe, writing for *The Studio*, commented: "This the most interesting departure from the usual smoking room *décor* is marked by the unity, the consistency—down to the last detail—which informs the whole" (1931: 41). However, for John de la Valette, the modernist critic and Honorary Organizing Secretary of the 1935 Exhibition of British Art in Industry at the Royal Academy, the room was not of suitable design for an ocean liner. He commented in his Royal Society of Arts speech in April 1936: "An improved post-war, even post-slump, example of this style is to be found in the *Empress of Britain*. The main lounge and drawing room are hardly distinguishable from those of a sumptuous hotel, and even Mr Edmond Dulac's Cathay Lounge seems a place on shore rather than in a ship" (1936: 714). The *Empress of Britain* was sunk whilst in service off the west coast of Ireland in 1940, but was replaced by a brand new ship of the same name in 1956. This was the ship which the leading designer of interiors of cruise ships, Joe Farcus, refurbished when he started working for Carnival Cruises in the 1990s after leaving the offices of Miami-based commercial architect *par excellence*, Morris Lapidus (Friedman 2010). Farcus was the lead architect for the global Carnival Cruises ship business, and understood what most modernist critics and previous ship line owners had not, that "flights of unpractical fancy" are key to attracting passengers to ocean liner or cruise ships in equal measure, and that it is vital that the interior designers should be involved from the first planning stages. Farcus was key to the process of ship design, and was included from the earliest stages, possibly contributing in no small part to the commercial success of Carnival Cruises (Motter and Pearl 2013). He has even included Oriental touches, including the Passage to India Lounge on the *Fascination* in 1994, complete with two model elephant heads. The global dominance of Carnival Cruises and their physical dominance over heritage sites such as Venice is perhaps part of another debate (Votolato 2011: 253–256).

This chapter has explored the Oriental style on board transnational transport through contrasting transitive spaces. It has explored the ways in which the Orient, often a destination for British ocean liners, was marginalized in the living and leisure spaces on board ship. The Oriental style was in evidence, in the cases of William de Morgan and Elsie MacKay, which demonstrate a fruitful transnational dialog. However, due to the nature of the liner as opposed to cruise journey, and the specific peripatetic situation of the passengers, Oriental spaces on P&O ships tended to be marginalized by a more prevalent and comforting representation of British national identity. The transnational voyages of these ships traced the lines of power of the British global hegemony throughout the nineteenth and early twentieth centuries. As power began to shift from Empire to Commonwealth, so representations of the Orient became more common. This chapter situates the Oriental interior within the discourse of transnational economic and political power. As air travel replaced travel by ocean liner, so cruise ships superseded ocean liners. *The Empress of Britain* includes an early Oriental-style interior. This could be explained by the ship's emphasis on the trans-Atlantic route, rather than the route eastwards. This was also a

Canadian-owned ship, designed to double as a cruise ship during the winter months. This more overt use of the Oriental style could be seen as a subtle appropriation of global power. It marked the time when the British Empire was waning, exercised by the ocean liner. The age of the cruise ship marked a new era of North American sailing for leisure, as aeroplanes replaced ships for the physical transport of business, officials and employees. The Oriental has entered mainstream interior design on more recent, design-driven cruise ships as the language of transnational design has became far more multi-national.

Acknowledgements

Thank you to John Graves, Curator of Ship History, National Maritime Museum, and Daniel Davies, AHRC Collaborative Doctoral Award candidate, National Maritime Museum and Middlesex University, for help with this chapter.

Notes

1 Britain's empire during this period was particularly important in "the East"—the Indian subcontinent, the "Far East," that is, Hong Kong and Australia/New Zealand, hence the number of British shipping lines that serviced that region. Though the lure of the East for the British did not start with Queen Victoria being bestowed with the title "Empress of India," fascination with the region was nevertheless fueled by its accessibility by ship in the period under discussion.

2 It should be stressed that these ships are different to cruise ships; ocean liners serviced particular lines between ports for trade, mail delivery and the transport of passengers. Cruise ships are a later innovation, and are designed purely for leisure use.

References

A Madras Officer (1846), *The Ocean and The Desert,* Vol. 1, London: T. C. Newby.
Anderson, C. (1966), "Interior Design of Passenger Ships," *Journal of the Royal Society of the Arts,* 114: 477–493.
"The Bentick" (1843), *Illustrated London News,* August 12.
Brooker, G. (2013), *Key Interiors since 1900,* London: Lawrence King.
Dawson, P. and B. Peter (2010), *Ship Style: Modernism and Modernity and Sea in the 20th Century,* London: Conway.
Friedman, A. (2010), *American Glamour and the Evolution of Modern Architecture,* New Haven and London: Yale University Press.

Huxtable, S. A. (2013), "Whistler's Peacock Room and the Artist as Magus," in L. Glazer and L. Merrill (eds.), *Palaces of Art, Whistler and the Art Worlds of Aestheticism*, Smithsonian Institution Scholarly Press: 67–81.

Motter, P. and L. Pearl (2013), "Meet Joe Farcus, Ship Architect," *Cruisemates*, March 5. http://www.cruisemates.com/articles/feature/farcus06.cfm [Accessed August 7, 2014].

Nochlin, L. (1989), "The Imaginary Orient," in *The Politics of Vision: Essays on Nineteenth-Century Art and Society*, New York: Harper and Row: 33–59.

Penner, B. and C. Rice (2013), "The Many Lives of Red House," in P. Sparke and A. Massey (eds.), *Biography, Identity and the Modern Interior*, Farnham: Ashgate: 23–35.

Potvin, J. (2005), "Vapour and Steam: The Victorian Turkish Bath, Homosocial Health, and Male Bodies on Display," *Journal of Design History*, 18(4): 319–333.

Rice, C. (2007), *The Emergence of the Interior: Architecture, Modernity, Domesticity*, London: Routledge.

Ulrich, K. (1998), *Monarchs of the Sea*, London: I. B. Tauris.

Valette, J. de La (1936), "The Fitment and Decoration of Ships: From the 'Great Eastern' to the 'Queen Mary'," *Journal of the Royal Society of Arts*, May 22: 705–726.

Votolato, G. (2011), *Ship*, London: Reaktion Press.

Wealleans, A. (née Massey) (2006), *Designing Liners: A History of Interior Design Afloat*, Oxford: Routledge.

White Star Line (1911), *Royal Mail Triple-Screw Steamers "Olympic" and 'Titanic,"* Liverpool: The Liverpool Printing and Stationery Co.

Wolfe, F. (1931), *Empress of Britain: The Decoration of a Liner*, 102: 20–43.

Websites

http://www.demorgan.org.uk/collection/galleon-tile-panel [Accessed August 4, 2014]

http://foucault.info/documents/heterotopia/foucault.heterotopia.en.html [Accessed July 31, 2014]

15

Posturing for Authenticity: Embodying Otherness in Contemporary Interiors of Modern Yoga

Lauren Bird

In an article entitled "The Most Beautiful Yoga Studios in New York City" from January 2012, online magazine *Well&Good NYC* outlines the parameters that define a "pretty" yoga studio—something, the authors claim, that is undeniably important to one's practice. Design details, they insist, are key in creating the necessary "vibe" of a yoga studio, whether that may be a "vibe for easily soothing the mind or energizing the spirit" (*Well&Good NYC* 2012). The environmentally friendly—or "eco-chic," as the industry terms it—features of these studios are fastidiously detailed in every paragraph of the article. The practice room of Montreal-based HappyTree Yoga [Figure 15.1] looks not unlike these idealized studios: austere nearly to the point of industrial, with open, whitewashed walls and wood floors, abundant and atmospheric natural light, and earthy accents like plants or colorful fabrics often characterize spaces of modern yoga in North America. Countless other images exist in this mold, many representative of the current design trends for spas and, to a lesser degree, gym spaces. Much like a spa, the space is serene and tranquil, and will receive on average fifty clients a day who, forgoing the gym, will use the yoga studio instead to bend, relax, stretch and sweat for their physiological

FIGURE 15.1 Yoga practice room, HappyTree Studio, Montreal. Photo courtesy: Asbed.com\Lumisculpt. Used with permission of HappyTree Yoga.

wellbeing. Health and bodily refinement, in this space, is a distinctly luxurious upper- and middle-class undertaking.

Like other studios, however, HappyTree's practice room features a collection of decorative objects one is unlikely to find in a gym or spa setting. On the wide platform of the windowsill, a statue of Ganesha (the elephant-headed Hindu god) sits next to Shiva, the lord of yoga. From a sculpture of seated Saraswati, the goddess of knowledge, strong Indian incense wafts through the room. Flowers are ritualistically offered to the statues, and above them a strange New Age pictorial amalgamation featuring a multiplicity of religious symbols and icons—including a Jewish star of David, a Hindu *chakra* motif,[1] and a Christian cross—overlooks the scene [Figure 15.2]. This is the altar of the practice room, and though they are overwhelmingly present in the majority of Western studios, altars are rarely prayed to or acknowledged during a typical modern postural yoga session; moreover, their meaning or purpose is almost never made explicit. The fact that images of Hindu deities, statues of the Buddha and New Age icons litter the windowsills of most commercial Western yoga studios, while crucifixes, for example, do not hang in the hallways of commercial gyms or spas, points to the hybrid, multi-layered nature of the spaces housing these objects. Despite many contemporary yoga studios primarily serving as spaces for secular group fitness, traditional fitness clubs and gymnasia nonetheless do not feature religious iconography or even decorative aspects within their interior spaces. What, then, allows the interior spaces of yoga studios to not

FIGURE 15.2 Altar space of the yoga practice room. Promotional image from HappyTree online gallery. Photo courtesy: Asbed.com\Lumisculpt. Used with permission of HappyTree Yoga.

only emphasize a highly Orientalized and exoticized design program, but simultaneously exist in a modern, secular context as spaces of fitness and health? Through the case study of HappyTree Yoga, an urban Montreal-based yoga studio, this chapter intends to examine the space of modern yoga as a site that, through the visual and material elements of its interior, evokes an ahistorical Orient as the repository of metaphysical wellbeing, wherein the authenticity of a studio and the practice it offers are often signaled by the presence of an Orientalizing and exoticizing design program. Images and objects in these spaces, I argue, reinforce how the modern postural yoga studio is designed as an escape from, or antidote to, the stresses of modern Western lifestyle through the integration of spirituality and the wisdom of the Orient with Western socio-cultural norms of health and bodily regulation. The fact that yoga studios come in an overwhelmingly standardized mold—from the features of the practice hall to the way in which they are decorated—reinforces the supposition that the yoga studio is a very carefully contrived space in its bid to provide authenticity to practitioners. While this particular work uses the specific setting of HappyTree to explore the link between Oriental ornamentation and the perception of authenticity in yogic interiors, it may also serve as an archetypal example of the vast majority of yoga studios, and may thus be more broadly understood as symptomatic of how yoga is envisioned in the popular Western imagination rather than a single studio's aesthetic inclination.

HappyTree features many of the objects characteristic of such settings: among others, prominently on display are a wealth of statues of Hindu deities, called *murtis*; Tibetan prayer flags; images of the Buddha; paintings and prints of *mandalas* or *yantras*;[2] and the ubiquitous symbol of yoga in the West: the Sanskrit *Om* syllable. Borrowing from Penny Sparke the precept that interiors can also be understood and analyzed by ensembles of objects within them (Sparke 2008: 11–12), I wish to argue that while these objects all contain individual histories and meanings, grouped together they create the characteristic pan-Asian pastiche of exoticism found in both studios that claim to follow certain guru and stylistic lineages[3] and studios, like HappyTree, that offer instructional classes not specific to any particular lineage of yoga.

In considering the interior as more than a physical space or amalgamation of objects, I ground my theoretical investigation of the interior as both at once perceived and experienced (Rice 2007, 2013). In defining the modern interior, Charles Rice proposes a reading of space as a physical, lived reality based in the materials of the built environment itself, but also as an image, a "reverie or imaginal picture [. . .] which could transform an existing spatial interior into something other" (2007: 2). To explore the yogic interior is to examine the duality of its presentation: its modern aesthetic and place in popular culture as a healthy and increasingly mainstream form of fitness, and its presentation of a sensorial experience that recalls its Eastern origins through both visual and haptic elements. In the case of the studio, this doubleness is expressed through the studio's physical layout, material culture and the way it proposes to leave urban reality and transport practitioners into an imaginary and ultimately immaterial, exoticized landscape. At once starkly modern and highly Orientalized, HappyTree presents a space that both prominently displays objects of Indian religiosity and yet remains silent on the actual histories of narratives of these objects, using them instead as representations of the interior as outside of modernity: an imagined landscape. Situated on an above-ground floor, the studio both metaphorically and literally lifts the practitioner up and above the bustle of the urban landscape and into what HappyTree calls, "a sunny and candlelit oasis designed to help you leave the city behind" (HappyTree Yoga 2014).

Five thousand years of authenticity

Originally the religious and ascetic practices of sages and holy men, only by a conscious legitimization process through the gatekeepers of science and rationality did yoga penetrate and incorporate itself into a Western worldview. It did so primarily in the late nineteenth century as an anti-colonial, eugenically inclined physical practice of Indian nation-building, maintaining a link to ancient ascetic and religious rites and practices that were factually tenuous at best but vigorously reinforced by Orientalists at the time. Barely a century old, yoga as it is practiced today in commercial studios or gyms is heavily based on gymnastic and callisthenic exercises and postures referred to as *asana*. Developed in conjunction with the European physical culture movement and re-imagined as a tool for anti-colonial Hindu nationalism, the popular *asana*-based practices found in today's modern postural yoga styles, such as Ashtanga and Bikram Yoga, are overall devoid of any direct reference to yoga's complex history and frame it, rather simplistically, as an unbroken five-thousand-year-old lineage of knowledge.

As Joseph Alter (2004, 2005), Elizabeth De Michelis (2005) and Mark Singleton (2008, 2010) have shown, what is contemporaneously referred to as Modern Postural Yoga differs greatly from what was practiced a little over a century ago in India, let alone several millennia. In considering yoga's transcultural history, Beatrix Hauser (2013) has suggested that the formulation of yoga today cannot simply be attributed to modernity or globalization, or as absolutely contingent on India's history of British colonialism.[4] More than non-linear, Hauser proposes a fragmented, almost nebulous course of development. As she states:

> Imagining the development of yoga as a family tree with Indian roots, a substantial trunk of "tradition," and several more or less globalized branches is a modern trope for a complex formation that more appropriately resembles a huge banyan tree with several intermingled aerial roots that make it difficult to recognize where the tree begins and

where it ends, how it is absorbed by other plants, and that it may, in fact, be the product of multiple distant origins.

(Hauser 2013: 11)

My aim is not to suggest that certain yogic branches are more authentic than others. Rather, I wish to argue that the typical displays of objects and decorative elements in the vast majority of contemporary Western yoga studios act as signifiers for a studio space's authenticity in so far as they present a material and visual link to yoga's (non-specific and sometimes historically inaccurate) Oriental origins, regardless of what *kind* of yoga is practiced in these spaces. Without these elements, the practice of modern yoga is easily reducible to a challenging workout, a therapeutic exercise or a coping mechanism for stress, among other things.

In his work on contemporary conceptions of yoga's premodern past, Joseph Alter has argued that it is precisely "this 'other' history [. . .] which both undermines and authorizes the idea of yoga as medicine [. . .] and this tension between pragmatic rationalism and esoteric magic . . . makes it powerful" (Alter 2005: 119). I would suggest that it is not only yoga itself, but the exoticized studio interior that produces the allure and authority of this Other history. Despite its contemporary grounding in modern medicine and the cult of the body beautiful, the studio is alluring precisely because it seems to offer this alternative mode of being in the world and in the body, outside of Western hegemony. Richard King suggests that "the current wave of postmodern anxiety about the foundations of Western civilization is partly a consequence of historicist and reductionist analysis being applied reflexively to the West" (King 1999: 157–158). Colin Campbell echoes this in his treatise on Easternization (2007), which he defines as the rise of the annexation and heroization of Eastern cultures as the answer to the ills of Western civilization. The yoga studio subtly suggests through its Oriental material culture that the panacea of health may be found in invoking and performing the rites, however interpreted, of yoga as a "healing ritual of secular [eastern] religion" (De Michelis 2005: 248). The objects in this space, then, are no longer assembled in a pastiche of *objets d'art* in a cabinet of curiosities or museum setting. Instead, they are agentic in representing a solution to the postmodern anxiety King suggests, and which begin, albeit slowly, to move out of the historicist and reductionist discourse of "traditional" Orientalism as defined by Edward Said (1978). Or as King defines it, a "negative" Orientalism that does not leave room for resistance, hybridity or "Orientalist discourses for anti-colonial purposes" (King 1999: 68).

Without attributing blatantly negative or positive attributes to the Orientalism that has characterized yoga's development, Singleton's contribution to the study of modern yoga has been particularly important in identifying the invention, construction and performance of yoga traditions since the height of Orientalism in India, from the mid-nineteenth century to the present. Singleton has termed this preoccupation with a conscious and careful establishing of authoritatively "classical" elements in yoga "constructive Orientalism" (2010: 87–90). As he suggests, this network is a result of the Orientalist project—in India and beyond—of the nineteenth century which goes beyond a conceptual framing and encompasses a literary and visual discernment for the purpose of a canonical selection and validation of how India's classical heritage should be defined and what it would comprise. His work on constructive Orientalism informs my own analysis and proposition that markedly foreign and exotic objects and images within yoga studios act as signifiers of these authentic aspects of yoga. This, alongside the idea of the actual architectural physicality of the studio and its ability to affect one's state of embodiment characterizes the interior's "doubleness" (2008: 2). This doubleness is reflected in yoga's construction as traditional and its actual performance as modern: if one understands the physical movements of yoga as exterior insofar as they are embodied and tactile, the interior experience of yoga becomes linked to the mental, the mystic and the transcendent. Such a modern and highly medicalized engagement with a subject constructed as premodern and thus irrational allows for the marked ambivalence that characterizes yoga studios. The interior, then, is neither only spatial nor only representational. Rather, it is a place between "reverie and reality" (Rice 2013: 103).

Authentically sacred and sacredly authentic

In his work on the history of the modern interior, Rice argues that the subject's negotiation of an interior is "psychologically charged [. . .] through the medium of objects and furniture" (2013: 3). The full effect of the space relies on its "doubleness"—on one hand, the physical and material reality of the space; and on the other, the interior as "an image, one that can be imagined and dreamed, and inhabited as such" (2007: 2). Significantly, he suggests this doubleness involves the "interdependence between image and space, with neither sense being primary" (2007: 2). The yoga studio's physical space is, as I wish to show, extremely modern and highly regulated in so far as it receives, conditions and is agentic in its practitioners' formulations of their own bodies during practice. It is, however, also the image of the Orient itself. Spatially immediate and conceptually distant, as much as the yoga studio folds bodies it also folds time, overlapping modern medicine onto the image of an ancient, pure and mythologized tradition, explicitly linking the space as one through which the true benefits of yoga's esoteric past may emerge and manifest. In this sense, the practitioner is "caught between material and immaterial registers [. . .] a material space that produces de-realized experiences" (Rice 2013: 13).

A promotional image [Figure 15.3] from HappyTree's 2010 advertising campaign exemplifies this conceptualization of the interior as both material

FIGURE 15.3 Promotional image from HappyTree online gallery. Photo courtesy: Asbed.com\Lumisculpt. Used with permission of HappyTree Yoga.

and immaterial: in the foreground, the image features one of HappyTree's teachers physically aiding and adjusting a client on his mat, and positioned (intentionally) beside the two of them in the background is the same print seen in Figure 15.2, moved from the wall and now the centerpiece of the studio's altar. Doubling as spatial reality and two-dimensional representation of the space, the single image contains multiple meanings and suggestions, evoking at once the sort of space that is both corporeally inhabitable but also dematerialized through the possibilities created by its own image. The space of the interior, "never wholly separate from its imagistic considerations" (Rice 2013: 13) is neither entirely physical or imaginary—such representations allow it to be framed as both, with the potential for corporeal habitation while capturing the immateriality of the interior through, in this case, photographic means: its representation, clearly marked through the presence of the art object, as one that encloses an Other history. Bodies silhouetted by the print echo the ambivalence of reverie and reality, wherein the space rests somewhere between physical architecture and the imagined links it conjures of other worlds and states of being through its Oriental décor.

Out of the temple and into the studio

Not unlike yogic practices themselves, symbols of Indian religiosity, such as the aforementioned *murtis* and Sanskrit letters have their own complex histories linked to both yoga and to the European penchant for collecting and exhibiting non-European *objects d'arts* in an entirely decontextualized fashion. There is perhaps no greater symbol of Indian religiosity than the *Nataraja*, Shiva as the Lord of Dance. Dating back to the Cola period (eighth century CE), the image of Shiva dancing silhouetted by a flaming ring, with one leg raised and serpentine locks flying, is perhaps an even more ubiquitous representation of yoga than the Sanskrit *Om* syllable. In order to understand the role of constructive Orientalism in the creation of authenticity in yogic interiors, I will briefly consider the research of Matthew Harp Allen (1997) on the "revival" of classical art in twentieth-century India through the example of Rukmini Devi, Indian dance and the ubiquitous *Nataraja*.

The queen of modern Indian dance, Rukmini Devi (1904–1986), is credited with reviving (or reinventing, depending on how one approaches it) *bharatnayam*, or classical Indian dance. Previously an art form reserved largely for temple life, Devi is credited with bringing what was conceived of as classical Indian dance to spaces of secular performance. She also brought with her onstage the icon of the *Nataraja*: in her own words, the "intention was that dance, now abolished in the temple, should create the temple atmosphere on the stage" (Allen 1997: 79). In doing so, Devi created the same spiritual resonance present in the temples she herself rejected, moving Indian dance out of a realm of religiosity and into one of secularity without relinquishing the visual culture of temple interiors (1997: 79). This act shaped a connection to Indian religiosity that fit snugly within the parameters of the Orientalist project in colonial India—a "second-order religiosity," which involved a dislocation and subsequent relocation of religious objects and a translation of their meaning (Singleton 2008: 90). This, as Allen's research demonstrates, was a conscious process of both legitimizing the art's historical tradition while simultaneously reinventing it. Though the *Nataraja* was historically never associated with dance or Indian nationality, it is due to Devi's popularization of the icon that it is now widely regarded as the quintessential symbol of Indian culture. Much like the Shiva *Nataraja*, the *murtis* that grace the altar space of HappyTree serve as a connection to the "classical" in yoga, and thus the authentic, as well as "a focus of devotion and inspiration for practitioners" (Singleton 2008: 90). According to Tapati Guha-Thakurta, this selection process for an authentic aesthetic was the case for much of India's indigenous art forms:

> The new nationalist ideology of Indian art, its aesthetic self-definitions and its search for a "tradition" had strong roots in Orientalist writing and debates. British Orientalism produced and structured much of its notion of an Indian art tradition. While it had provided the core of historical knowledge and archeological expertise on the subject, it would also stand at the helm of the aesthetic reinterpretation of Indian art during the turn of the century.
> (Guha-Thakurta 1992, in Allen 2007: 69)

Despite this, I would suggest most practitioners of yoga and studio owners who decide which objects are displayed and how the studio is decorated would not identify themselves as Orientalists. At the same time, I do not wish to suggest that appropriating symbols of various East and South-East Asian cultural and religious histories is a harmless exercise by curious and aesthetically appreciative Westerners. Rather, it is worth noting that while such objects are displayed as markers of difference in yoga studios—reinforcing yoga's authenticity as a non-Western practice—such practices are often undertaken without critical self-reflection by studio owners and remain rooted in longstanding imbalances of colonial power and dominance.

Richard King has argued that, despite Hindu reformers and Western apologists having only the intention of bettering indigenous people's lives according to their own values, Orientalism as modernization and Orientalism as Westernization cannot and should not be regarded as separate undertakings (King 1999: 153). By erasing the vein of colonial resistance that gave birth to modern yoga, the yoga studio romanticizes the practice's origins and history without acknowledging indigenous agency in developing and revolutionizing modern yoga. This strain between the desire to present yoga as modern in the contemporary studio setting but hold aloft the ideal of a foreign, otherworldly source is visible in the tension between the studio as a space of health, hygiene, and fitness, and its highly exoticized decorative program.

While the majority of yoga-related research from a sociological or anthropological standpoint takes into account practitioner perspectives on embodiment or the physiological effects of yoga,[5] few take into consideration practitioners' experiences of the places and spaces where they practice. One of the only works that concerns itself (albeit briefly) with practitioners' reactions to studio aesthetics, Sacha Mathew's field research (2011) on Indian religiosity in contemporary yoga considers three popular Montreal yoga studios. At Sattva Yoga Shala, for example, the walls are covered with paintings of Hindu deities, the windowsills of the practice room are lined with small statues of more deities—including two of the aforementioned *Natarajas*—and the wall is covered with a *yantra* (or sacred geometric diagram). While one of his interviewees from Sattva expressed an appreciation of the overtly Hindu décor because it was the "cultural part not found in gyms" (Mathew 2011: 55), another student expressly disagreed. He claimed not to be a "spiritual guy," and thus the ornamentation made him uncomfortable (Mathew 2011: 55). Moreover, Mathews stresses that, while the majority of the practitioners he interacted with knew virtually nothing about what the various art objects represented, they did feel it was an important aspect that gave respect to yoga's origins (2011: 71). Many of them did not, however, view yoga as a religion (Matthews 2011: 53), an important point that recalls the argument that spirituality and Eastern philosophy are not regarded by the West as institutionalized, structured and historically specific religions.[6] Because of the explicitly *non*-Hindu engagement with yoga in his fieldwork, Mathew suggests that it renders not only the practice itself but the abundance of Hindu iconography non-threatening, as practitioners essentially knew nothing about the images themselves, aside from their association with "the East" in all its imagined homogeneity.

While HappyTree offers a workshop on Hindu mythology in its teacher-training program, it otherwise remains silent on the presence of these objects; though studio owner Melanie Richards describes at length in an interview for this research that the ensembles of objects, particularly at the altar, are assembled in reaction to the pervasive secularization of yogic spaces. In deciding to devote a space to an altar in the practice room, Richards emphasizes the desire to give practitioners a "focal point" during practice, and that it is a matter of being "less afraid of bringing spirituality into the studio." When students are not facing the mirrors for practice, they face the altar, and in doing so, the altar becomes both a locus of sacrality within the room as well as a point of control, from which the teacher's authority issues, symbolically both receiver and transmitter of yoga's authenticity. This authenticity is relayed verbally and physically as the teachers position themselves at the point of authority through instruction and through their physical positioning in the room, standing in front of and silhouetted by the altar space itself.

While, according to Richards, the altar is meant to evoke the sacrality of the practice space, as the *Om* and prayer flag garland above the door signal, the other decorative elements are consciously chosen in so far as they maintain the exoticism of the decorative program but are not the focus of quasi-religious attention as the altar is. Along the main hallway in HappyTree that leads practitioners between the practice room and the changing rooms, the walls feature several works of art. On one side, minimalist ink drawings of anthropomorphic figures in various yoga poses, donated to the studio by artist Meier Kaur, line the wall above a cushioned alcove. Opposite, a large-scale commissioned work by S. Jowett, one of HappyTree's own clients, is prominently featured: titled *Tree Mandala*, it is a large silver tree from which the traditional iconography of the subtle body *chakras* emerge [Figure 15.4]. In keeping with the Orientalizing aesthetic, the end of the hall features a sculpture of a multi-faced golden Buddha head next to purple and white drapery decorated in *mandala* motifs. The presence of these elements are part of an effort to, as Richards defines, "give the hallway a little magic." Richards explains how the *chakras* of *Tree Mandala* are a sacred visual element that she hopes impact students as they pass through the hallway space, awakening what she describes as a "certain feeling." Decoration in the hall is part of a greater effort to unite the space of the lounge and practice hall with the rest of the studio, both on a visual level and on a more "energetic" level. She explains, "that [it] was my spiritual mentor who noticed [the space] was cut off—how everything was so beautiful out in

FIGURE 15.4 Tree Mandala commissioned by S. Jowett for HappyTree Yoga Studio, 2012. Mixed media, 4' × 4'. Photograph used with permission of the artist, Barbara Duarte de Lima.

front and then as soon as you went down the hall [. . .] it just turned into a regular space, there was nothing beautiful or inspiring about it. So that people are going in or out of the locker room and there's that feeling of sacred in the space." Dislocated from religion and relocated into the secular interior of the modern yoga studio, these decorative elements nonetheless surpass their purpose as visually pleasurable objects and become an attempt to evoke a more numinous experience.

In conducting semi-structured interviews with clients of the studio, it became evident that a vast majority of them attributed either an increased sense of authenticity in connection to the objects or a heightened perception of what many chose to identify as "spirituality." One student remarked that "the paintings in the studio are yoga inspired, which add to this feeling of authenticity for its clients." Another suggested the objects carry even more potency if one is introduced to their meaning, therefore allowing the practitioner to "better embody them." One in particular, a teacher in training who identified as being "deeply spiritual," suggested that without a deity, "the place is not infused or initiated with the presence of the divine," and that a *murti* acts as "a divine guide that opens and helps everybody practice yoga more deeply."

Overwhelmingly, it appears the very presence of these objects allows practitioners to engage in more than physical exercises or modern, secular *techniques du corps*. Instead, students may experience something "deeper," part of what David Morgan terms "felt life-belief" (2010: 56–58), in which objects with religious or spiritual value are experienced by practitioners through emotions or sentiments rather than merely decorative accents. In considering this, I wish to propose overlapping the interior as image of the Other with Walter Benjamin's notion of the interior as "long experience" (*Erfahrung*), founded, as Rice relays, on "an appeal and a connection to tradition, and the accumulation of wisdom over time" (Benjamin 1999: 731; Rice 2007: 11). From physical objects that embodied such immaterial notions of history and tradition, a feeling of long experience could perhaps be grasped and, like the nineteenth-century domestic interior, the yoga studio's refuge of long experience exists to counteract the "short experience" (*Erlebnisse*) of the city, modernity, and all its immediately jarring and alienating experiences (Benjamin 1999). HappyTree creates these moments of interior refuge not through its own traditional objects but through objects of Other traditions, extending the long experience to one not only of time, but of place. If the interior indeed doubles as both material reality and an image that is not necessarily rooted in real time, then there is a certain "mortification" of the past that takes place in the representation of the interior not only as image, but as *past* image, indeed in this case as the "illumination of a forgotten past" (Rice 2007: 35), one that is at times remembered as authentic, hybrid or altogether Other.

Conclusion

More recent research, particularly work in the fields of sociology and anthropology, have come to show that most casual practitioners who use these spaces know little to nothing about yoga's esoteric history, or how it arrived in the West, but find the exoticized aesthetics of yoga studios to either be disturbing in the way they recall another culture or useful insomuch as they substantiate and pay homage to the roots of yoga. It is these sensory cues—the presence of religious objects, the smell of burning incense, the sound of traditional Indian music—that recall and identify the imaginary Orient from which many of these practitioners draw their ideas of yoga's history in the first place. Claims such as those of the Take Back Yoga initiative that insist modern Western yoga is inauthentic, or that the religious objects in yoga studios have lost their power due to the commercial or secular nature of the space—a "conscious delinking of yoga from its Hindu roots" (Hindu American Foundation 2013)—deny and ignore the studio's ability to function as commercial and secular, yet as a sacred space *apart* from the consumer culture that characterizes the postindustrial landscape. Perhaps as a result of yoga's long and complex history, it seems whatever modality of embodiment one chooses—or perhaps conforms to—in the setting of the yoga studio is, in some way or another, embroiled in a discourse of authenticity. How many *murtis* are there in a practice room? How faithfully to the original is a posture or breathing technique taught and performed?

As postmodernism has tried to show time and again, authenticity within a grand and singular narrative is highly exclusionary and ripe for deconstruction. In a similar way, if one is to judge the space of modern yoga for a perceived authenticity, it should be judged, as Geoffrey Samuel suggests, "on its own terms, not in terms of its closeness to some presumably more authentic Indian practice" (in Singleton and Byrne 2008: 6). Practitioners are then as concerned with their own authenticity as they are with the practice they engage in, and it is "clear that for many, yoga is seen as the privileged site of an authenticity otherwise unavailable or deficient in their daily experience and is felt to provide [. . .] a more 'authentic' way of being" (in Singleton and Byrne 2008: 6). Whether the presence of a statue beside the mat of a teacher imbues the interior space with an aura of numinous authenticity, or the image of a guru authenticates the idea of lineage, or an emphasis on healing one's body brings them into a state of authentic wellbeing and integration is negotiated differently by each body and each individual.

As stated in the introduction, this chapter did not set out to define how *authentic*, however problematically defined, the space of yoga and HappyTree in particular is. It set out, instead, to understand how authenticity may be constructed, displayed, embodied and experienced in a setting that is hybrid at its core. Certain facets of the yoga studio remain problematic: while Orientalism, colonial discourse and cultural appropriation are all features of these studios that require thorough self-reflection by both the consumers and producers of such narratives, the studio nonetheless remains a site ripe with possibilities. By acknowledging the history of yoga in all its complexity and embracing the myriad of ways it is experienced, physically, spatially and visually, studios may begin to offer a more genuine access to yoga, and providing authenticity rather than posturing for it.

Notes

1 "From at least the end of the of the first millennium CE, yogic and Tantric traditions in India began to evolve the idea of an alternative anatomy, which mapped the 'subtle body' (*sukshma sharira*) as a locus of spiritual energies and points of graduated awakening —*chakras* (wheels) or *padmas* (lotuses)— arranged along a vertical axis (*sushumna*) through a network of channels (*nadis*)" (see Reddy 2013: 275). Simplified *chakra* forms are common visual tropes in modern yoga studios and are used to illustrate yoga's connection to psychosomatic and spiritual understanding of the body.

2 *Mandalas* and *yantras* are geometric or circular symmetrical design patterns traditionally used in Eastern mysticism and part of both traditional Hindu and Buddhist iconography. They can refer to a specific deity or to a general concept or representation, such as symbolically representing the harmony of the universe.

3 As part of their decorative scheme, these studios often bear the portraits of the founders of their lineages. Ashtanga Yoga Montreal and the Centre de Yoga Iyengar de Montréal are both examples of this. HappyTree Yoga's practice room currently displays two dozen small portraits of individuals deemed important to the exportation of yoga to the West.

4 I use De Michelis' term of "Modern Postural Yoga" in this case to denote specifically the type of yoga—physical-based instructional classes that sometimes involve breathing and meditation exercises—practiced in most contemporary commercial yoga studios in the West. As De Michelis notes, however, there are myriad forms of yoga that have developed and are currently practiced worldwide, including styles based solely on meditation rather than posture, as well as styles that directly engage with other religious practices, such as Christianity or Judaism (see Mathew 2011: 74–76). Throughout this chapter, I refer to modern or contemporary yoga as signifying the posture-based instructional classes typical of commercial North American studios.

5 For a summary and assessment on the current state of academic research on contemporary forms of yoga, see especially K. Baier (2012), "Modern Yoga Research: Insights and Questions," presented in conjunction with the conference proceedings of *Yoga in Transformation: Historical and Contemporary Perspectives on a Global Phenomenon*, University of Vienna, Austria, available for access at http://modernyogaresearch.org/wordpress/wp-content/uploads/2012/04/Baier-Modern-Yoga-Research-Review-2012.pdf. See also Newcombe, S. (2009) "The Development of Modern Yoga: A Survey of the Field", *Religion Compass*, 3(6): 986–1002.

6 This transformation of "esoteric traditions into a philosophy geared to everyday spiritual concerns" can be linked to the work of the Theosophist Society in late nineteenth- and early twentieth-century India (see Fuller 2001: 80–81).

References

Allen, M. H. (1997), "Rewriting the Script for South Indian Dance," *The Drama Review*, 41(3): 63–100.

Alter, J. S. (2004), *Yoga in Modern India: The Body between Science and Philosophy*, Princeton: Princeton University Press.

Alter, J. S. (2004), "Modern Medical Yoga: Struggling with a History of Magic, Alchemy and Sex," *Asian Medicine*, 1(1): 119–146.

Benjamin, W. (1999), *The Arcades Project*, trans. H. Eiland and K. McLaughlin, Cambridge and London: The Belknap Press of Harvard University Press.

Campbell, C. (2007), *The Easternization of the West: A Thematic Account of Cultural Change in the Modern Era*, Boulder: Paradigm Publishers.

De Michelis, E. (2005), *A History of Modern Yoga: Patañjali and Western Esotericism*, London: Continuum.

Fuller, R. C. (2001), *Spiritual, But Not Religious: Understanding Unchurched America*, Oxford: Oxford University Press.

Guha-Thakurta, T. (1992), *The Making of a New Indian Art: Aesthetics and Nationalism in Bengal, c. 1850–1930*. Cambridge: Cambridge University Press.

"Your Downtown Montreal Yoga Studio," *HappyTree Yoga Online*. http://happytreeyoga.com [Accessed November 20, 2013].

Hauser, B. (2013), "Introduction: Transcultural Yoga(s). Analyzing a Traveling Subject," in B. Hauser (ed.), *Yoga Traveling: Bodily Practice in Transcultural Perspective*, Heidelberg, Springer.

Hindu American Foundation, "Take Back Yoga: Bringing Light to Yoga's Hindu Roots," *Take Back Yoga*. http://www.hafsite.org/media/pr/takeyogaback [Accessed March 25, 2013].

King, R. (1999), *Orientalism and Religion: Postcolonial Theory, India and "the Mystic East"*, London and New York: Routledge.

Mathew, S. (2011), *Indian Religion and Western Yoga Practices*. MA thesis, Department of Religions, Concordia University.

Morgan, D. (2010), "Materiality, Social Analysis, and the Study of Religion," in D. Morgan (ed.), *Religion and Material Culture: The Matter of Belief*, London and New York: Routledge.

Reddy, S. (2013), "Medical Yoga," in *Yoga: The Art of Transformation*, exhibition catalog, Smithsonian Institute, Washington.

Rice, C. (2007), *The Emergence of the Interior: Architecture, Modernity, Domesticity*, London and New York: Routledge.

Rice, C. (2013), "Rethinking Histories of the Interior," in G. Brooker and S. Stone (eds.), *From Organization to Decoration: An Interior Design Reader*, London and New York: Routledge.

Singleton, M. (2008), "The Classical Reveries of Modern Yoga: Patanjali and Constructive Orientalism," in M. Singleton and J. Byrne (eds.), *Yoga in the Modern World: Contemporary Perspectives*. London: Routledge.

Singleton, M. (2010), *Yoga Body: The Origins of Modern Posture Practice*, Oxford: Oxford University Press.

Singleton, M. and J. Byrne (2008), "Introduction," in M. Singleton and J. Byrne (eds.), *Yoga in the Modern World: Contemporary Perspectives*, London: Routledge.

Sparke, P. (2008), *The Modern Interior*, London: Reaktion Books.

"New York City's Most Beautiful Yoga Studios," *Well and Good NYC*. http://www.wellandgoodnyc.com/2012/01/02/new-york-citys-most-beautiful-yoga-studios-2/#new-york-citys-most-beautiful-yoga-studios-1 [Accessed November 23, 2013].

INDEX

Adam, Robert 133, 242, 246
Ageron, Charles-Robert 195
Ahmed, Sarah 9, 10, 14
Aitchison, George 127, 135
Alayrac-Fielding, Vanessa 128
Aldrich, Robert 59, 61, 62, 72
Allen, Matthew Harp 259
Alter, Joseph S. 255, 256
Ameri, Amir H. 54, 55, 228
Anderson, Anne 95
Anderson, Colin 238, 240–1, 244–5
Arita kilns 180
    Japanese export figure of a lion-dog (1670–1690) 179–80
    model of a lion-dog (1660–1690) 179–80
Asplund, Karl 152, 156
Aristotle 113
Armani, Giorgio 13
Armstrong, Thomas 139
Aubin, Penelope 97–8, 101–7
Auslander, Leora 189
Autry, Gene 85
Avcioglu, Nebahat 54

Bacon, Francis 69
Baer, Nancy van Norman 147
Baier, Karl 265
Bailey, Ann 181
Baker, Malcolm 44
Ballaster, Ros 97, 99, 101, 103, 165
Banfield, Ann 25
Barmé, Scot 82
Barthes, Roland 78, 119, 124
Baudrillard, Jean 23, 78–9, 83, 88, 147
Bayer, Patricia 199
Beaulieu, Annette Leduc 120
Beaulieu, Jill 7, 11, 93
Bédard, Camille 166

Beer, Gillian 28
Bekkaoui, Khalid 98
Bell, Quentin 25
Benjamin, Roger 159
Benjamin, Walter 48, 53, 263
Benton, Charlotte 192
Bertin, André 190, 191
Bhabha, Homi 6, 204, 216
Bie, Oskar 50
Bird, Lauren 167
Birnir, Adda 4
Blair, Sheila S. 54
Bloom, Jonathan M. 54
Bode, Wilhelm von 44, 45, 48, 50–1
    Room 9 in the Kaiser-Friedrich-Museum (1904) 48, 51
Boijen, William Bouwens der 115
    Musée Cernuschi (1873–1874) 113–14, 115
Bolton, Andrew 8
Boone, Joseph Allen 61–3, 67, 69, 72, 73, 94–5
Borie, Jean 113
Börlin, Jean 95, 148–9, 151, 156–8
    Dervishes (1920) 148–9
Borman, Tracy 177, 185
Bowles, Carington 172
    A monument dedicated to posterity in commemoration of [the] incredible folly transacted in the year 1720 (c.1764) 172
Bowrey, Thomas 178
Bradshaw, David 35
Bradshaw, Peter 80–1
Brandon, James R. 85
Bredbeck, Gregory 31
Bridgman, Frederick Arthur 21
Briffa, Emmanuel 166, 223–4, 227, 231

Brooker, Graeme 236
Brown, Bill 128
Bruno, Giuliana 228
Bryson, Norman 62, 73
Burbridge, Frederick William 215
Burke, Edmund 129
Burne-Jones, Georgiana 134
Burt, Ramsay 148
Buscombe, Edward 81–2
Byrne, Jean 264

Camard, Florence 199
Cameco Capitol Arts Centre, 221
Camille, Michael 151
Campbell, Colin 256
Campbell, Louise 128, 130, 141
Caracciolo, Peter L. 108
Carlos, Ann M. 171
Carswell, John 170
Castle, Terry 61, 72
Cavafy, Constantine P. 62, 65–8, 72–3
Çelik, Zeynep 53
Cernuschi, Henri 95, 112–16, 119–22, 124–5
Champollion, Jean-François 226
Chang, Ting 113
Chaudey, Gustave 113
Chaussé, Alcide 219, 222, 224
    Empress Theatre (1927) 219–20, 222–31
Cheang, Sarah 14, 141
Childe, Theodore 137
Chippendale 132, 213
Christie, Manson and Woods 135
Church, Frederick Edwin 208
Churchill, Winston 171
Clarke, Kenneth 73
Clason, Isak Gustaf 145
    Hallwyl Palace (1898) 145
Clunas, Craig 129
Codell, Julie F. 11
Cohen-Rose, Sandra 223
Collcutt, Thomas Edward 241
Colomina, Beatriz 12
Conant, Martha Pike 108
Connoisseur 139, 140
    "No. I- Mr. Jarvis's Collection" (1901) 140

Cooper, Anthony Ashley, Earl of Shaftesbury 98–9, 108
Cooper, H. J. 203
Copley, Anthony 33
Corner, Edred John Henry 212
Corrigan, Karina 175
Cowles, Virginia 170
Craciun, Adriana 108
Crane, Walter 241
Crinson, Mark 5, 7, 165–6
Cruikshanks, Eveline 172
"Curio" 140

Dacre, Charlotte 97–8, 104–8
Dale, Richard 170, 171
Dardel, Nils 95, 145–8, 151–2, 156–61
    Crime passionnel (1921) 157
    Reception (1921) 158
Daudet, Alphonse 115, 125
Davies, Daniel 250
Da Vinci, Leonardo 113, 118
Dawson, Philip 236
Décoration Intérieur Moderne 197
Demaison, M. 113–14
De Michelis, Elizabeth 255–6, 265
DeMille, Cecil B. 85
Department of Islamic Art, Metropolitan Museum of Art 42
Despatys, Pierre 114
    Photograph of the Great Buddha Hall (n.d.) 114
Deutsch, Ludwig 21
Devi, Rukmini 259
D'Ezio, Marianna 94
Digges, West 134
Dixon, Charles Edward, R. I. 237
    Orient Line to Australia (c.1912) 237
Doane, Mary Ann 87
Dobie, Madeleine 93, 189
Dorn, Marion 241
Dufrêne, Maurice 197
Dulac, Edmund 246–8
    Cathay Lounge (1931) 246–8
Du Maurier, George 128, 130
    A Disenchantment (1876) 130
Dunn, Henry Teffry 134
    Dante Gabriel Rossetti and Theodore Watts—Dutton in the

Dining Room (?) at 16 Cheyne Walk (1882) 134
Dunn, James A. 105, 107
DuPlessis, Robert S. 173
Dupré, Louis 67
   Voyage à Athènes et à Constantinople (1824) 67
Duret, Théodore 113, 120

Eastwood, Clint 82
   The Outlaw Josey Wales (1976) 82
Eberson, John 220–1, 222, 224
Edgeworth, Maria 108
Edwards, Holly 10, 14, 53 165, 226
Edwards, Jason 128
Eidlitz, Leopold 208
El-Zein, Amira 97
Empress Cultural Centre 223
Esmein, Suzanne 120, 122

Falize, Lucien 112
Farcus, Joe 248
   Passage to India Lounge (1994) 248
Fellion, Courtney 77, 80
Figueiredo, Peter de 133
Fleming, Victor 85
   Gone with the Wind (1937) 85
Ford, John 85
Forster, E. M. 22, 25–33, 35–6
Foucault, Michel 219, 227
Fouquières, André Becq de 125
Freeman, Michael 13, 14
Frelinghuysen, Alice Cooney 181
Friedman, Alice T. 248
Fuller, Robert C. 265
Fuss, Diana 12–13, 15

Gaillard, Emmanuelle 8
Galland, Antoine 39, 53, 94, 97–8, 101, 107–8
Garber, Marjorie 61–2, 69, 73
Geczy, Adam 8
Geffroy, Gustave 118
Gendron, Joffre 231
Gentile, Kathy Justice 106
Gere, Charlotte 208
Germain, Betty 172
Gérôme, Jean-Léon 3, 93
Godwin, Edward William 133

Golan, Romy 195, 198
Goldin, Amy 43
Gollapudi, Aparna 104
Goncourt, Edmond de 95, 112, 116–19, 121–2, 124–5
Goncourt, Jean de 95, 112, 116, 118
Gonse, François 115
Gonse, Louis 114–15, 121
Goupil, Albert 48–9, 155
   Oriental room (1888) 48–9, 155
Gouws, Dennis S. 23
Grabar, Oleg 46, 52–3
Graven and Mayger 221
   Fisher Theatre (1928) 221
Graves, John 250
Grier, Katherine C. 208
Grosrichards, Alain 102–3
Guha-Thakurta, Tapati 259

Hall, Ben M. 221, 230–1
Hamling, Tara 175
Handley, Stuart 172
HappyTree Yoga 252–3, 255, 258
   Altar space (n.d.) 253
   Promotional image (2010) 258
   Yoga practice room (n.d.) 252
Harrison, Rachel 81
Hassard, Annie 215
Hauser, Beatrix 255–6
Haweis, Mary Eliza Joy 135, 214
Hayton, David W. 172
Haywood, Eliza 97, 107
Herbert, Henry, 9th Earl of Pembroke 185
Hernandez, Felipe 6, 7
Herzog, Charlotte 220
Hibberd, Shirley 214
Hindu American Foundation 263
Hobbs and Chambers 137
Hockney, David 23, 59–60, 62–73
   According to the Prescriptions of Ancient Magicians (1966) 66
   The Beginning (1966) 67
   Gregory Watching the Snow Fall, Kyoto, Feb 21, 1983 (1983) 62, 69, 71
   In Despair (1966) 67
   Illustrations for Fourteen Poems from C. P. Cavafy (1966–67) 65

In an Old Book (1966) 67–8
In the Dull Village (1966) 62, 66
Mark, Suginoi Hotel, Beppu (1971) 62, 69–70
One Night (1966) 67
Tea Painting in an Illusionistic Style [Typhoo Tea] (1961) 62–4, 70
Two Boys Aged 23 or 24 (1966) 66
Hodgson, Mrs Willoughby 133
Hogarth, William 170–1
    The South Sea Scheme (1720) 170–1
Hollingsworth, A. T. 128–9, 134
Hoppot, Julian 171
Hornstein, Shelley 231
Hoskins, Lesley 208
Howard, David S. 181
Howard, Deborah S. 42
Howard, Henrietta 170, 177, 185
Hughes, Linda K. 35
Hughes, Robert 69
Humbert, Jean-Marcel 226–8, 232
Hunt, William Holman 66
    Lantern-Maker's Courtship (c.1860) 66
Huxtable, Sally-Anne 240
Huysman, Joris-Karl 119

Inaga, Shigemi 113
Ingrassia, Catherine 170
Ingres, Jean Auguste Dominique 93, 206
Institut de Tokyo 122
Inventories of the South Sea Directors 165, 169, 173–4, 181, 184
Iqbal, Razia 52

Jaffer, Amin 175
James, Henry 127–8, 129
Jeckyll, Thomas 139
Jodidio, Philip 51, 55
Johnson, Hugh 181
Johnson, Johnnie E. V. 171
Jones, A. H. 247
Jones, Inigo 133
Jones, Jonathan 11, 12, 72
Jones, Owen 42, 207, 212
Jowett, S. 261
    Tree Mandala (2012) 261

Kabbani, Rana 11, 61
Karan, Donna 13
Kaur, Meier 261
Kelmscott Manor and Estate Conservation Management Plan 136
Kelvin, Norman 136
Kerr, Robert 129
Khoo, Olivia 80, 82
Kidd, William 214
Kiernan, Victor Gordon 60
Kinerk, Michael D. 221
King, Anthony D. 204
King, Richard 256, 260
Kive, Solmaz Mohammadzadeh 22, 155
Klonk, Charlotte 44, 45, 51, 54
Knapp, Gottfried 230
Knight, Ellis Cornelia 108
Knipp, Christopher 108
Knox and Webb 241
Koda, Harold 8, 69
Kolomeir, Harriet T. 221, 224, 230, 231
Komaroff, Linda 40
Krafft, Hugues 95, 112, 119–25
    Jardin miniature (c.1885) 123
    Midori-no-sato (1883) 121–3
    "Zashiki" et "toro" (c.1885) 121
Kroger, Jens 40, 50
Kuniyoshi, Utagawa 69

Lago, Mary 35
Lamb, Charles 128
Lanken, Dane 224, 231–2
Lant, Antonia 226, 231
Largillière, Nicholas 182
Lapidus, Morris 248
Laurencin, Marie 160–1
Lavery, John 247
    Empress Room (n.d.) 247
Lawrence, T. E. 73
Le Brun, Charles 182
Le Corbeiller, Clare 181
Lee, S. Charles 220
Lefebvre, Henri 5, 9
Lefeuvre, Jean 229
    First-class stairway of the *Champollion* (1924) 228, 229

Léger, Fernand 160
Leigh, Vivian 85
Leighton, Frederic 12, 95, 127–30, 135–7, 141, 207, 240
    Arab Hall (1881) 12, 95, 127, 207, 240
Leleu, Jules 197
Lemere, Bedford 138
    Peacock Room (1877) 12, 129, 135, 137–9, 240
Lemaire, Gerard-Georges 72–3
Leon, Sergio 80, 85
    The Good, the Bad and the Ugly (1966) 85
Leti, Giuseppe 113
Lewis, Glen 82
Lewis, John Frederick 65, 66
    A Frank Encampment in the Desert of Mount Sinai, 1842 (1856) 65
    A Lady Receiving Visitors (The Reception) (1873) 66
    Hareem Life, Constantinople (1857) 66
    The Mid-day Meal (1875) 65
Lewis, Reina 93–4
Lévitan 187–8, 197–8, 200
    Furniture catalog (1931) 187, 188
    Furniture catalog (1933) 197–8, 200
    Furniture catalog (1935) 197
Lindahl, Ingemar 151–2
Liste Officielle des Exposants 197
Litzenburg, Thomas V., Jr. 181
Livingstone, Marco 65, 69, 73
Loew, Marcus 220
Loftie, Martha Jane 135
Loftie, William John 134
Loos, Adolf 154, 156
Loti, Pierre 12
Lowe, Lisa 6, 7
Lucie-Smith, Edward 65
Lukas, Scott A. 226

Mack, Robert L. 108
MacKenzie, John M. 8, 10–11, 72, 159, 236, 241, 244
Mackintosh, John 69
MacKay, Elsie 243, 244–5, 248
    First Class Smoking Room (1929) 244, 245–6

The Verandah Café (1929) 235, 243, 244–5
Macleod, Diane Sachko 11
Magne, Henri-Marcel 193–4
    An ideal bedroom set (1925) 194
Mahdi, Musin 108
Makdisi, Saree 104, 108
Manet, Édouard 67, 113
    Olympia (1863) 67
Maré, Rolf de 95, 145–60
Marks, Emmanuel Murray 131–2, 137–9
Marsh, Jan 134, 139
Martin, Fredrik Robert 48, 50
Martin, Richard 8, 69
Martineau, Jocelyne 221
Martin's Collection (1897) 50
Massey, Anne 167
Mathew, Sacha 260–1, 265
Matisse, Henri 159
Maurel, André 113
McKee, Alison L. 87
McWilliams, Mary 52
Mellor, Anne 108
Meniaud, Jean 195
Mernissi, Fatema 66
Merrill, Linda 135, 137, 139
Meyer-Riefstahl, Rudolf 40
Meynell, Wilfrid 136
    "A Portion of the Dining Room" (1881) 136
Miller, Barbara Stoler 35
Miller, Frank 105
Milles, Jeremiah 184
Minear, Richard H. 69
Ministère du Commerce et de l'Industrie 190
Mitchell, Timothy 21–2, 54
Moleworth, Elizabeth 170
Montagu, Mary Wortley 21, 98, 100–2, 106, 107
Montesquiou, Robert de 119, 121
Moore, Andrew 174, 184
Morgan, David 263
Morgan, William de 240–1, 248
Morgenthaler, Hans 55
Morris, May 136, 137

Morris, William 42, 129, 132, 135–7, 139, 206–7
   Kelmscott House 129, 135–7, 207
   Trade Card (n.d.) 132
Morrison, Craig 220, 226
Morse, Edward Sylvester 115
Morton, Patricia 195, 198–9
Mosse, Richard 1–4
   Breach (2009) 1–4
Motter, Paul 248
Mouveau, Georges 148–9
   Dervishes (1920) 148–9
Mozart, Wolfgang Amadeus 232
   The Magic Flute (1791) 232
Mudge, Jean M. 182
Myzelev, Alla 15

Näslund, Erik 147, 149–50, 152, 158
Naylor, Gillian 207
Neal, Larry 171
Necipoğlu, Gürlu 54
Neiswander, Judith A. 133
Newcombe, Suzanne 265
Nochlin, Linda 2–3, 236
Nordau, Max 128, 154, 156
Nussbaum, Felicity 108

O'Doherty, Brian 54–5
Olivier, Marcel 196
O'Rorke, Brian 241
Ostwald, Michael J. 23
Oueijan, Naji B.108
Oxford English Dictionary 73, 232

Pang, Oxide 81
Paris, W. Francklyn 192
Pastore, Chaela 189
Pater, Jean-Baptiste 182
Pater, Walter 130
Paxton, Joseph 210
   Crystal Palace (1851) 210
   Palm houses 210
Pearce, Nick 132
Pearce, Susan M. 147
Pearl, Linda 248
Pei, I. M. 55
Pelletier, Louis 222, 232
Peltre, Christine 72
Pennell, Elizabeth Robins 131

Pennell, Joseph 131
Penner, Barbara J. 236
Periton, Diana 116
Peter, Bruce 236
Petitpas, Julien 191, 196
Pfister, Manfred 99
Picart, Bernard 176
   A true picture of the famous skreen describ'd in the Londn. journal no. 85 (1721) 176
Picasso, Pablo 160
Pierson, Stacey 130–1
Pilkington, Mary 108
Pinkney, Tony 137
Pisarro, Camille 113
Poiret, Paul 13
Pollock, Griselda 152
Pollock, Sheldon 30
Potvin, John 55, 242
Poussin, Nicholas 182
Pratt, Mary Louise 11
Preziosi, Donald 53
Printz, Eugène 198–9
Prou, René 197
Proust, Marcel 12, 121

Raffaelli, Jean François 117
   Portrait of Edmond de Goncourt (n.d.) 117
Ramírez, Juan Antonio 83
Rand, Edward Sprague 215
Rapp brothers 221
Reddy, Sita 264
Reed, Christopher 95, 129
Reeve, Clara 99, 108
Régamey, Félix 121
Reitlinger, Gerald 128, 131, 179
Rice, Charles 12, 236, 254, 257–8, 263
Richards, Charles Russell 192, 193
Richards, Jasmine 84, 86
   Digital reconstruction of *Tears of the Black Tiger*'s "duel" scene (n.d.) 84
   Digital reconstruction of *Tears of the Black Tiger*'s "hallway" scene (n.d.) 86
Richards, Melanie 261
Richards, Sarah 182
Riding, Christine 61

Roberts, Mary 7, 11, 93
Robinson, Basil William 42
Robinson, William Heath 247
    Knickerbocker Bar (n.d.) 247
Roessel, David, 35
Romanets, Myrana 108
Rosenbaum, Stanford Patrick 25
Rossetti, Dante Gabriel 129, 131–4, 137, 139, 141
    Trade Card (n.d.) 132
Rossetti, William Michael 134
Rousseau, Jean-Jacques 101
Roxburgh, David 48, 54
Royal Architectural Institute of Canada 224
Ruhlmann, Jacques-Emile 197–9
Ruskin, John 42, 79
Russell, Hilary 222
Rutherford, Jonathan 204, 216
Rydell, Robert W. 192

Said, Edward W. 5, 9, 11–12, 26, 52, 59–61, 63, 69, 72, 78, 88, 93, 101, 188, 204, 206, 216, 222, 227, 256
Saisselin, Rémy G. 137
Salway, Oliver 46
Sanzio, Raphael 175, 183
Sarre, Friedrich Paul Theodor 40, 47, 48
    Exhibition of Masterpieces of Muhammedan Art (1910) 40, 47
    Room 9, the Kaiser-Friedrich-Museum (1904) 48, 51
Sasanatieng, Wisit 23, 77–8, 80–1, 83, 85, 87–8
    Making *Tears of the Black Tiger* (2000) 83
    Tears of the Black Tiger [Fa Thalai Jone] (2000) 23, 77–8, 79–84, 86–8
Sato, Tomoko 204
Schinkel, Karl Friedrich 232
Schotland, Sara D. 108
Sconce, Jeffrey 82
Searle, Adrian 62
Semper, Gottfried 54, 155, 158, 160–1
Sextro, Laura 166
Shalem, Avinoam 42
Shanks, Edward 27, 35

Sheridan, Frances 97, 102, 108
Siddal, Lizzie 134
Silverman, Debora L. 124
Singleton, Mark 255–7, 259, 264
Sontag, Susan 119
Sornette, Didier 171
Sparke, Penny 166, 254
Spencer, Robin 139
Sprengel, David 156–8
Stangos, Nikos 63, 73
Stanley, Tim 42, 54
Staynes, P. A. 247
Stein, Roger B. 129, 141
Stephens, Virginia 25
Stephenson, Andrew 128, 141
Stevenson, John James 241
Sutton, Damian 82, 85
Suzuki, Junji 121
Swift, Jonathan 172

Tallis, John 39
Tang, Leilei 171
Taveneaux, Antoine 34
    Lakshmana Temple (n.d.) 11
Taylor, Mark 23
Temin, Peter 171
Tillinghast, Richard 54
Travail du Bois 190, 191, 196
Troelenberg, Eva M. 40, 46, 52
Tromans, Nicholas 60, 65–6, 73
Troy, Jean de 182

Ulrich, Kurt 236

Valentine, Maggie 220
Valette, John de la 248
Van Alphen, Ernst 62, 67, 73
Vargas, Victor 22
Varley, Lynn 105
Vaux, Calvert 208
    "Olana" (1872) 208
Voth, Hans-Joaquim 171
Votolato, Greg 236, 248

Waagen, Friedrich 44, 54
Wagner, Richard 230
Walker, Emery 135
Walsh, Justyn 170–1
Walter, Marc 8

Wantanabe, Toshio 204
Warhol, Andy 119
Waring and Gillow 211
Waring, Samuel James 211–12
   Palmyra 211–13
Warner, Marina 40, 53
Watson, Rosamund Marriott 130, 135
Watteau, Antoine 182
Watt, William 133
Watts, Theodore 134
Wayman, Dorothy G. 115
Wayne, John 85
Webb, Peter 72, 73
Webb, Philip 136
Webber, Byron 133
Weber, Stefan 54, 55
Weeks, Emily M. 59, 60, 66, 69, 72
Weichel, Eric 165, 166
Whistler, James Abbott McNeill 12, 129, 131–2, 134, 137–9
   The Blue Girl (c.1875) 139
   Trade Card (n.d.) 132
Whitehead, Christopher 43–4, 54

White Star Line 243
Wigley, Mark 160
Wild, Antony 203
Wilde, Oscar 73, 124, 133
Wilhelm, Dennis W. 221
Williams, Henry T. 215
Williamson, George Charles 131, 137–9
Wilmotte, Jean-Michel 51
   Museum of Islamic Art (2008) 51
Wilson, Timothy 177
Windover, Michael 227–8
Wolfe, Elsie de 205–6, 208–9, 212, 216
Wolfe, Frida 247–8
Wollen, Peter 159
Wood, Barry D. 40, 42, 47
Woolf, Virginia 22, 25–6
Woolf, Leonard 25

Yeats, W. B. 26
Yeazell, Ruth 97

Zola, Émile 118

www.ingramcontent.com/pod-product-compliance
Lightning Source LLC
Chambersburg PA
CBHW050136240426
43673CB00043B/1683